Societal Stress and Law

Larry D. Barnett

Societal Stress and Law

Springer

Larry D. Barnett
Wilmington, DE, USA

ISBN 978-3-031-30874-1 ISBN 978-3-031-30875-8 (eBook)
https://doi.org/10.1007/978-3-031-30875-8

This Springer imprint is published by the registered company Springer Nature Switzerland AG
The registered company address is: Gewerbestrasse 11, 6330 Cham, Switzerland

To
Linda Rae, my wife and friend

Preface

As a (retired) law school professor, I have long accepted that the institution of law has social effects that are unplanned, and even some that are unwanted, but I assumed that such side effects were an unimportant sideshow to the social benefits of law. My experience in the field of law tested these beliefs, however, and I have come to question their accuracy. In particular, I think that we must entertain the distinct possibility that the number of law-induced social side effects is sizeable and that many of the side effects are sociologically significant. That few scholars acknowledge and pay attention to such side effects is thus regrettable, particularly since the institution of law occupies a prominent place in modern nations. My hope is that the present book will promote scholarship that seeks to identify and explain unwanted, unanticipated social effects that stem from law.

The skepticism that I gradually developed regarding law is the foundation for the present book, but it was the election of Donald J. Trump as president of the United States in November 2016, and the substantial number of votes he received in his bid for re-election four years later, that prompted me to write the book. Through his statements and actions, Mr. Trump may be the most socially divisive president[1] and the most self-serving president[2] since the installation of the first president of the country more than two hundred years ago.[3] Moreover, Mr. Trump is the only

[1]Gregory Eady et al., Brookings Institution, *Comparing Trump to the Greatest — and the Most Polarizing — Presidents in U.S. History* (reporting data obtained in a survey conducted during the period December 2017 to January 2018 of members of the Presidents & Executive Politics Section of the American Political Science Ass'n; reporting findings obtained with a response rate of 53 percent), https://www.brookings.edu/blog/fixgov/2018/03/20/comparing-trump-to-the-greatest-and-the-most-polarizing-presidents-in-u-s-history (last visited Aug. 25, 2022).

[2]Elizabeth A. Cobbs et al., Historians on Trump: We've Never Seen Anything Like This, CNN Opinion (Oct. 4, 2019), https://www.cnn.com/2019/10/02/opinions/trump-impeachment-unprecedented-cobbs-longley-osgood-suri/index.html (last visited Aug. 25, 2022).

[3]George Washington became the first U.S. president on April 30, 1789. Lindsay M. Chervinsky, *The Historical Presidency: George Washington and the First Presidential Cabinet*, 48 Presidential Stud. Q. 139, 139 (2018).

U.S. president to be impeached twice by the House of Representatives,[4] and he condoned, if not instigated, the violent assault on the U.S. Capitol in January 2021—an assault whose goal was to overturn the state-certified vote counts in the November 2020 election for president and vice president of the United States. Mr. Trump and his followers were potentially to American society what a wrecking ball is to a building, and their rise and persistence must be explained. Law, in my view, contributed to the political support for Mr. Trump in 2016 and 2020, even though it was not the sole (or even the main) reason for this support.

Besides being a lawyer, I am also a sociologist, and I believe that sociology can explain how the institution of law generated support for Mr. Trump. In my view, this support arose not by chance or through personalities but was, instead, due to overarching sociological conditions and forces that were responsible for developments over a lengthy period in, inter alia, American law. Specifically, I hypothesize that these conditions and forces collectively, albeit gradually, worked to increase society-level stress and that the stress, in turn, provoked a strong reaction in the political arena that scholars largely failed to anticipate. The reaction, which included electorate support for Mr. Trump, is popularly called a "culture war" that is being waged over whether societal engineering is appropriate for the federal courts as well as for the federal legislature, i.e., Congress. Because the foregoing developments are inherently sociological, I utilize sociological tools to account for them.

Although I cannot avoid subjectivity in naming specific instances in the institution of law that created political support for Mr. Trump and cannot rank the instances that I name in terms of their contribution to this support, the following merit consideration. In my view, the instances that I list in the following paragraphs generated society-level stress and thereby influenced voters in the 2016 and 2020 presidential elections. Not all of the law-related developments that did so, however, are on the list. I cite here only the instances that I believe were most likely to have had an impact on the support garnered by the candidates of the Republican Party in these two elections. The instances listed, I should mention, are among those that are pertinent to the long-term direction of social change in American society.

Because of its temporal proximity to the November 2016 election, the first instance on my list is Obergefell v. Hodges in which the U.S. Supreme Court held that, under the due process guarantee and the equal protection guarantee of the Fourteenth Amendment to the Constitution, governments in the country must allow a same-sex couple to marry if they allow an opposite-sex couple in equivalent circumstances to marry.[5] The ruling, which eliminated the ability of legislators and hence voters to determine whether marriage should be available only to opposite-sex couples,[6] was announced by the Court on June 26, 2015;[7] the general election, in which Mr. Trump won a majority of the electors in the Electoral College, took place

---

[4] U.S. Const. art. 1, § 2 cl. 5.

[5] Obergefell v. Hodges, 135 S. Ct. 2584, 2604–05 (2015).

[6] *Id.* at 2642 (Alito, Scalia & Thomas, JJ., dissenting).

[7] J. Sup. Ct. U.S., Oct. Term 2014, at 919.

sixteen months later, i.e., on November 8, 2016.[8] The proximity of the ruling to the election makes the ruling a plausible influence on the outcome of the election since nearly two out of five adults in the United States during this period thought that law should *not* permit same-sex couples to marry.[9] These adults obviously comprised a sizeable group, and some if not many of them would have been swayed by the ruling to vote for Mr. Trump,[10] who had said in early 2016 that he would be inclined, if elected, to fill vacancies on the Court with judges likely to reverse the ruling.[11]

However, Americans who at the time of the 2016 election were unhappy with what the Supreme Court had done on social matters undoubtedly did not object to just the ruling on same-sex marriage. Constitution-based rulings of the Court that socially unsettled sizeable segments of the U.S. public appeared earlier. Abortion was also a matter on which such rulings touched a raw social nerve and undoubtedly alienated numerous voters whose beliefs aligned with those of Mr. Trump. In a series of cases that started in 1973, the Court held that governments in the United States do not have a free hand under the Constitution to restrict access to abortion.[12] Notably, prior to the 2016 election, one out of every five U.S. adults thought that abortion should be unlawful under "all circumstances."[13] Mr. Trump expressed a not-dissimilar position,[14] a position that would have swayed many voters in the 2016 election: Two out of every five registered voters who favored Mr. Trump in 2016 considered abortion to be an issue that would be "very important" to them in

[8] FED. ELECTION COMM'N, FEDERAL ELECTIONS 2016, at 23, 190, 191 (2017), https://www.fec.gov/introduction-campaign-finance/election-and-voting-information/federal-elections-2016 (last visited Aug. 25, 2022).

[9] GALLUP, INC., GALLUP HISTORICAL TRENDS: LGBT RIGHTS [3] (2022), https://news.gallup.com/poll/257705/support-gay-marriage-stable.aspx (last visited Aug. 25, 2022).

[10] In May 2015, more than one-third of U.S. adults who believed that law should not allow same-sex marriage stated that they would vote for a particular candidate for a "major" office only if the candidate held the same belief. This percentage was appreciably higher than in 2004 and 2008. Justin McCarthy, Gallup Inc., *Record-High 60% of Americans Support Same-Sex Marriage* (2015), https://news.gallup.com/poll/183272/record-high-americans-support-sex-marriage.aspx (last visited Aug. 25, 2022).

[11] Ramesh Ponnuru, *President Trump and Same-Sex Marriage*, NAT'L REV., June 1, 2018, https://www.nationalreview.com/corner/president-trump-views-on-same-sex-marriage (last visited Aug. 25, 2022).

[12] JOHN E. NOWAK & RONALD D. ROTUNDA, CONSTITUTIONAL LAW 1029–78 (8th ed. 2010). In addition, see Whole Woman's Health v. Hellerstedt, 136 S. Ct. 2292 (2016).

[13] GALLUP NEWS SERV., GALLUP POLL SOCIAL SERIES: VALUES AND BELIEFS quest. 12 (2022), https://news.gallup.com/poll/393104/pro-choice-identification-rises-near-record-high.aspx (last visited Aug. 25, 2022).

[14] Tyler Pager, *Trump Breaks His Silence on Supreme Court Abortion Ruling*, POLITICO, June 30, 2016 (reporting that Mr. Trump remarked during an interview that, as president, he would nominate justices to the U.S. Supreme Court who would interpret the Constitution in ways that curbed the availability of lawful abortion), https://www.politico.com/story/2016/06/trump-abortion-supreme-court-224984 (last visited Aug. 25, 2022).

deciding for whom they would vote.[15] Their support for Mr. Trump was not in vain. As President, Mr. Trump nominated three justices to fill vacancies on the U.-S. Supreme Court, and the Court subsequently withdrew its recognition of a right to abortion stemming from the national Constitution.[16]

Given that the Constitution has broad significance to Americans,[17] rulings by the U.S. Supreme Court that interpret its provisions may not have been the sole Constitution-pertinent source of societal stress that alienated segments of the U.-S. population and affected the outcome of the November 2016 contest for president. Another such source may have been social conflict over the Equal Rights Amendment during 1972–1982,[18] the period that Congress specified for states to decide whether the amendment should be added to the Constitution.[19] The proposed amendment, which would have invalidated government-made distinctions grounded on sex, was opposed by one-fourth to one-third of all the U.S. adults[20] and was unable to gain the approval of a sufficient number of states during 1972–1982. The effort to incorporate the amendment into the Constitution did not, however, disappear after 1982. Instead, the effort continued, including in the years leading up to the 2016 election.[21] The prospect of having the amendment in the Constitution could have had an impact on voting in the 2016 presidential election if the social conflict over ratification during 1972–1982 left a residuum of societal stress that amplified the societal stress from the pre-election effort to keep the amendment viable. The residuum could also have exacerbated the sociological impact of concurrent or subsequent U.S. Supreme Court rulings on the portions of the American public that thought the rulings jeopardized conventional aspects of social life.

I realize, of course, that the thesis I advance in this book is at variance with popular views regarding law and will not sit well with some politically driven segments of the U.S. population, including a sizable segment of the professoriate and student body at many U.S. colleges and universities. I can only hope that the thesis and the evidence provided by the book for it will be considered when

---

[15] Pew Res. Ctr., 2016 Campaign: Strong Interest, Widespread Dissatisfaction 32, 65 (2016) (reporting results from a nationwide sample of adults surveyed during June 2016).

[16] Dobbs v. Jackson Women's Health Org., No. 19-1392, slip op., 2022 WL 2276808 (2022) (overturning Roe v. Wade, 410 U.S. 113 (1973)).

[17] Larry D. Barnett, Societal Agents in Law: A Macrosociological Approach 13–15 (2019).

[18] *See* Donald T. Critchlow & Cynthia L. Stachecki, *The Equal Rights Amendment Reconsidered: Politics, Policy, and Social Mobilization in a Democracy*, 20 J. Pol'y Hist. 157, 171, 172 (2008) (describing the political conflict over ratification during 1972–1982 as "acrimonious" and observing that the conflict influenced politics in the United States for "decades").

[19] Barnett, *supra* note 17, at 143–44. Disagreement exists over whether the amendment can be validly ratified by states after the close of the Congress-designated ratification period. Thomas H. Neale, Cong. Res. Serv., The Proposed Equal Rights Amendment: Contemporary Ratification Issues 18–26 (CRS Report R42979) (2018).

[20] Rita J. Simon & Jean M. Landis, *Women's and Men's Attitudes About A Woman's Place and Role*, 53 Pub. Opinion Q. 265, 275 (1989). Notably, the percentage that opposed the amendment was larger in the later years of the 1972–1982 period than in the early years. *Id.*

[21] Neale, *supra* note 19, at 2–3, 16–18.

evaluating how law affects social life. Law has a large presence in America, and *all* of its consequences need to be taken into account.

In closing, I want to acknowledge the resources for scholarship at Widener University libraries. In particular, I am indebted to the Wolfgram Memorial Library for its online databases in the social sciences and to the Delaware Law School Library for its online databases in law. I also want to thank members of the staff of the Delaware Law School Library for their diligence in obtaining items whose full text was not available in the online databases. Christy D'Antonio, a member of the library staff, was particularly helpful and merits special mention. No author completes a work of scholarship locked in a tower—ivory or otherwise—and the foregoing immeasurably facilitated my writing of the present book. Any and all deficiencies in the book are, of course, solely my responsibility.

Wilmington, DE, USA
November 2022

Larry D. Barnett

Contents

List of Figures

List of Tables

Chapter 1
Societal Stress: Theory, Meaning, and Measurement

1.1 Concepts and Knowledge

> Every now and then a [person's] mind is stretched by a new idea or sensation, and never shrinks back to its former dimensions.[1]

A new concept has the ability to alter thinking about a phenomenon and provide a fuller understanding of the phenomenon, but to do so, it must first be adopted and applied. Openness to neglected and unknown concepts, therefore, is a prerequisite to the benefit(s) that these concepts may provide. Such openness, of course, entails flexibility, but flexibility differs in degree between individuals as well as between societies. Not surprisingly, where individuals and where societies fall on the flexibility–inflexibility continuum has been found to be consequential: For an individual, greater flexibility increases innovativeness;[2] for a society, greater flexibility enhances societal viability[3] and fosters economic growth.[4] Since societies are

[1] Oliver Wendell Holmes, Sr., *"The Deacon's Masterpiece: Or the Wonderful 'One-Hoss-Shay'"*, *in* The Autocrat of the Breakfast-Table 256 (J. M. Dent & Sons, Ltd., 1970) (1858), https://archive.org/details/autocratofbreakf00holm. The word "person's" has been substituted for the word "man's" in order to bring the passage into line with present-day social values.

[2] Asta A. Georgsdottir et al., *The Role of Flexibility in Innovation*, *in* International Handbook on Innovation 180, 181–84 (Larisa V. Shavinina ed., 2003).

[3] *See* Marlene Sway, *Economic Adaptability: The Case of the Gypsies*, 13 Urb. Life 83, 85, 97 (1984) (studying several local Gypsy communities in the United States, Yugoslavia, and the British Isles; concluding that the communities, by virtue of their flexibility, were able "to remain economically and culturally independent").

[4] Nation-level economic growth is promoted by, inter alia, "economic freedom," a manifestation of individualization and its accompanying ideology of individualism. Mohammed Ershad Hussain & Mahfuzul Haque, *Impact of Economic Freedom on the Growth Rate: A Panel Data Analysis*, 4(2) Economies art. 5, March 2016, at 1, 10. Flexibility is conceptually related to individualization and individualism, but as sociological variables, societal flexibility and individualization/individualism are distinct phenomena. Michael Minkov. *A Revision of Hofstede's Model of National*

L. D. Barnett, *Societal Stress and Law*,
https://doi.org/10.1007/978-3-031-30875-8_1

composed of institutions[5] and vary in substance, an institution can differ in flexibility between societies at a particular point in time and between points in time within a particular society. Such differences are important for what happens in the institution.[6]

The societal institution that is devoted to knowledge production (and hence to scholarship) is directly relevant to the instant book, because the book deals with one field of study in that institution and with a concept that, I believe, merits attention by scholars in the field. Of course, whether and the extent to which a concept is applied in a field depends on, inter alia, how well the concept captures aspects of at least one phenomenon pertinent to the field. Acceptance of a concept also depends on the flexibility of the field. Notably, the macrosociology of law—the field that is of interest to the present book—scores low on flexibility.[7] Even if that characterization is incorrect as a general matter, the particular concept on which the instant book focuses may encounter substantial resistance in some quarters where, despite its ring of familiarity and comfortable fit in a macrosociological framework, certain conclusions to which the concept leads may be unwelcome.[8]

To contextualize any such resistance, the book follows a path that is important in the knowledge-generating institution. Indeed, the path is essential in every field of study in that institution. A field in the knowledge-generating institution necessarily

---

Culture: Old Evidence and New Data from 56 Countries, 25 Cross Cultural & Strategic Mgmt. 231, 251 fig. 6, 252 fig. 7 (2018).

Individualization/individualism, like flexibility, has been found to stimulate innovation in technology and science. Mark Zachary Taylor & Sean Wilson, *Does Culture Still Matter? The Effects of Individualism on National Innovation Rates*, 27 J. Bus. Venturing 234, 237–39, 245 (2012); Andrzej Bukowski & Seweryn Rudnicki, *Not Only Individualism: The Effects of Long-Term Orientation and Other Cultural Variables on National Innovation Success*, 53 Cross-Cultural Res. 119, 126–27, 134–35, 138–39, 143–44 tbl. 3, 149 tbl. 5 (2019). In bringing about economic growth, societal flexibility and individualization/individualism may thus work through innovation in technology and science. Societal flexibility and individualization/individualism have social effects, too. *See* Larry D. Barnett, Societal Agents in Law: A Macrosociological Approach 106–07 (2019) [hereinafter SAIL vol. 1] (positing that increases in individualization/ individualism are accompanied by decreases in stereotypes in social life and involve, by implication, greater societal flexibility); Ronald Inglehart, *Mapping Global Values*, 5 Comp. Sociol. 115, 131–34 (2006) (finding that individualization and individualism promote and strengthen democracy).

[5] See the text accompanying *infra* notes 55 & 56.

[6] Thomas A. DiPrete et al., *Work and Pay in Flexible and Regulated Labor Markets: A Generalized Perspective on Institutional Evolution and Inequality Trends in Europe and the U.S.*, 28–30 (Leibniz Inst. for the Soc. Sci., Discussion Paper 109, 2003), available in the Social Science Open Access Repository at https://www.ssoar.info/ssoar/handle/document/11213; Theresa Gunn & Joshua Shackman, *A Comparative Analysis of the Implications of the Islamic Religion on Corporate Capital Structures of Firms in Emerging Market Countries*, 7 Int'l J. Islamic & Middle E. Fin. & Mgmt. 277, 284–85 (2014).

[7] Allan V. Horwitz, *Resistance to Innovation in the Sociology of Law: A Response to Greenberg*, 17 Law & Soc'y Rev. 369, 382 (1983).

[8] See the text accompanying *infra* notes 112 to 117.

employs concepts,[9] and by considering and using new concepts, it can fulfill its mission, viz., to enlarge the store of substantive knowledge about the subjects that are central to the field. Without question, the institution as a whole has succeeded in materially expanding available knowledge.[10] Importantly, this expansion has been accompanied by, and has probably been responsible for, the emergence of new specialized fields within the institution.[11] The increase in fields has, in turn, enhanced the ability of every field to advance: A field in a multi-field setting can bring in and adapt concepts from other fields, and the numerical growth of fields has, consequently, expanded opportunities for scholars in every field to cross disciplinary lines and draw concepts from fields outside their own. Since the development and acceptance of novel concepts facilitates (and may often be critical to) progress in the knowledge-creating institution,[12] crossing the boundaries of fields can lead, and has led, to gains in knowledge.[13]

In this book, I use a concept in one field and modify it for another. The two fields, however, are not similar; indeed, they are in entirely different branches of the knowledge-producing institution. In particular, I borrow a concept from the field of physiology, where the concept has gained scientific status and helped to make sense of what happens to individuals.[14] I put the concept into the field of

[9] Herbert Blumer, *Science Without Concepts*, 36 AM. J. SOCIOL. 515 (1931).

[10] Peter Vinkler, *The Institutionalization of Scientific Information: A Scientometric Model (ISI-S Model)*, 50 LIBR. TRENDS 553, 554–56 (2002); Caroline S. Wagner & Dae Joong Kim, *The Price of Big Science: Saturation or Abundance in Scientific Publishing?*, 1 POL'Y & COMPLEX SYS. 108, 112 fig. 2, 120 fig. 6 (2014).

[11] *See* G. W. Trompf, *The Classification of the Sciences and the Quest for Interdisciplinarity: A Brief History of Ideas from Ancient Philosophy to Contemporary Environmental Science*, 38 ENVTL. CONSERVATION 113, 122 (2011) (describing the growing number of specialized fields in universities as having "entered a phase of critical overload").

[12] *See* Albert Einstein, *Ernst Mach*, 17 PHYSIKALISCHE ZEITSCHRIFT 101, 102 (1916), *reprinted in* 6 THE COLLECTED PAPERS OF ALBERT EINSTEIN: THE BERLIN YEARS: WRITINGS, 1914–1917, at 141, 142 (Alfred Engel trans., 1997) ("Concepts that have proven useful in ordering things can easily attain an authority over us such that we ... take them as immutably given. They are then rather rubber-stamped as a 'sine-qua-non of thinking' and an 'a priori given,' etc. Such errors make the road of scientific progress often impassable for long times.").

[13] Shiji Chen et al., *Exploring the Interdisciplinary Evolution of a Discipline: The Case of Biochemistry and Molecular Biology*, 102 SCIENTOMETRICS 1307, 1309, 1312–1313 & fig. 1, 1315–16 & fig. 5 (2015) (studying change over the 1910–2012 period in citations to other fields by publications within the field of biochemistry and molecular biology); Alan L. Porter & Ismael Rafols, *Is Science Becoming More Interdisciplinary? Measuring and Mapping Six Research Fields Over Time*, 81 SCIENTOMETRICS 719, 724, 728, 741 (2009) (studying change over the 1975–2005 period in citations to journals in other fields by publications in biotechnology-applied microbiology, electrical-electronic engineering, mathematics, research-experimental medicine, neuroscience, and atomic-molecular-chemical physics).

[14] Sandor Szabo et al., *The Legacy of Hans Selye and the Origins of Stress Research: A Retrospective 75 Years After His Landmark Brief "Letter" to the Editor of* NATURE, 15 STRESS 472 (2012). *See generally* William P. Butz & Barbara Boyle Torrey, *Some Frontiers in Social Science*, 312 SCI. 1898, 1899 (2006) (naming biology as one of a half-dozen "areas of innovation" that are benefitting social science).

macrosociology, where I adapt and apply it in an attempt to understand what happens to the institution of law in a society. Broadly speaking, then, the book is about whether a concept that arose in one area of scientific endeavor is beneficial to a very different area of scientific endeavor.

1.1.1 The Concept of Societal Stress

As I use the word here, a *concept*—i.e., "an idea of a class of objects, a general notion or idea"[15]—aids the production of knowledge by connecting seemingly disparate observations and, in revealing a common feature of the observations, puts the observations in a distinct light.[16] Accordingly, just as adding a concept to the intellectual tools of an individual person can benefit the individual, adding a concept to a field of scholarship can benefit the field. To be exact, new concepts can help to make the world understandable. Concepts are thus central in a knowledge-generating enterprise, and without new concepts, the enterprise may mimic a perpetual spinning top, moving endlessly in circles and never getting ahead.

The instant book comes within macrosociology as a field of study and focuses on the concept of *societal stress* as it pertains to the content of law, i.e., the wording of the proscriptions and prescriptions that are adopted and enforced by government. The institution of law, I contend, is not a freestanding component of a modern (or, indeed, any) society,[17] and since a society is a system, the institution of law in a society does not haphazardly alter its promulgated rules for social behavior.[18] In my view, the law content of a society is, instead, due to the macro-level forces that shape the society, and it evolves in response to change in the nature, magnitude, and direction of these forces.[19] Unfortunately, the foregoing position is seldom found in the United States, where individualism is honored [20] and law content is usually

[15] 3 Oxford English Dictionary 653 (2d ed.1989) (def. 2.a. of "concept").

[16] Gerhard Schurz, *Common Cause Abduction: The Formation of Theoretical Concepts and Models in Science*, 24 Logic J. of the IGPL 494, 495–96 (2016).

[17] For evidence that this proposition applies to non-modern societies, see John Hines, *Social Structures and Social Change in Seventh-Century England: The Law Codes and Complementary Sources*, 86(233) Hist. Res. 394, 395 (2013).

[18] Larry D. Barnett, Explaining Law: Macrosociological Theory and Empirical Evidence 8–13 (2015) [hereinafter Explaining Law]. In SAIL vol. 1, *supra* note 4, at 80–86, I consider the distinction between a social activity and a non-social activity, the criteria that determine whether a particular social activity is significant to a society, and possible sources of information on the criteria that are applied in making the determination.

[19] Law in the Western world has retained rather than replaced its prevailing paradigm when the content of law has undergone modification. Geoffrey Samuel, *Have There Been Scientific Revolutions in Law?*, 11 J. Comp. L. 186, 187, 188–89, 212–13 (2016) (concluding that historically the key ideas in European law have stayed the same). That paradigms in law are stable over time may be explained by persistence of the types of societal forces responsible for law content.

[20] Explaining Law, *supra* note 18, at 191, 252–53.

considered to be a "bottom-up," individual-driven phenomenon. In my thinking, however, law content is a "top-down" phenomenon and, therefore, is fruitfully examined within a macrosociological framework. Notably, law content on key forms of social behavior displays discernible patterns in the United States, [21] and a substantial body of empirical evidence backs the conclusion that overarching sociological forces are responsible for the patterns that exist in the content of American law.[22]

In a nutshell, the present book seeks to advance our understanding of the differences that exist in what law says and does not say regarding core social activities—differences that exist between jurisdictions at a single time point as well as within a jurisdiction over time. In pursuit of its goal to understand the content of law, the book employs the concept of *societal stress*, i.e., society-level stress (or, to use a synonym, *social stress*) as the lens for studying jurisdiction and temporal differences in law. In employing the concept, the book makes six assumptions:

(1) A society, like an individual, is subject to stress;
(2) Societal stress can result from, inter alia, the advocacy or adoption of new law content;
(3) Because every society is a system and hence inclines toward equilibrium, a society will be destabilized by society-level stress;
(4) Societal destabilizations from society-level stress happen in spurts rather than gradually because such destabilizations take place when thresholds for the occurrence of stress are passed;
(5) Stress-induced destabilizations of a society will prompt the society to take steps to increase stability or at least avoid further reductions in stability; and
(6) The steps that a society takes to combat the consequences of societal stress may include maintaining or altering law content to safeguard social cohesiveness.

The foregoing assumptions, being interrelated, form a set that is the foundation for the approach to law that is taken in this book. Although the book uses the United States to illustrate its thesis, I believe that the assumptions in the set apply to all structurally complex societies that are democracies, and they may also apply to societies that are neither structurally complex nor democratically governed. The

---

Individualism differs from collectivism in four ways: Individualism posits that (i) each human being possesses an identity that is unique rather than an identity that is based on a group and (ii) all human beings have the same intrinsic worth. Additionally, individualism posits, as ideals, (iii) independence of each human being rather than interdependence among human beings and (iv) pursuit of personal goals rather than pursuit of group goals. Harry C. Triandis, *Individualism and Collectivism: Past, Present, and Future*, *in* THE HANDBOOK OF CULTURE AND PSYCHOLOGY 35, 36 (David Matsumoto ed., 2001).

[21] SAIL VOL. 1, *supra* note 4, at 161–67, 172–74 (identifying eras in U.S. Supreme Court interpretations of the national constitution).

[22] *Id.* at 91–116 (using the findings of empirical research to formulate propositions that link specific macrosociological variables to the content of law in structurally complex, democratically governed nations).

assumptions, furthermore, are not without a basis in theory. In particular, they rest on structural-functionalism theory, which is summarized in *infra* Sect. 1.2.[23]

1.1.2 The Nature of Societal Stress

The concept of societal stress is not entirely absent from social science research,[24] but it has not been extensively used in that research either. As a result, the concept has yet to be applied systematically by scholars who study law, and the core attributes of societal stress have yet to be identified. In an ideal world, of course, these attributes, which constitute the referent of the concept of societal stress, would be known before law-interested scholars tried to ascertain whether the concept is helpful in their work. However, not only are the attributes of societal stress presently unknown; unearthing the attributes faces a formidable obstacle, namely, the underlying concept of "stress" lacks a generally agreed-upon definition.[25] Still, the newness of the concept of societal stress justifies an attempt to locate the referent of the concept. Even if the attempt ends in failure, the attempt may generate curiosity about the concept and spur its application in law-relevant scholarship. A concept without an unequivocal definition can have a place in scholarship.[26] Indeed, the absence of a consensus on a definition of "stress" has not kept scholars from employing the concept of stress,[27] and employing it often.[28]

---

[23] Under the assumptions, a society is coextensive with a law-designated jurisdiction. Therefore, a law-designated jurisdiction such as the United States is deemed to have a society, and because the United States is geographically subdivided into smaller law-designated jurisdictions (i.e., states), each sub-jurisdiction has a society.

[24] See especially Louis M. Terrell, *Societal Stress, Political Instability, and Levels of Military Effort*, 15 J. Conflict Resol. 329 (1971).

[25] Lawrence E. Hinkle, Jr., *Stress and Disease: The Concept After 50 Years*, 25 Soc. Sci. & Med. 561, 561 (1987) (pointing out that the concept of stress lacks a widely accepted definition that permits identification of "when the state [of stress] exists" in individual organisms and in human societies); Paul D. Bliese et al., *Stress and Well-Being at Work: A Century of Empirical Trends Reflecting Theoretical and Societal Influences*, 102 J. Applied Psychol. 389, 390 (2017) (observing that the concept of stress has "multiple meanings"); Am. Inst. of Stress, *What is Stress?* (2022) (contending that a practicable definition of stress is impossible to formulate), https://www.stress.org/what-is-stress.

[26] Jack M. C. Kwong, *Why Concepts Can't Be Theories*, 9 Phil. Explorations 309, 310 (2006).

[27] Hinkle, *supra* note 25, at 561.

[28] An indicator that the concept of stress receives considerable attention from scientists is that the Norwegian Register for Scientific Journals, Series and Publishers lists thirteen currently published journals whose title includes the word "stress" in English or another language. The Register is online at https://kanalregister.hkdir.no/publiseringskanaler/Forside?request_locale=en (last visited Aug. 26, 2022). Additional evidence of the frequent use in science of the concept of stress is provided by Michel Le Moal, *Historical Approach and Evolution of the Stress Concept: A Personal Account*, 32 Psychoneuroendocrinology 53 (2007) (reporting that, during the last three decades, the concept of stress was referenced in over 200,000 biomedical publications).

I begin the search for the central attributes of societal stress by pointing out that the attributes must involve *society-level* stress rather than individual-level stress; must be confined to the sociological substance of society-level stress and hence exclude the sociological triggers and effects of such stress; must be measurable as a continuum that can differ in amount between societies at a single point in time as well as within a society at different points in time; and must allow a range of empirical markers of society-level stress without being so ambiguous that acceptable quantitative indicators of society-level stress cannot be devised. With these criteria in mind, I draw on and extrapolate from existing stress-relevant scholarship, and formulate three meanings of societal stress using the attributes that I identify. As will be apparent, the three meanings overlap to a not-insignificant extent. The considerable overlap in the meanings bolsters the argument that the concept of societal stress has utility in social science because it references properties that are similar to each other and hence form a set.[29] The concept, in other words, has a discernible referent. Notably, all of the three meanings are implicit in ancient Greek works that employ the term "homeostasis," i.e., "steady state," to capture a key to the human condition, and the continued existence of the idea expressed by the term supports the utility of the idea.[30]

Under the first meaning (meaning #1), society-level stress is what a society develops when, and to the degree that, it lacks the ability to accomplish an objective. The first meaning thus considers society-level stress to be an accompaniment of, and to be tied to, a shortage of a societal resource relative to a societal goal.[31] The limiting resource may be of any type—including financial, technological, or social—but society-level stress may be greater when a certain type of resource is involved than when another type of resource is involved. The goal that is an element of society-level stress presumably has a greater impact on the amount of stress when the societal importance of the goal is higher than when it is lower. The goal, of course, may vary in societal importance from one time point to another in a society, and may also vary in societal importance from one society to another.

Under the second meaning (meaning #2), society-level stress is what a society develops when, and to the degree that, it encounters a requirement that it did not anticipate and does not control, i.e., when it fails to deal with a situation or an event

[29] *See* John Gerring, *What Makes a Concept Good? A Criterial Framework for Understanding Concept Formation in the Social Sciences*, 31 Polity 357, 367 tbl. 1, 373–74 (1999) (proposing eight criteria that determine whether a concept is useful in social science; describing the criterion of "coherence" as the close relationship between the properties listed for a concept; and contending that coherence may be the all-important criterion).

[30] George P. Chrousos et al., *Introduction: The Concept of Stress and Its Historical Development*, *in* Mechanisms of Physical and Emotional Stress 3, 3, 4 (George P. Chrousos et al. eds., 1988). Stress has thus been defined as the felt presence of a threat to homeostasis, i.e., as the felt clash between forces that promote, and forces that upset, "balance, equilibrium, or harmony." *Id.* at 3, 4.

[31] *See* Terrell, *supra* note 24, at 331.

to which adaptation is necessary.[32] The second meaning, in other words, considers societal stress to be a corollary of, and to be linked to, a society-level push that calls for a society-level adjustment when the society is not expecting to make the needed adjustment and is unable at the moment to react suitably and adjust. Under the third meaning (meaning #3), stress is what a society develops when, and to the degree that, two or more structural elements of the society fit together less than perfectly and/or when an imperfect fit exists between the society and its outside environment. The third meaning, accordingly, regards societal stress as a phenomenon that occurs when a society is maladjusted, internally and/or externally, and hence operating below its optimal level.

In summary, three meanings can be formulated for the concept of societal stress. Specifically, societal stress can be seen as the society-level condition that emerges when societal wherewithal does not allow a society to reach its objectives (meaning #1), as the society-level condition that is present when a society is ineffective in dealing with demands placed on it (meaning #2), and/or as the society-level condition in which a society is maladjusted internally and/or in relation to its physical or social setting (meaning #3). Under all of these meanings, society-level stress can rise and fall in amount, can continue for either a short period or a long one, and can impel societal change as well as opposition to societal change. For aspects of social life in a society that differ between themselves in where they stand on the scale of social values in the society, societal stress is likely to be greater in amount and more persistent over time when it involves aspects that are high on the scale than when it involves aspects that are low on the scale. In short, each of the three meanings of societal stress acknowledges that societies exhibit variability in amounts of social stress, and envisions that increases in these amounts raise, linearly or nonlinearly, the pressure for and resistance to societal change. Change and opposition to change in the content of law, therefore, are more probable when this content addresses a feature of social life that is highly prized and important than when it addresses a feature that is not.

1.1.3 An Illustration of Societal Stress: Political Support for Donald J. Trump

In recent decades, the United States has experienced what has been labeled a "culture war" in the political arena, i.e., a dispute over the principles that should govern "best social practices" in government.[33] This dispute illustrates society-level stress and is

---

[32] J. M. Koolhaas et al., *Stress Revisited: A Critical Evaluation of the Stress Concept*, 35 Neuroscience & Biobehavioral Reviews 1291, 1298 (2011).

[33] Michael Barone, *Revisiting a Transformational Speech: The Culture War Scorecard*, Am. Conservative, May 30, 2018, https://www.theamericanconservative.com/articles/revisiting-a-transformational-speech-the-culture-war-scorecard. The cited article discusses a speech by Patrick

not a mirage: The existence of a "culture war" in the United States is supported by empirical data[34] and contributed to the election in 2016 of Donald J. Trump as president of the United States;[35] it is probably responsible, too, for a substantial portion of the sizeable number of votes received by Mr. Trump in his race for re-election in 2020. Notably, among all voters in the 2016 election, fully one in every 8.5 cast their ballot for Mr. Trump with the belief that the "most important factor" in choosing the president in that year was the appointment of justices to the U.-S. Supreme Court.[36] Not surprisingly, then, a key objective of the administration of President Trump was to populate the federal courts with judges whose philosophy was consistent with the philosophy of his backers, i.e., a philosophy that resists employing the judicial branch of government to try to remedy social problems.[37] Logically, this objective would have emerged from federal appeals-court rulings that struck down state-level legislation and government policy that were favorable to traditional arrangements in American social life. The rulings, by invalidating state law and policy under provisions of the federal Constitution, kept states from choosing their own path on the topics of the invalidated legislation/policy. The rulings evidently motivated many voters to support Mr. Trump, and the number of

---

Buchanan; for the full text of this speech, see Patrick Joseph Buchanan, *Culture War Speech: Address to the Republican National Convention (17 August 1992)*, Voices of Democracy: The U.S. Oratory Project, http://voicesofdemocracy.umd.edu/buchanan-culture-war-speech-speech-text.

[34] Pew Res. Ctr., The Partisan Divide on Political Values Grows Even Wider 3 (2017) (using data gathered in national surveys of adults in the United States during the years 1994 to 2017; finding that the mean difference between Democrats and Republicans in having conservative beliefs regarding ten political issues more than doubled from 1994, when the mean difference was 15 percentage points, to 2017, when the mean difference was 36 percentage points), http://www.people-press.org/2017/10/05/the-partisan-divide-on-political-values-grows-even-wider.

[35] Nazita Lajevardi & Marisa Abrajano, *How Negative Sentiment toward Muslim Americans Predicts Support for Trump in the 2016 Presidential Election*, 81 J. Pol. 296, 297, 301 (2018) (using regression to analyze data from five sample-surveys of U.S. residents; finding that, net of other factors, hostility toward Muslims was "strongly correlated with support for Trump"). The "culture war" includes enmity toward Muslims. Rhys H. Williams, *Immigration and National Identity in Obama's America: The Expansion of Culture-War Politics*, 42 Canadian Rev. Am. Stud. 322 (2012).

[36] Twenty-one percent of all voters interviewed in election-day exit polls in November 2016 stated that "supreme court appointments" were "the most important factor" in choosing between the ballot-listed candidates for president; in this group, 56 percent voted for Mr. Trump. Jane Coaston, *Polling Data Shows Republicans Turned Out for Trump in 2016 Because of the Supreme Court*, Vox, June 29, 2018, https://www.vox.com/2018/6/29/17511088/scotus-2016-election-poll-trump-republicans-kennedy-retire (last visited Aug. 27, 2022).

Therefore, $.21 \times .56 = .1176 \times 100 = 11.76$ percent of all voters in the election backed Mr. Trump because they were concerned with the types of individuals who become justices of the U.S. Supreme Court. The foregoing percentage represents one out of every 8.5 voters in the 2016 U.S. presidential election ($100 \div 11.76 = 8.5$).

[37] Hans A. von Spakovsky & Elizabeth Slattery, Heritage Found., *Commentary: The Rule of Law in Trump's First 100 Days* (2017), https://www.heritage.org/courts/commentary/the-rule-law-trumps-first-100-days (last visited Aug. 27, 2022).

such voters would have helped to affect the outcome of the 2016 election and the extent of support for Mr. Trump in the 2020 election.

In light of the emphasis placed on changing the philosophical bent of the federal judiciary, mention should be made that the Trump Administration had considerable success: The U.S. Senate confirmed three nominations made by President Trump to the Supreme Court and 54 nominations made by President Trump to the region-specific federal circuit appeals courts; only three out of the previous twelve U.-S. presidents who were in office since the end of World War II placed more judges on the Supreme Court and only four placed more judges on the region-specific circuit appeals courts.[38] These picks would have been in line with the political philosophy of Mr. Trump and, therefore, of those who voted for him.[39]

1.2 Structural-Functionalism Theory

Should one of the proposed meanings of societal stress be preferred over the others? A negative answer to the question is suggested by an early but still-influential theory in anthropology and sociology. The theory—structural functionalism—has had a "profound" impact on the social sciences[40] and "continue[s] to ramify through ... social science theorizing."[41] Structural-functionalism theory remains important in the social sciences because it captures mainstays of social life and because it more accurately portrays social life than any theory that centralizes conflict.[42] By avoiding the position that social conflict is dominant in social life, structural functionalism does not carry, let alone embrace, political agendas, and it is thereby less likely to produce subjective assessments of the social desirability of existing societal arrangements and happenings. Such agendas and assessments, which during the 1960s

38 United States Courts, Judgeship Appointments by Presidents, https://www.uscourts.gov/judges-judgeships/authorized-judgeships/judgeship-appointments-president (last visited Sept. 9, 2022). Under the U.S. Constitution, judges for the federal courts are nominated by the President; nominees take office if confirmed by the Senate. U.S. CONST. art. II, § 2.

39 U.S. presidents generally, in nominating federal-court judges, favor individuals who have a political philosophy similar to their own. Brandon Rottinghaus & Chris Nicholson, *Counting Congress In: Patterns of Success in Judicial Nomination Requests by Members of Congress to Presidents Eisenhower and Ford*, 38 AM. POL. RES. 691, 709–10 (2010); Tajuana D. Massie et al., *The Timing of Presidential Nominations to the Lower Federal Courts*, 57 POL. RES. Q. 145, 153 (2004).

40 Anthony R. Welch, *The Functionalist Tradition and Comparative Education*, 21 COMP. EDUC. 5, 5 (1985).

41 Carl Patrick Burrowes, *The Functionalist Tradition and Communication Theory* 4 (paper presented at the 1993 annual meeting of the Ass'n for Educ. in Journalism & Mass Communication).

42 Michael Meacham, *A Review of the Equality Movement: Problems and Directions for Both Sexes*, 31 GENDER ISSUES 83, 96–97 (2014).

began to displace objectivity in the scholarship of numerous sociologists,[43] have compromised the credibility of sociologists[44] and the status of their discipline within the community of sciences.[45] Political agendas have also become embedded in the law-and-society school.[46] Structural functionalism, in short, is a potential antidote to the pursuit of political ends that has taken hold in sociology[47] and cognate social-science fields. It may, therefore, help to build confidence in these disciplines.

Because structural functionalism theory remains useful to sociology, it can contribute to the conclusions reached by sociologists in their scholarship on law. Accordingly, I sketch the theory here. Notably, all of the three meanings of societal stress that I have proposed are compatible with the theory and, as *infra* Sect. 1.3 shows, are expressed in U.S. law. Among these three meanings, accordingly, one meaning is not clearly superior to the others in scholarship that focuses on the macrosociology of law.

What are the core teachings of structural functionalism?[48] As its name implies, structural functionalism focuses on the organizational constituents (i.e., structure) of a society and on the service (i.e., function) that each constituent performs for a society. According to structural-functionalism theory, the organizational constituents of a society are neither randomly present nor without roles in the society; instead, the constituents are connected to one another, normally work to fulfill

---

[43] Seymour Martin Lipset, *The State of American Sociology*, 9 SOCIOL. FORUM 199, 207 (1994).

[44] Members of the American Sociological Association, in a sample survey conducted in 2003, were found to be overwhelmingly "left wing" in political orientation. Daniel B. Klein & Charlotta Stern, *Sociology and Classical Liberalism*, 11 INDEP. REV. 37, 42, 46, 51 (2006). Sociologists and their scholarship are likely viewed as less credible because they are dominated by an ideology of political liberalism. Nathan Cofnas et al., *Does Activism in Social Science Explain Conservatives' Distrust of Scientists?*, 49 AM. SOCIOLOGIST 135, 139, 140, 145–46 (2018) (listing examples in which individual scientists and professional associations of scientists mischaracterized research findings in presentations to law-writing bodies so that the findings would support a politically liberal agenda; and hypothesizing that this liberal bias has caused politically conservative Americans to discount conclusions drawn by scientists). Notably, confidence in science declined between the mid-1970s and 2010 among politically conservative U.S. adults but not among politically liberal or moderate U.S. adults. Gordon Gauchat, *Politicization of Science in the Public Sphere: A Study of Public Trust in the United States, 1974 to 2010*, 77 AM. SOCIOL. REV. 167, 172, 175 fig. 1, 176–77 & tbl. 2, 182 (2012).

[45] EXPLAINING LAW, *supra* note 18, at 246–47.

[46] SAIL VOL. 1, *supra* note 4, at 8–10.

[47] Jonathan H. Turner, *"Is Public Sociology Such a Good Idea?"*, 36 AM. SOCIOLOGIST 27 (2005). *Accord*, Lipset, *supra* note 43, at 207, 212–13, 215–16 (contending that the discipline of sociology is being threatened by severe internal divisions that have accompanied an increasing emphasis on political activity for the purpose of promoting social justice). The politicization of sociologists has been described as the reason that sociology is in a "parlous state" and is "a self-destructive discipline." Lipset, *supra* note 43, at 199, 218. Politicization has been and remains prominent among academic sociologists. Ilana Redstone Akresh, *Departmental and Disciplinary Divisions in Sociology: Responses from Departmental Executive Officers*, 48 AM. SOCIOLOGIST 541, 557–58 (2017).

[48] The key propositions of structural-functionalism theory are identified and discussed in Ronald Fletcher, *Functionalism as a Social Theory*, 4 SOCIOL. REV. 31, 33, 38, 43 (1956).

societal needs,[49] and in their operation tend to complement one another. In the eyes of structural functionalism, then, a society is a self-maintaining system and inclined to avoid or minimize internal strife, i.e., a society favors "homeostasis, or equilibrium," and thus usually remains "'in some sort of steady state, either a static or moving stability . . . .'"[50] A society is in a steady state when, over a lengthy period, it either stays unchanged, or changes in a given direction at a pace or by an amount that is roughly constant over time. A likely reason for the existence of a steady state is that a society, being a system, contains feedback loops.[51]

The proposition that a human society normally is in a steady state and acts when necessary to increase its stability should not be surprising, because a society, being a system, requires a relatively high degree of cohesion among its organizational constituents (system integration) and among its people (social integration).[52] A society thus changes in order to keep or raise the level of internal cohesiveness that the society must have in order to survive and solve problems.[53] The predilection of a society for cohesiveness is illustrated by mergers of local governmental units in a nation. When such mergers happen, they are built on social ties rather than on political or economic similarities between merging jurisdictions.[54] Otherwise stated, mergers of local governments occur as they do because, in preserving social connections, they are responding to the societal push for cohesiveness.

What qualifies as an organizational constituent of a society? Under structural functionalism, a constituent is a social institution,[55] i.e., a recognizable pattern of behavior that is prominent in, important to, and valued by the society in which it

---

[49] Societal need, as I formulate the concept, is discussed in EXPLAINING LAW, *supra* note 18, at 96–98; LARRY D. BARNETT, THE PLACE OF LAW: THE ROLE AND LIMITS OF LAW IN SOCIETY 302–07 (2011) [hereinafter THE PLACE OF LAW].

[50] Jenni McIntyre, *The Structural-Functional Approach to Family Study*, in EMERGING CONCEPTUAL FRAMEWORKS IN FAMILY ANALYSIS: WITH A NEW INTRODUCTION FOR THE 1980S, at 52, 59 (F. Ivan Nye & Felix M. Berardo eds., 1981). *See also* S. N. Eisenstadt, *Functional Analysis in Anthropology and Sociology: An Interpretative Essay*, 19 ANN. REV. ANTHROPOLOGY 243, 244 (1990) (observing that societies are conceptualized by structural-functionalism as "bounded systems with certain basic 'societal prerequisites' in the absence of which they would disintegrate").

[51] Sylvia Walby, *Complexity Theory, Systems Theory, and Multiple Intersecting Social Inequalities,* 37 PHIL. SOC. SCI. 449, 454–55, 463–64 (2007) (treating societies as systems, and noting that a system has feedback loops). For evidence of societal steady states resulting from feedback loops, see Giselinde Kuipers, *How National Institutions Mediate the Global: Screen Translation, Institutional Interdependencies, and the Production of National Difference in Four European Countries*, 80 AM. SOCIOL. REV. 985, 987, 1001, 1003, 1008 (2015).

[52] David Lockwood, *Social Integration and System Integration*, *in* EXPLORATIONS IN SOCIAL CHANGE 244 (George K. Zollschan & Walter Hirsch eds., 1964).

[53] Robert G. Perrin, *The Functionalist Theory of Change Revisited*, 16 PAC. SOCIOL. REV. 47, 55 (1973).

[54] Yosef Bhatti & Kasper M. Hansen, *Who 'Marries' Whom? The Influence of Societal Connectedness, Economic and Political Homogeneity, and Population Size on Jurisdictional Consolidations*, 50 EUR. J. POL. RES. 212, 226 tbl. 4, 228 (2011).

[55] Fletcher, *supra* note 48, at 33.

exists.[56] An unmistakable institution in a nation is government and the rules (i.e., law) that government promulgates. Because the institutions of a society are interlocked and affect one another, macro-level conditions and happenings outside the institution of government/law will be detectible inside the institution of government/law.[57] There should, then, be no surprise that all of the meanings of societal stress that were proposed in *supra* Sect. 1.1.2 are embedded in opinions that courts in the United States have written to make known the rationales that they employed when deciding cases.

For sociologists, the rationales that are explicitly recorded in court opinions not-infrequently offer valuable insights into the societal underpinnings of law. A key activity of courts in the United States is to remove uncertainties in the wording of constitutions and statutes. This activity occurs in the course of settling disputes, and when a dispute involves an uncertainty in a provision of a constitution or a statute, the judiciary through its opinions can reveal the ideas on which the provision is based.[58] At the same time, rulings by courts in the United States, by creating a "common law," permit law content in the country to accommodate new circumstances while continuing to embody the values of American society[59] and reinforce the trust of participants in their society.[60] In the words of the Supreme Court of Michigan, "[t]he common law is . . . incremental in adapting to society's changing circumstances, developing gradually to reflect our policies, customs, norms, and values."[61] The common law produced by courts, therefore, both benefits the societal system by responding to its needs and helps in the search for the societal underpinnings of law.

---

[56] EXPLAINING LAW, *supra* note 18, at 12 n.21, 154 n.27, 191.

[57] An illustration is furnished by the case of Marbury v. Madison, 5 U.S. (1 Cranch) 137 (1803). In *Marbury*, the U.S. Supreme Court construed the national Constitution and concluded that the Constitution empowers the federal judiciary to decide whether an action by government complies with the provisions of the Constitution. *Marbury* is valuable as an example of the influence that society has on law because its interpretation of the Constitution is generally thought to be the most consequential of all such interpretations that the Court has rendered. Davison M. Douglas, *The Rhetorical Uses of Marbury v. Madison: The Emergence of a "Great Case"*, 38 WAKE FOREST L. REV. 375, 376 & n.2, 378, 380 (2003). Notably, judicial review of the constitutionality of government action was a widely accepted idea in the United States before *Marbury* was decided. Miguel Schor, *The Strange Case of* MARBURY *and* LOCHNER *in the Constitutional Imagination*, 87 TEX. L. REV. 1463, 1467–69 (2009).

[58] *See* SAIL VOL. 1, *supra* note 4, at 14–15 (discussing the reasons for "the sociological richness" of U.S. Supreme Court opinions that interpret provisions of the U.S. Constitution).

[59] Frank Partnoy, *Synthetic Common Law*, 53 U. KAN. L. REV. 281, 297–98 (2005). *Accord*, Robert B. Thompson, *Piercing the Veil: Is the Common Law the Problem?*, 37 CONN. L. REV. 619, 623 (2005).

[60] John A. Makdisi, *The Islamic Origins of the Common Law*, 77 N.C. L. REV. 1635, 1700 (1999). For a discussion of the sociological importance of trust in government and of beliefs in the fairness of law, see THE PLACE OF LAW, *supra* note 49, at 61–63, 404, 443 n.89.

[61] Rafaeli, LLC v. Oakland County, 952 N.W.2d 434, 460 (Mich. 2020).

1.3 The Expression in Law of the Concept of Societal Stress

Let me turn now to court opinions that express the central ideas in the three meanings that I have proposed for societal stress. The appearance of the meanings in the reasoning of judges is evidence that the concept of societal stress is pertinent to the account that macrosociology can supply of the content of law: Court opinions would not incorporate the meanings unless societal stress played a role in law. While the opinions that I cite are from courts in the United States, judges in other nations, through their opinions, may be able to shed light on the macrosociological origins of the law content in those nations,[62] especially when the nations are similar to the United States in social structure and culture.

Of particular note, the reasoning in the opinions that I cover in Sect. 1.3 is consistent with structural-functionalism theory. The United States, as evidenced by the wording of the preamble to its national Constitution,[63] is grounded on the philosophy that the population and government of the country are committed to furthering the commonweal. American courts manifest this philosophy because they replace law that is hampering social life and causing social injustice:

> [T]he function of law is to help solve social problems. Law is life; it deals with the relationship of human beings and must concern itself with everyday problems whether they are labeled social or legal. It does no good to verbalize about the court's inherent power to update the law and then not act when there is a need crying for satisfaction.[64]

The above passage underscores a key sociological function of law as an institution, viz., to assist society in meeting its needs.[65] In the words of another court, a society employs law "to . . . sustain its moral equilibrium."[66] The content of U.S. law, therefore, can be expected to behave in accordance with structural-functionalism theory, and can be understood using this theory and its concepts.

---

[62] *See* Chisuse v. Director-General, Dep't of Home Affairs, 2020 SACLR LEXIS 23 ¶18 (S. Afr.), where the Constitutional Court of South Africa wrote that the "duty [of courts] to provide reasons [when they hold legislation to be unconstitutional] is a vital strut to the Judiciary's legitimacy in our constitutional democracy, which is based on a culture of justification."

[63] U.S. Const. pmbl. ("We the People of the United States, in Order to form a more perfect Union, establish Justice, insure domestic Tranquility, provide for the common defence, promote the general Welfare, and secure the Blessings of Liberty to ourselves and our Posterity, do ordain and establish this Constitution for the United States of America").

[64] Hutchens v. Hankins, 303 S.E.2d 584, 598 (N.C. Ct. App. 1983) (quoting Garcia v. Hargrove, 176 N.W.2d 566, 573 (Wis. 1970)) (Hallows, C.J., dissenting), *review denied*, 305 S.E.2d 734 (N.C. 1983). *Accord*, People v. Dist. Ct. of San Juan, 60 D.P.R. 222 (P.R. 1942) (motion for rehearing) ("The law seeks to be practical in its functioning and to discard everything that might be useless and that might unnecessarily hinder its primary purpose, which is the furtherance of justice.")

[65] David Rabban, *The Historiography of the Common Law*, 28 Law & Soc. Inquiry 1161, 1183–84 (2003).

[66] State v. Peck, 773 N.W.2d 768, 782 (Minn. 2009).

Meaning #1 describes societal stress as the society-level condition that develops when the society cannot reach one or more of its goals with what it has available for achieving the goal(s). Goals differ in the degree to which they are important to a society, of course, and all else being equal, greater society-level stress presumably stems from an unattained goal that is more socially important than from an unattained goal that is less socially important. Among the goals of a society, justice occupies a high rank because, as one court has written, a society has a "deep-seated need to see justice triumphant."[67] Meaning #1 is thus implicitly present in passages of court opinions that acknowledge the achievement of justice as essential to a society and that condemn societal arrangements and events that do not provide social fairness:

- "Our [judicial] system relies for its validity on the confidence of society; without a belief by the people that the system is just and impartial, the concept of the rule of law cannot survive."[68]
- "The purpose and function of law is to resolve disputes and to facilitate a structure for the organization of a just society—in a word, to provide justice."[69]
- "The highest standards of public morality and the inexorable requirements of good conscience rest upon the Government in its dealings with its citizens. … The Government must be neither reluctant nor evasive in correcting wrongs inflicted upon a citizen. By so doing it demonstrates to the people of the world the fairness and justice of our form of society and law. The government need not sheepishly confess error; it must be stalwart and forthright in its recognition of injustice. By so doing, faith and confidence in our system of law will be maintained."[70]
- When prosecuting a defendant for an alleged commission of a crime, "[t]he United States Attorney is the representative not of an ordinary party to a controversy, but of a sovereignty whose obligation to govern impartially is as

[67] United States v. Gupta, 904 F. Supp.2d 349, 355 (S.D. N.Y. 2012), *aff'd*, 747 F.3d 111 (2d Cir. 2014), *cert. denied*, 575 U.S. 962 (2015).

[68] People ex rel. Clancy v. Super. Ct., 705 P.2d 347, 351 (Cal. 1985). *Accord*, State v. Garcia-Ongay, 490 P.3d 1, 9 (Idaho 2021) (referencing "the Judiciary's mission to provide access to justice through the timely, fair, and impartial resolution of cases"); Williams v. Pennsylvania, 136 S. Ct. 1899, 1909 (2016) ("Both the appearance and reality of impartial justice are necessary to the public legitimacy of judicial pronouncements and thus to the rule of law itself"). *See also* Planned Parenthood of Southeastern Pennsylvania v. Casey, 505 U.S. 833, 865 (1992), where the U.-S. Supreme Court wrote that its "power lies … in its legitimacy, a product of substance and perception that shows itself in the people's acceptance of the Judiciary as fit to determine what the Nation's law means and to declare what it demands."

[69] Rubanick v. Witco Chem. Corp., 593 A.2d 733, 741 (N.J. 1991) (quoting Howard T. Markey, *Needed: A Judicial Welcome for Technology — Star Wars or Stare Decisis?*, 79 F.R.D. 209, 210 (1978)).

[70] Abo v. Clark, 77 F. Supp. 806, 811 (N.D. Cal. 1948), *modified on other grounds*, 186 F.2d. 766 (9th Cir.), *cert. denied*, 342 U.S. 832 (1951).

compelling as its obligation to govern at all; and whose interest, therefore, in a criminal prosecution is not that it shall win a case, but that justice shall be done."[71]

Meaning #2 explicates societal stress as the society-level condition that results from a situation or event to which the affected society must react. For such situations and events—i.e., situations and events that are unexpected and (as yet) uncontrolled—the amount of societal stress is likely to be a function of the degree to which an effective society-level reaction is necessary but does not occur. Meaning #2 is implicitly recognized by courts in the following opinions:

- "We live in a changing world where the law must respond to the demands of a modern society."[72]
- "The common law is not static, but is a dynamic and growing thing and its rules arise from the application of reason to the changing conditions of society. Flexibility and capacity for growth and adaption is its peculiar boast and excellence."[73]
- "[T]he common law adapts to changing circumstances to advance notions of fair play and equity."[74]
- "The distinguishing characteristic of the common law is that it expands or contracts to meet the changing conditions of the social and economic order .... The law is dynamic; it must approach certainty, but it can never stand still. It is of all things an instrument of expanding life, and its principles must be so applied as to bring within its compass new situations that constantly develop in the progress of changing times and conditions[.]"[75]

Meaning #3 asserts that societal stress is the society-level condition that involves an inadequate fit by the society to its internal circumstances or its external environment. Society-level stress is likely to increase, ceteris paribus, as the inadequacy of the fit intensifies and persists. Among the internal circumstances of a society to which the society and its law must adapt are change in cultural ideals and social-

---

[71] Berger v. United States, 295 U.S. 78, 88 (1935).

[72] John Donnelly & Sons, Inc. v. Outdoor Advertising Bd., 339 N.E.2d 709, 717 (Mass. 1975).

[73] McCormack v. Oklahoma Publ'g Co., 613 P.2d 737, 740 (Okla. 1980) (reproducing the second sentence from Hurtado v. California, 110 U.S. 516, 530 (1884)). *See also* Matos-Rivera v. Flav-O-Rich, 876 F. Supp. 373, 377 (D. P.R. 1995) (the common law "permits the law to evolve and adapt to the marked political, economic, and social changes in a society"); Spinelli v. Gaughan, 12 F.3d 853, 856 (9th Cir. 1993) ("the common law is not static. By its nature, it adapts to changing circumstances ... ."). See the text that accompanies *supra* notes 58 to 60 for a definition and explanation of the "common law."

[74] State ex rel. Schmidt v. Nye, 440 P.2d 585, 589 (Kan. Ct. App. 2019). *Accord*, Power Marketing Direct, Inc. v. Foster, 938 So.2d 662, 675 (La. 2006) (court rulings must be "in keeping with ... our notions of fair play and equity"); Hill v. Sibley Mem'l Hosp., 108 F. Supp. 739, 741 (D. D.C. 1952) ("Courts should ever be alert to widen the circle of justice to conform to the changing needs and conditions of society").

[75] Chamberlain v. Chamberlain, 155 So. 136, 137 (Fla. 1934).

economic problems. Meaning #3 is thus illustrated by the following passages in court opinions:

- "To enforce the Constitution's protection of human dignity, this Court [the U.S. Supreme Court] looks to the evolving standards of decency that mark the progress of a maturing society."[76]
- Law "is not static, but is endowed with vitality and a capacity to grow. It never becomes permanently crystallized but changes and adjusts itself from time to time to new developments in social and economic life in order to meet the changing needs of society. The law must have some flexibility. In a sense it must be behind the times, because before the law changes or develops new rules, the conditions requiring the modifications must acquire some degree of permanency."[77]
- During the 1930s, when the United States faced "baffling economic and sociological problems growing out of a nation-wide depression," government at both the federal level and the state level utilized legislation and policy "to avert catyclysmic [sic] changes which were thought to threaten the equilibrium and tranquility of our society."[78]

To summarize, the three formulations of the concept of societal stress[79] are recognizable in U.S. common law, and they can probably be found in law documents of other nations that, like the United States, are structurally complex and democratically governed. However, the presence of the concept in the law of societies does not end our inquiry. Instead, it leads to another question: Can we compare the amount of societal stress in two or more societies at a single time point and in a single society at two or more time points? The question requires one or more quantitative indicators of societal stress. In Sect. 1.4, to which I turn next, I consider empirical indicators that potentially manifest society-level stress and that may permit the measurement of differences in the amount of such stress between societies and between points in time within a society.

---

[76] Hall v. Florida, 572 U.S. 701, 708 (2014) (internal quotation marks omitted). *See* Michael Buchhandler-Raphael, *Drugs, Dignity, and Danger: Human Dignity as a Constitutional Constraint to Limited Overcriminalization*, 80 Tenn. L. Rev. 291, 296 (2013) (describing human dignity as "a recurrent theme" in U.S. Supreme Court interpretations of the national Constitution). Approval of the notion of human dignity first appeared in a majority opinion of the U.S. Supreme Court in January 1952. Rochin v. California, 342 U.S. 165, 174 (1952).

[77] Belt v. Hamilton Nat. Bank, 108 F. Supp. 689, 690 (D. D.C. 1952), *aff'd*, 210 F.2d 706 (D.C. Cir. 1953). *See also* Arwine v. Bannan, 346 F.2d 458, 469 (6th Cir. 1965) ("a necessary and proper evolution of the living law [is] to meet the changing needs of society" (quoting Cameron v. State, 112 So.2d 864, 873 (Fla. Dist. Ct. App. 1959)), *cert. denied*, 382 U.S. 882 (1965); Merit Oil Co. v. Dir. of Div. of Necessaries of Life, 65 N.E.2d 529, 532 (Mass. 1946) ("The field for the legitimate exercise of the police power [by the legislature] is coextensive with the changing needs of society"); Tuttle v. Buck, 119 N.W. 946, 947 (Minn. 1909) ("It must be remembered that the common law . . . has been determined by the social needs of the community which it governs. . . . Manifestly it must change as society changes . . . .").

[78] Wood v. Lovett, 313 U.S. 362, 372, 376 (1941) (Black, J., dissenting).

[79] See the paragraphs accompanying *supra* notes 30 to 32.

1.4 Empirical Indicators of Societal Stress

Concepts are vital in every field of scholarship, including science. They are the ingredients of theory,[80] and theory is the vehicle that allows scientists to achieve the ultimate goals of the scientific enterprise, namely, to explain what already exists and predict what will exist in the future. The concept of mass has thus been helpful to physics as a science,[81] and the concept of societal stress may advance macrosociology as a science. Nonetheless, a concept by itself does not explain or predict. As pointed out earlier, a concept is a category of phenomena, and its role in scholarly work is to bring together multiple phenomena that on the surface are disparate in character but share a nonobvious, yet identifiable, attribute.[82] This attribute is the referent of the concept, and when concepts are put into an "if–then" statement that links an earlier-in-time conceptualized attribute to a later-in-time conceptualized attribute, explanation and prediction become possible—the earlier-in-time attribute explains and predicts the later-in-time attribute.[83] Since "if-then" statements comprise formal theory, concepts are the building blocks for and the components of theory in science. It is through concepts, therefore, that science is able to explain and predict.

A concept, however, must be measured if it is to be useful to scientists. Since the referent of a concept is an identifiable attribute that is an abstraction from what the concept encompasses, the referent is not itself observable and hence is not itself measurable. To measure the referent of a concept, scientists must use an indicator that logically captures the essence of the referent and empirically gauges either the amount of the referent (if the referent varies quantitatively) or the condition of the referent (if the referent varies qualitatively).[84] An indicator, in other words, is an instrument for a concept. In social science, an indicator that is employed for different historical eras must be measurable in each era,[85] and in the case of research that covers two or more societies, an indicator must be measurable in each society. Social science studies of the states of the United States must thus have empirical data for indicators in every state.

[80] Gerring, *supra* note 29, at 381.

[81] Max Jammer, Concepts of Mass in Classical and Modern Physics 2–3 (Dover Pubs. 1997) (1961).

[82] See the text accompanying *supra* notes 15 & 16.

[83] *See* Victor Gijsbers, *Understanding, Explanation, and Unification*, 44 Stud. Hist. & Phil. Sci. Pt. A 516, 521 (2013) (recognizing two types of understanding, namely, (i) understanding from awareness that a set of phenomena share at least one characteristic and thus form a category; and (ii) understanding from awareness that a set of phenomena form at least one cause-effect sequence).

[84] For an indicator to capture the amount of the referent of a concept, it must be measured with an ordinal scale, an interval scale, or a ratio scale. An indicator captures the condition of the referent of a concept when it is measured with a nominal scale. Scale levels are described in Larry D. Barnett, Societal Agents in Law: Quantitative Research 6 (2019) [hereinafter SAIL vol. 2].

[85] Kenneth C. Land & Alex C. Michalos, *Fifty Years After the Social Indicators Movement: Has the Promise Been Fulfilled?*, 135 Soc. Indicators Res. 835, 861–62 (2018).

The above discussion presupposes, of course, that an indicator has been chosen for a concept. What should determine, or at least significantly contribute to, this choice? The question takes us to theory, because the choice of an indicator for a concept ought to be guided by theory that is pertinent to the concept.[86] In this regard, however, the concept and possible indicators of society-level stress face two obstacles—the connection between theory and indicators is undeveloped in sociology,[87] and macrosociology has yet to build a sizeable body of theory on society-level stress and its relationship to law content. The situation in macrosociology should not be surprising since the macrosociology of law as a field of study is in an early stage of development. Consequently, a choice of indicators to measure societal stress is unavoidably tentative, and extensive testing of specific potential indicators of society-level stress will be required before any indicator achieves a secure place in the macrosociology of law.

Let me take a step in the search for useful indicators of society-level stress by proposing three possible quantifiable indicators. I consider these possibilities to be generic indicators in the sense that each may be useful for a range of societal settings and for a range of social forms. Readers should keep in mind, however, that the indicators named do not constitute a final or exhaustive list; indeed, one or all of the named indicators may eventually be discarded and replaced by other indicators. In addition, readers should note that all of the indicators on my list involve the removal of people from, or the addition of people to, a population. Other processes can undoubtedly furnish indicators of societal stress, but on logical grounds, a process that takes current participants out of social arrangements or puts new participants into social arrangements has the potential to be disruptive, with the probability and severity of disruption becoming greater as the process grows in magnitude and persists over time. Each of the indicators that I propose, accordingly, is consistent on its face with the idea of societal stress.

A caution is necessary at this point. Specifically, theorists and researchers in the macrosociology of law will have to settle on the exact manner in which the indicators should be used. A given indicator can differ between two or more jurisdictions at one point in time and can differ in one jurisdiction at two or more points in time. With a quantitative indicator, cross-jurisdiction comparisons and cross-time comparisons will thus be made, but *how* the comparisons should be done will have to be decided. The most useful comparisons will probably be based on (1) the absolute difference between absolute amounts, i.e., ($amount_1 - amount_2$), and/or (2) the relative difference between absolute amounts, i.e., ($amount_1 \div amount_2$). Empirical research will be necessary to ascertain the best way to compare indicator amounts across jurisdictions and across time, and ascertain the way(s) that is (are) suitable for a specific indicator and/or a specific law topic. The possibility cannot be dismissed that a particular kind of comparison, while appropriate for one indicator, will be

---

[86] Ivar Frønes, *Theorizing Indicators: On Indicators, Signs and Trends*, 83 Soc. Indicators Res. 5, 6, 13, 19–20 (2007).

[87] Land & Michalos, *supra* note 85, at 861.

inappropriate for another indicator and that a particular kind of comparison, while appropriate for one law topic, will be inappropriate for another law topic.

Let me turn to the data for the indicators, which are discussed in reference to the United States because of my familiarity with American society and sources of data on that society. I assume, however, that each indicator will be useful for all nations that, like the United States, are structurally complex and democratically governed; each indicator is also assumed to be useful for all U.S. states. These assumptions will, of course, have to be empirically tested to determine whether they are warranted.

Three quantifiable indicators, I believe, should be considered for the concept of society-level stress.[88] Each indicator is expressed in rates rather than raw numbers, and its magnitude can thus be compared across jurisdictions and across time.

1.4.1 Rate of Incarceration for Crime

In its broadest construction, the incarceration rate for crime covers inmates of the prisons and jails of every level of government in the United States. The numerator of the rate consists of the number of persons who, at a given point in time, are in the custody of a government (federal, state, or local) for an alleged or proven crime; the denominator of the rate is the numerical size of the resident population of the applicable jurisdiction at the same point in time. The rate is measured as the number of persons in custody per 100,000 residents. Data on the incarceration rate in the United States start in the middle of the nineteenth century.[89]

---

[88] Immigration is not suggested as an indicator for two reasons. First, total immigration includes unlawful immigration as well as lawful immigration. However, the scale of unlawful immigration into the United States during recent decades can be estimated just roughly, and over longer periods of time is unknown. See notes 37 and 38, the text that accompanies them, and the Appendix in Chap. 1 of LARRY D. BARNETT, DEMOGRAPHY AND THE ANTHROPOCENE (2021) [hereinafter DEMOGRAPHY AND THE ANTHROPOCENE]. A potential alternative to immigration is the presence in the total U.S. population of individuals who were born outside the United States. However, estimates of foreign-born persons exhibit considerable variation over time, and the estimates can be highly inaccurate at certain times. Jennifer Van Hook et al., *Recent Trends in Coverage of the Mexican-Born Population of the United States: Results from Applying Multiple Methods Across Time*, 51 DEMOGRAPHY 699, 719–20 (2014).

Second, if the criterion for choosing an indicator of societal stress is the movement of people into and out of a population, immigration should be an indicator only if emigration, too, is an indicator. In the alternative, immigration and emigration should be combined into a single indicator, viz., net immigration. Unfortunately, data are severely limited regarding the number of resident U.S. citizens and U.S.-resident non-citizens who emigrate from the United States each year. *See* LAURA B. SHRESTHA & ELAYNE J. HEISLER, CONG. RES. SERV., THE CHANGING DEMOGRAPHIC PROFILE OF THE UNITED STATES 11 (2011) (pointing out that, in 1957, "methodological difficulties" ended the gathering of data on emigration from the United States), https://crsreports.congress.gov/.

[89] Estimates of incarceration rates in the United States are available in:

What warrants the use of crime-incarceration rates as an indicator of society-level stress? At least two justifications can be advanced. The first is that incarceration for crime, by taking the incarcerated individuals out of their physical environment, disrupts the social life of the persons with whom the incarcerated individuals were interacting. The second justification arises from quantitative research on the relationship between the crime-incarceration rate and the crime rate. Although incarceration for crime is on the surface entwined with crime—incarceration for crime presumes the prior occurrence of crime—the incarceration rate has been found to be related to the violent-crime rate at only some points in time rather than at all points in time,[90] and is not, in the long run, a function of the property-crime rate.[91] Moreover, with a constant crime rate, the incarceration rate in a population can rise or fall in response to change in the prevalence of persons in the population who have in the past been convicted of felonies.[92] Because the incarceration rate for crime is not invariably tied to the rate of crime, the two rates have no necessary connection and are separate phenomena that can operate independently of one another. Since the crime-incarceration rate stands on its own and is comfortably within the meaning of the concept of societal stress, it is a plausible indicator of such stress.

- Margaret Werner Cahalan & Lee Anne Parsons, Historical Corrections Statistics in the United States, 1850–1984, at 30 tbl. 3-3, 32 tbl. 3-4, 77 tbl. 4-2 (NCJ–102529) (1986), https://www.bjs.gov/content/pub/pdf/hcsus5084.pdf.
- Bureau of Just. Stat., Bulletin: State and Federal Prisoners, 1925-85, at 2 tbl. 1 (NCJ-102494) (1986) (covering inmates of state and federal prisons; omitting inmates of local-government jails) https://www.ncjrs.gov/pdffiles1/Digitization/102494NCJRS.pdf.

Annual incarceration rates after the period covered in the preceding sources are published in the yearly *Prisoners Series* of the U.S. Bureau of Justice Statistics; the publications are available online at https://www.bjs.gov/index.cfm?ty=pbse&sid=40.

See also Patrick A. Langan et al., Bureau of Just. Stat., Historical Statistics on Prisoners in State and Federal Institutions, Yearend 1925-1986, at 5–13 tbl. 1 (reporting yearly numbers of inmates in state and federal prisons) (NCJ-111098) (1988), https://www.bjs.gov/index.cfm?ty=pbdetail&iid=3745.

[90] Michael C. Campbell et al., *Historical Contingencies and the Evolving Importance of Race, Violent Crime, and Region in Explaining Mass Incarceration in the United States*, 53 Criminology 180, 188–89, 194–95 & tbl. 2 (model 2), 199 (2015); Michael C. Campbell & Matt Vogel, *The Demographic Divide: Population Dynamics, Race and the Rise of Mass Incarceration in the United States*, 21 Punishment & Soc'y 47, 55, 59 tbl. 2, 61 tbl. 4 (2019). As measured in these studies, violent crime was limited to assault, homicide, rape, and robbery. Campbell et al., *supra*, at 191; Campbell & Vogel, *supra,* at 57.

[91] William Spelman, *Crime, Cash, and Limited Options: Explaining the Prison Boom*, 8 Criminology & Pub. Pol'y 29, 32 tbl. 1, 34–35, 37–39 tbl. 2, 56–58 tbl. 4 (2009).

[92] Ryan D. King, *Cumulative Impact: Why Prison Sentences Have Increased*, 57 Criminology 157, 162–64, 173 (2019).

1.4.2 Suicide Rate

Suicide—which is defined in the United States as "[d]eath caused by self-directed injurious behavior with any intent to die as a result of the behavior"[93]—has proven to be an empirically troublesome subject for epidemiologists and demographers who study causes of mortality. Accurate data on the incidence of suicide have been hard to compile, with analyses of suicide frequencies in government-published vital statistics concluding that the frequencies in these publications are undercounts.[94] At a particular time point and in a particular jurisdiction, therefore, the number of suicides per 100,000 population, i.e., the suicide rate, is higher than that reported in official vital statistics. Not surprisingly, incorrect data on suicide can create a problem for studies in the macrosociology of law. Specifically, the extent to which suicide is underreported may differ at one time point between jurisdictions and/or over time within a jurisdiction.[95] If these differences exist and are sizeable, wrong conclusions will be drawn from the suicide rate as an indicator of the amount of societal stress. The suicide rate as a measure of society-level stress can, in short, be problematic.

Nonetheless, the limitations of suicide-rate data should not be an automatic bar to relying on the data for studies of societal stress. One reason for using the suicide rate in these studies is that the phenomenon of suicide logically fits under the concept of society-level stress. The rate of suicide, simply put, intuitively makes sense as an indicator of the amount of societal stress. A second and closely related reason for considering the suicide rate as a gauge of societal stress is that suicide has a strong empirical tie to social life. Even though a suicide results from the action of an individual human being, the *rate* of suicide responds to changes in jurisdiction-level attributes and is not simply a function of individual-level attributes. For example, age-standardized suicide rates among men and women in western European nations

---

[93] Alex E. Crosby et al., Centers for Disease Control & Prevention, Self-Directed Violence Surveillance: Uniform Definitions and Recommended Data Elements 23 (2011), https://stacks.cdc.gov/view/cdc/11997.

[94] Ingvild Maria Tøllefsen et al., *The Reliability of Suicide Statistics: A Systematic Review*, 12(9) BMC Psychiatry, Feb. 14, 2012, at 1, 2, 8–9 & tbl. 2. For additional evidence that government-reported data on suicide understate the incidence of suicide, see: Shelly S. Bakst et al., *The Accuracy of Suicide Statistics: Are True Suicide Deaths Misclassified?*, 51 Soc. Psychiatry & Psychiatric Epidemiology 115, 115–16, 121 (2016) (analyzing data for 2005 and 2008 on cause of death in Tel Aviv, Israel); Alexandra Tragaki & Konstantinos Lenos, *Suicide Rates in Greece: Comparing Mortality Data with Police Reporting Statistics and Investigating Recent Trends*, 51 Finnish Y.B. of Population Res. 61, 63, (2017) (comparing vital statistics records and police records on suicides in Greece from 1990 onward).

[95] *See* David P. Phillips & Todd E. Ruth, *Adequacy of Official Suicide Statistics for Scientific Research and Public Policy*, 23 Suicide & Life-Threatening Behav. 307, 309, 315 tbl. 1, 317–18 (1993) (using computerized death certificates to study deaths in California that occurred during the period 1966–1990; concluding that erroneous assignments of suicides to other causes of death differed between California counties dichotomized on the basis of their population and varied in extent across five-year time periods for the state as a whole.)

have been found to vary inversely with the nation-level percent change in gross domestic product per person and with the nation-level ratio of children below age five to women 15–49 years old.[96] Suicide rates in these countries, in other words, go down when national economic growth and the presence of children go up. Suicide, therefore, is part of the society in which it occurs and unavoidably a societal phenomenon.

However, the above are not the only reasons that macrosociologists who focus on law content should think about including the suicide rate as an indicator of society-level stress. An additional reason is that researchers are not confined to just one indicator of such stress. They have the option of employing the suicide rate along with another indicator (or other indicators) of society-level stress. Indeed, the credibility of conclusions that involve societal stress will be bolstered by consistent results from more than one indicator. A consideration in this regard, however, is that the rate of suicide differs between demographic groups. For example, the suicide rate for men is not the same as the suicide rate for women, and variation over time in this sex differential correlates dissimilarly with the suicide rate for each sex—the correlation of the sex differential with the suicide rate for men is positive (albeit weak), and the correlation of the sex differential with the suicide rate for women is negative.[97] The suicide rate thus does not behave identically in both sexes, opening up the possibility that sex-specific suicide rates may have to be used. If so, studies of social stress will need to avoid a sex-undifferentiated suicide rate in favor of the suicide rate among males and the suicide rate among females. Similarly, age-specific suicide rates may have to be employed in measuring the amount of societal stress. The suicide rate varies by age, and its magnitude at a particular age differs materially from one time period to another.[98] As a consequence, the suicide rate at certain ages may be more accurate as an indicator of societal stress at a given point in time than the suicide rate at other ages, and the suicide rate at certain ages may be more accurate during particular periods than during other periods. If so, the suicide rate as a gauge of societal stress will need to be age-specific as well as period-specific.

---

[96] Antonio Rodríguez Andrés, *Income Inequality, Unemployment, and Suicide: A Panel Data Analysis of 15 European Countries*, 37 Applied Econ. 439, 440, 442–43, 446 tbl. 3, 448 tbl. 5 (2005) (using data on fifteen Western European nations for the period 1970–1998). *But see* Sylwia J. Piatkowska, *Socio-Economic Development, Economic Fluctuations, and Age-Specific Suicide: A Cross-National Test of the Durkheim, Henry and Short, and Ginsburg Theories*, 59 Sociol. Q. 471, 477–79, 485–87 & tbl. 3, tbl. 4 (2018) (using data on seventeen Western European nations for the period 1956–2012; finding that the manner in which country-level economic growth and childbearing are measured affects whether these variables are found to be related to age-specific suicide rates).

[97] Phillips Cutright & Robert M. Fernquist, *The Relative Gender Gap in Suicide: Societal Integration, the Culture of Suicide, and Period Effects in 20 Developed Countries, 1955-1994*, 30 Soc. Sci. Res. 76, 86–87 (2001).

[98] Robert M. O'Brien & Jean Stockard, *A Common Explanation for the Changing Age Distributions of Suicide and Homicide in the United States, 1930 to 2000*, 84 Soc. Forces 1539, 1540 fig. 1a, 1552 (2006).

1.4.3 Total Fertility Rate

The total fertility rate ("TFR"), as its name implies, is a gauge of the level of childbearing in a human population, but unfortunately what it measures is often misinterpreted. Because the TFR may be a useful indicator of societal stress, I begin by describing in detail what the TFR tells us and how it is calculated.

In general terms, the TFR is an estimate of the average *lifetime* number of live births among the females in a population who in a particular year enter the age range for childbearing. The estimate is based on the age-specific fertility rates of females in the population who are, during the year for which the TFR is calculated, in the childbearing phase of their lives. The TFR is thus often computed for a given year from the number of live births in that year per 1000 females at each age in the age range 15–49, the age range within which females may be assumed to bear children.[99] Because the TFR assumes that the number of live births that occur in a particular year per 1000 females at every age remains the same in future years, it is necessarily a *projection* of average lifetime childbearing by the group of females who reached childbearing age in that year. Of course, the foregoing assumption will be wrong because age-specific fertility rates are not constant over time, and the change that takes place in age-specific fertility rates will produce year-to-year differences in the TFR.

For the population for which the TFR is computed, then, the TFR is a gauge of eventual childbearing by females in the population who come of childbearing-age in a given year, and it does not measure the final fertility of this cohort.[100] Importantly, changing rates of childbearing over a particular time period have a much more pronounced impact on the TFR for a given year than on the completed fertility of women in this year, i.e., the fertility of women who in this year turned fifty years of age. Additionally, the TFR, being a function of age-specific fertility rates, is unaffected by shifts over time in the age distribution of women in the population.[101] As a

[99] Births occur to females who are younger than age fifteen and to females who are older than age forty-nine, but these births are a miniscule share of all births. In the United States during calendar year 2019, for example, females who were under age fifteen had a total of just 1,787 live births and females who were over age forty-nine had a total of just 1,073 live births; among females of all ages, the total number of live births was 3,747,540. Joyce A. Martin et al., *Births: Final Data for 2019*, NAT'L VITAL STAT. REP., vol. 70, no. 2 (March 23, 2021), at 4, 15 tbl. 3. Females below age 15 and females aged 50+ thus produced just (1,787 + 1,073) = (2,860 ÷ 3,747,540) = 0.0008 × 100 = 0.08 percent of births in the United States during 2019.

[100] *See* John Bongaarts, *The End of the Fertility Transition in the Developed World*, 28 POPULATION & DEV. REV. 419, 421–22 & tbl. 1 (2002) (comparing the completed fertility rate of women born in 1960 to the average total fertility rate in 1980–1994 for each of thirty-two developed nations).

[101] Stephanie J. Ventura et al., Centers for Disease Control, *Revised Birth and Fertility Rates for the United States, 2000 and 2001*, 51(4) NAT'L VITAL STATISTICS REP., Feb. 6, 2003, at 1, 4.

Table 1.1 Calculation of the Total Fertility Rate (Example for Age Range 10–49)

(column 1) Age range	(column 2) Number of births per 1000 females: mean of age range	(column 3) Number of births per 1000 females: all ages in age range
10–14	1.4	7.0
15–19	59.9	299.5
20–24	116.5	582.5
25–29	120.2	601.0
30–34	80.8	404.0
35–39	31.7	158.5
40–44	5.5	27.5
45–49	0.2	1.0
	$\Sigma = 416.2$	$\Sigma = 2081.0$

result, the TFR is an appealing demographic measure of the level, and of temporal shifts in the level, of childbearing in a population.[102]

In sum, the TFR offers us information about human reproduction, and reveals the number of children that the average female in a society will bear by age 50 if she lives to age 50 and, while growing older, experiences the fertility rate that existed at each age in the calendar year in which she entered her childbearing period.[103] Table 1.1 shows how the TFR is computed and therefore may help in understanding and interpreting the TFR.[104] The first of the three columns in the example lists the five-year age ranges of childbearing-age females; the second column provides the average fertility rate in the United States in 1990 for each five-year age range, i.e., the average number of births per 1000 U.S. females who were in each of the designated age ranges in 1990;[105] the third column, which is based on the second column, reports the fertility rates for all of the ages within each age range. The third column thus provides the age-specific fertility rates for U.S. females in 1990.

[102] John Bongaarts & Griffith Feeney, *On the Quantum and Tempo of Fertility*, 24 Population & Dev. Rev. 271, 271–72 (1998).

[103] U.N. Population Div., Dep't of Econ. & Soc. Aff., *World Fertility Report 2012: Age-Specific Fertility Rate, Total Fertility and Mean Age at Childbearing*, at 1 (2013) (defining the total fertility rate as "the mean number of children a woman would have by age 50 if she survived to age 50 and were subject, throughout her life, to the age-specific fertility rates observed in a given year"), https://www.un.org/en/development/desa/population/publications/dataset/fertility/wfr2012/MainFrame.html (follow "Metadata" hyperlink and then select "Age-specific fertility rate, Total fertility, Mean age at childbearing"). The TFR is based on live births. See Population Reference Bureau, Glossary of Demographic Terms (2019), https://www.prb.org/glossary. The TFR thus excludes stillbirths, which are instances that involve "the death or loss of a baby before or during delivery"; stillbirths occur in approximately one percent of all pregnancies in the United States. Centers for Disease Control & Prevention, *What is Stillbirth?* (2019), https://www.cdc.gov/ncbddd/stillbirth/facts.html.

[104] For another example, see Arthur Haupt et al., Population Reference Bureau's Population Handbook 10–11 (6th ed. 2011).

[105] Column 1 and column 2 are from Ventura et al., *supra* note 101, at 8–9 tbl. 2 & n.2 (using births to women of all races through age 49).

Because every age range in the example includes five years, the rates in the third column are the rates in the second column multiplied by five. As the third column reveals, the TFR, expressed as the mean number of lifetime live births projected for 1000 U.S. females who came of childbearing age in 1990, was 2081,[106] or 2.081 per female.

Why is the TFR potentially useful as an indicator of societal stress? The modernization of a society is evidenced by, inter alia, a sizeable decline in the scale of childbearing in the society. Indeed, social science considers the TFR a (but not the sole) defining difference between a modern society and a non-modern society—the former is characterized by a relatively low TFR and the latter by a relatively high TFR.[107] Societal stress is logically an accompaniment of the extensive social change involved in modernization and is thus useful for understanding the large reduction in the TFR that is a prominent aspect of modernization. Societal stress is also helpful for understanding the reduction that occurs in the TFR due to a socially destabilizing economic event[108] and a higher female labor-force participation rate.[109] On their face, a major shock to the economy and a substantial alteration in sex roles imply society-level stress. The TFR, accordingly, is attractive as a potential quantitative indicator of the social stress that occurs in societies.

1.5 Drivers and Consequences of Societal Stress

I begin Sect. 1.5 by calling attention to a question that will face law-pertinent research that includes the variable of society-level stress. The question deals with how society-level stress arises or changes when it responds to its causes and how it acts when it brings about its effects. In particular, the question revolves around whether societal stress, as a consequence and as a driver, behaves in (1) a steady, gradual manner or (2) a sporadic, sudden manner. I believe that empirical research will find that (2) is much more frequent than (1). The outcome of this research will be important to scholarship on society-level stress as a sociological phenomenon. If and when (1) characterizes society-level stress, linearity exists between societal stress

[106] See *id.* at 7 tbl. 1.

[107] Ron Lesthaeghe, *The Unfolding Story of the Second Demographic Transition*, 36 Population & Dev. Rev. 211, 246 (2010); Dogan Hatun & David F. Warner, *Disentangling the Roles of Modernization and Secularization on Fertility: The Case of Turkey*, 41 Population Res. & Pol'y Rev. 1161, 1183–84 (2022). *See* Jennifer Johnson-Hanks, *Demographic Transitions and Modernity*, 37 Ann. Rev. Anthropology 301, 306–08 (2008) (identifying mechanisms that may link modernity to low fertility).

[108] Joshua R. Goldstein et al., *Fertility Reactions to the "Great Recession" in Europe: Recent Evidence from Order-Specific Data*, 29 Demographic Research 85, 92 (2013).

[109] Vinod Mishra & Russell Smyth, *Female Labor Force Participation and Total Fertility Rates in the OECD: New Evidence from Panel Cointegration and Granger Causality Testing*, 62 J. Econ. & Bus. 48, 60–61 (2010).

and its causes as well as between societal stress and its effects. If and when (2) characterizes society-level stress—i.e., if and when the reactions and actions of societal stress are irregular and abrupt—nonlinearity exists between societal stress and its causes as well as between societal stress and its effects. In either case, thresholds will be present.[110] Because thresholds are probably common in all human groups, including a society,[111] thresholds should be expected as the sociological sources of society-level stress work to alter the occurrence of such stress and as society-level stress operates to alter social life.

Several cautions, though, are in order here. First, a threshold of society-level stress may be determined by the specific sociological source that produces stress, and for a given aspect of social life, a threshold may differ from one source to another. Several sociological sources of societal stress, that is, may result in several thresholds of societal stress for a given aspect of social life. Second, for a particular sociological source of societal stress, a threshold of stress may be at a certain level when the source is rising or falling at one speed but be at another level when the source is rising or falling at another speed. Exactly where a threshold exists, in other words, may depend on the rate of change in a sociological source of stress. Third, identical thresholds of societal stress for multiple aspects of social life may not, when exceeded, be followed by the same frequency of stress in all of these aspects. Put otherwise, the frequency of societal stress that occurs when a threshold is reached may not be the same for every affected aspect of social life—societal stress may happen more often in the case of certain aspects than in the case of other aspects.

In the present book, I focus on what I believe to have been a—but certainly not the sole—driver of society-level stress in the United States since the middle of the twentieth century, namely, the actions of, and the substance of the rules of, the institution of law. Americans cannot be expected to escape social side effects from what law says and does not say, especially when law deals with society-significant social activities and arrangements. Notably, much of the content of U.S. law that has developed since the mid-twentieth century incorporates the social-political ideology that is currently popular in the social sciences,[112] especially sociology.[113] Given what is known about how humans perceive and react,[114] the professionals and

---

[110] Explaining Law, *supra* note 18, at 10, 53 & n.150; The Place of Law, *supra* note 49, at 231, 263–64, 465–66.

[111] For evidence that thresholds exist in social life, see: Gianmarco Alberti, *Modeling Group Size and Scalar Stress by Logistic Regression from an Archaeological Perspective*, 9(3) PLoS One, March 2014 (e91510) [no pagination in original]; Ron Johnston et al., *Rethinking the Analysis of Ethnic Residential Patterns: Segregation, Isolation, or Concentration Thresholds in Auckland, New Zealand?*, 34 Geographical Analysis 245 (2002).

[112] Cal. Ass'n of Scholars, A Crisis of Competence: The Corrupting Effect of Political Activism in the University of California 18, 23–24, 41 (2012), https://eric.ed.gov/?id=ED530869.

[113] Solon Simmons, *Ascriptive Justice: The Prevalence, Distribution, and Consequences of Political Correctness in the Academy*, 6(2) The Forum art. 8, at 1, 3, 9 tbl. 3b (2008).

[114] Jeremy A. Frimer et al, *Liberals and Conservatives are Similarly Motivated to Avoid Exposure to One Another's Opinions*, 72 J. Experimental Soc. Psychol. 1, 11 (2017). *Cf.* Eddie Harmon-Jones

students in the social sciences who espouse the currently reigning ideology may not regard the law content that embodies this ideology as responsible for society-level stress and for problems generated by such stress. Of particular relevance is that the promoters of the ideology that is in vogue on many university campuses in the United States have shown a distinct unwillingness in recent years to allow questions about the ideology.[115] They have, instead, insisted on "political correctness"[116] and favored suppression of what they deem to be politically incorrect statements[117] despite the endorsement by Americans of freedom of expression[118] and despite the harm that an insistence on "political correctness" is likely to inflict on the knowledge-creating institution in the United States.[119] My hope is that the instant book will help to persuade the disciples of the ideology that the content of law that embodies this ideology can have unwanted consequences, including negative reactions to and the eventual rejection of the content, and that these consequences can be manifestations of society-level stress.

In sum, an ideology-inspired practice now clashes with an ideal in a setting (higher education) where the importance of the ideal has long been recognized[120] and where the vast majority of scholarship originates. Because the clash includes efforts to suppress questions about the social-political ideology involved in the clash,

---

& Judson Mills, *Dissonance Theory and an Overview of Current Perspectives on the Theory*, *in* Cognitive Dissonance: Reexamining a Pivotal Theory in Psychology 3, 4, 6, 17 (Eddie Harmon-Jones ed., 2d ed. 2019) (reviewing cognitive dissonance theory; concluding that the theory has received support from empirical research).

[115] *E.g.*, Peter Wood, Nat'l Ass'n of Scholars, The Architecture of Intellectual Freedom (2016).

[116] Kenneth Lasson, *The Decline of Free Speech on the Postmodern Campus: The Troubling Evolution of the Heckler's Veto*, 37 Quinnipiac L. Rev. 1, 2–4, 93 (2018).

[117] *Free Speech Under Attack: Book Bans and Academic Censorship: Hearing Before the H. Subcomm. on Civil Rights and Civil Liberties of the House Comm. on Oversight and Reform*, 117th Cong. 1 (2022) (statement of Jonathan W. Pidluzny, Am. Council of Trustees and Alumni) (observing that "the problem of academic censorship has reached crisis levels — not so much in K-12 education but on our college and university campuses").

An indicator that intolerance based on ideology has become problematic in higher education in the United States is that, in September 2022, legislation was proposed in Congress to deny federal government funding to any university or college that uses "a political test" when deciding on faculty members to hire, promote, or tenure or when deciding on applications submitted by individuals who want to matriculate at the university/college. The proposed legislation defines a political test as "a method of compelling or soliciting . . . a statement of personal belief in support of any ideology or movement that — (A) promotes a specific partisan or political set of beliefs; (B) promotes a particular viewpoint on an issue of public controversy; or (C) promotes the disparate treatment of any individual or group of individuals on the basis of race or ethnicity." Restoring Academic Freedom on Campus Act of 2022, H.R. 8945, § 2, 117th Cong. (2022).

[118] Richard Wike & Katie Simmons, Pew Res. Ctr., Global Support for Principle of Free Expression, but Opposition to Some Forms of Speech 4, 6 (2015).

[119] Philip Hunter, *Is Political Correctness Damaging Science?*, 6 EMDO Rep. 405 (2005).

[120] Gordon E. Baker, *Thomas Jefferson on Academic Freedom*, 39 Bull. Am. Ass'n Univ. Professors 377, 378 (1953).

numerous colleges and universities are not facilitating innovation in scholarship. Specifically, the intolerance of the questions by adherents of the ideology undermines the social conditions that are necessary for critical thinking in scholarship. This point is illustrated by the free-speech guarantee of the First Amendment to the U.S. Constitution.[121] Under the free-speech guarantee, government in the United States cannot, without an overriding justification, block private citizens from disseminating messages that might lessen acceptance of a particular social-political ideology or require private citizens to disseminate messages that might encourage acceptance of a particular social-political ideology.[122] Indeed, the core goal of the First Amendment has historically been to bar government from favoring viewpoints of certain content and disfavoring viewpoints of alternative content.[123]

Because the First Amendment aims to keep government from differentiating social-political viewpoints in oral and written communications, a government-operated university, being subject to the First Amendment,[124] has limited authority to prohibit and penalize, and demand and reward, specific social-political viewpoints, at least when these viewpoints are suited to a type of activity that the university considers appropriate for its participants.[125] Scholarship by faculty members and their graduate students in government-run programs of higher education in

---

[121] "Congress shall make no law respecting an establishment of religion, or prohibiting the free exercise thereof; or abridging the freedom of speech, or of the press; or the right of the people peaceably to assemble, and to petition the Government for a redress of grievances." U.S. Const. amend. I. The First Amendment was approved by Congress and submitted to the states for their consideration in 1789; it was ratified by the requisite number of states and became part of the Constitution in 1791. U.S. House of Representatives, The Constitution of the United States as Amended, H.R. Doc. 110–50, at 13 (2007); 1 Stat. 21, 97 (1848).

[122] Iancu v. Brunetti, 139 S. Ct. 2294, 2298–99, 2302 (2019) (reviewing a provision of a federal statute pursuant to which a federal government agency rejected an application filed by a private party to register a trademark; concluding that the provision, which prohibited issuance of a trademark for "immoral … or scandalous matter," violated the First Amendment because the provision constituted "viewpoint-discriminatory law," i.e., created "viewpoint bias" in law). See the provision at 15 U.S.C. § 1052(a). Government action that curtails free speech on a social-political topic is constitutional under the First Amendment only when the action is "content neutral" and "narrowly tailored to serve a significant government interest" and has "left open ample alternative channels for communication of the information." Schenck v. Pro-Choice Network of W. N.Y., 519 U.S. 357, 369 (1997).

In a concurring opinion in *Iancu*, *supra*, a justice of the Court who endorsed the majority opinion characterized viewpoint discrimination as "poison to a free society" and observed that "such discrimination has become increasingly prevalent in" the United States. Iancu v. Brunetti, *supra*, at 2302 (Alito, J., concurring). *See also* Perry Educ. Ass'n v. Perry Local Educators' Ass'n, 460 U.S. 37, 62 (1983) (5-4 decision), where the four dissenting justices wrote that "[v]iewpoint discrimination is censorship in its purest form and government regulation that discriminates among viewpoints threatens the continued vitality of 'free speech.'"

[123] Joseph Blocker, *Viewpoint Neutrality and Government Speech*, 52 B.C. L. Rev. 695, 696 (2011).

[124] SAIL vol. 1, *supra* note 4, at 73 n.215 (explaining the application of the First Amendment to state and local governments).

[125] Christian Legal Soc'y v. Martinez, 561 U.S. 661, 685 (2010) (citing and quoting Rosenberger v. Rector & Visitors of Univ. of Virginia, 515 U.S. 819, 829–30 (1995)).

the United States, accordingly, is within the scope of the First Amendment constraint on viewpoint bias by governmental entities. Similarly, run-of-the-mill scholarship by faculty members and their graduate students at non-public universities in the United States is outside the reach of government regulation because the First Amendment allows government little latitude when acting to encourage or discourage advocacy by private parties.[126] In short, a university, whether public or private, is "a special place" in the United States[127] since its professoriate exists "to test ideas and to propose solutions, to deepen knowledge and refresh perspectives."[128] Moreover, this thesis is endorsed by a sizeable majority of Americans.[129] The U.-S. Supreme Court has thus recognized that a government in the United States that distinguishes between viewpoints in a university creates a problematic situation:

> Vital First Amendment speech principles are at stake here. The first danger to liberty lies in granting the State the power to examine publications to determine whether or not they are based on some ultimate idea and, if so, for the State to classify them. The second, and corollary, danger is to speech from the chilling of individual thought and expression. That danger is especially real in the University setting, where the State acts against a background and tradition of thought and experiment that is at the center of our intellectual and philosophic tradition.[130]

---

[126] Rosenberger v. Rector & Visitors of Univ. of Virginia, 515 U.S. 819, 828 (1995) ("In the realm of private speech or expression, government regulation may not favor one speaker over another. Discrimination against speech because of its message is presumed to be unconstitutional."); Members of the City Council of the City of Los Angeles v. Taxpayers for Vincent, 466 U.S. 789, 804 (1984) ("the First Amendment forbids the government to regulate speech in ways that favor some viewpoints or ideas at the expense of others," and while "the state may sometimes curtail speech when necessary to advance a significant and legitimate state interest . . . there are some purported interests — such as a desire to suppress support for . . . an unpopular cause, or to exclude the expression of certain points of view from the marketplace of ideas — that are so plainly illegitimate that they would immediately" be unacceptable when government employs its resources in a manner that affects the speech of private parties).

[127] Kincaid v. Gibson, 236 F.3d 342, 352 (6th Cir. 2001) (en banc) (also asserting, with respect to the First Amendment, that "[t]he university environment is the quintessential 'marketplace of ideas'"). *Accord*, Husain v. Springer, 494 F.3d 108, 121 n.11 (2d Cir. 2007), *cert. denied*, 552 U.S. 1258 (2008) (observing that a wide range of ideas is critical in universities for higher education to carry out its mission and that "particular vigilance" is thus appropriate to ensure that First Amendment rights are not suppressed by government at universities in the United States).

[128] Urofsky v. Gilmore, 216 F.3d 401, 428 (4th Cir. 2000) (Wilkinson, C.J., concurring), *cert denied*, 531 U.S. 1070 (2001).

[129] *See* Gallup, Inc., Free Expression on Campus: A Survey of U.S. College Students and U.S. Adults 14, 33 (2016) (reporting analyses of data obtained from a national sample of U.S. adults surveyed in 2016; finding that two out of three adults believed that institutions of higher education should allow students to encounter "all types of speech and viewpoints" even though some of the ideas advocated are "offensive").

[130] Rosenberger v. Rector & Visitors of University of Virginia, 515 U.S. 819, 835 (1995). The final sentence in the quoted passage makes clear that, in the United States, universities (and colleges) are considered to be places where diverse views are not only permitted but encouraged. *Accord*, Meriwether v. Hartop, 992 F.3d 492, 498 (6th Cir. 2021) (observing that "[t]raditionally, American universities have been beacons of intellectual diversity and academic freedom. They have prided themselves on being forums where controversial ideas are discussed and debated."). *See also* John

Briefly said, in the world of higher education, innovation in scholarship is a prominent ideal that favors the consideration of challenges to prevailing social-political ideologies. Given the societal benefits that can flow from innovation, such challenges should not be brushed aside.

1.6 Law Content as a Source of Societal Stress

Precisely when does law content in a jurisdiction produce and respond to societal stress in the jurisdiction? The Prohibition era in the United States provides an example and helps to underscore the utility of the concept of societal stress. The era, which spanned much of the first third of the twentieth century, emanated from public concern over the consumption of liquor by individuals[131] and involved significant changes in federal law. In particular, two amendments to the U.-S. Constitution define the Prohibition era: The first marked the start of the era, and the second, in repealing the first, marked the end.[132] Notably, when it acted to curb the use of intoxicating drinks, law had a socially significant side effect—it noticeably raised the homicide rate.[133] A plausible macrosociological interpretation of this side

Inazu, *The Purpose (and Limits) of the University*, 18 UTAH L. REV. 943, 947 (2018) (positing that a key function of a university is to "facilitat[e] disagreement across differences").

A government-funded and -operated university is a public forum, and as such it has, under the First Amendment, a highly circumscribed ability to advantage viewpoints that have a certain content and disadvantage viewpoints that have a different content. See Pleasant Grove City, Utah v. Summum. 555 U.S. 460, 469–70 (2008) (discussing government-owned property that is a "traditional public forum" and government-owned property that is a "designated public forum"; pointing out that, in both types of fora, the First Amendment imposes "the same strict scrutiny" on government restraints applied to private-party speech).

131 Jack S. Blocker, *Did Prohibition Really Work? Alcohol Prohibition as a Public Health Innovation*, 96 AM. J. PUB. HEALTH 233, 234–36 (2006).

132 The Eighteenth Amendment, which in January 1919 had been ratified by the constitutionally required number of states, banned "the manufacture, sale, or transportation of intoxicating liquors within, the importation thereof into, or the exportation thereof from the United States … for beverage purposes"; the Twenty-First Amendment, which in December 1933 had been ratified by the requisite number of states, repealed the Eighteenth Amendment but allowed each state to decide whether to prohibit "[t]he transportation or importation for delivery or use therein of intoxicating liquors." U.S. CONST. amend. XVIII, § 1; U.S. CONST. amend. XXI, §§ 1, 2. To implement the Eighteenth Amendment, federal legislation was adopted in October 1919. National Prohibition Act, Pub. L. No. 66-66, ch. 85, tit. III, § 21, 41 Stat. 305, 322–23 (1919).

133 Gary F. Jensen, *Prohibition, Alcohol, and Murder*, 4 HOMICIDE STUD. 18, 21–22 & fig. 1, 24, 29–31 (2000). *Accord*, Mark Asbridge & Swarna Weerasinghe, *Homicide in Chicago from 1890 to 1930: Prohibition and Its Impact on Alcohol- and Non-Alcohol-Related Homicides*, 104 ADDICTION 355, 355–56, 358, 360–61 (2009) (finding that Prohibition increased the rate of alcohol-unrelated homicides in Chicago).

The consumption of intoxicating beverages in the United States during the Prohibition era was materially curtailed only in the short run by law that was enacted to restrict the availability of intoxicating beverages. DEMOGRAPHY AND THE ANTHROPOCENE, *supra* note 88, at 59 & n. 44

effect is that social stress was generated when law moved to reduce the consumption of intoxicating beverages, and the greater social stress brought about an increase in homicides. That such stress was a product of the law seeking to combat intoxicating-beverage consumption is evidenced by the rescission of the law just a decade-and-a-half after it was adopted. Rescission was a response by American society to the social stress engendered by law and removed a source of that stress.

I turn next to two findings from empirical research on society and law, because I believe that the concept of societal stress helps to make sense of them. These findings are that (1) a substantial increase as well as a substantial decrease in the incidence of a society-important social activity alters the content of law[134] and (2) law content in a structurally complex and democratically governed nation does not, in the long run, materially affect how often individuals engage in society-significant social activities that the law content attempts to regulate. Both findings support the use of the concept of societal stress in macrosociology and in the sociology of law. Finding (1) is plainly linked to societal stress and need not be discussed further. In the case of finding (2), however, the connection to societal stress is not evident. Additionally, finding (2) is out of line with a widely held view of law. Accordingly, I examine this finding in depth.

Perhaps surprisingly, the thesis that law in a modern nation does not exert a major, lasting influence on the incidence of core social activities is backed by a substantial body of empirical research.[135] Because the thesis does not accord with

(summarizing and discussing Angela K. Dills et al., *The Effect of Alcohol Prohibition on Alcohol Consumption: Evidence from Drunkenness Arrests*, 86 Econ. Letters 279 (2005)).

[134] Explaining Law, *supra* note 18, at ch. 1 pts. 2, 3.

[135] *Id.* at 14–15, 55–58 app. B; Demography and the Anthropocene, *supra* note 88, at pt. 3.3.1; Larry D. Barnett, The Biosphere and Human Society: Understanding Systems, Law, and Population Growth ch. 3 pts. 3.2 & 3.4 (2023) (hereinafter The Biosphere and Human Society) (summarizing the findings of studies that investigated the effectiveness of law that sought to alter the incidence of abortion and the incidence of international migration); Paul H. Robinson & John M. Darley, *Does Criminal Law Deter? A Behavioural Science Investigation*, 24 Oxford J. Legal Stud. 173, 174–75, 197–204 (2004); Helmut Hirtenlehner & Per-Olof H. Wikström, *Experience or Deterrence? Revising an Old but Neglected Issue*, 14 Eur. J. Criminology 485, 486–89, 496–98 (2017). *Accord*, Ryan T. Motz et al., *Does Contact with the Justice System Deter or Promote Future Delinquency? Results from a Longitudinal Study of British Adolescent Twins*, 58 Criminology 307, 309, 314–15, 319, 323, 326, 333 (2020) (analyzing data on a representative sample of pairs of 18-year-old same-sex twins in Britain who had been born in England or Wales; studying within-pair differences in self-reported criminal conduct that resulted in contact with the institution of justice during the prior twelve months; finding that "contact with the justice system . . . promotes misbehavior" rather than lessens it), https://onlinelibrary.wiley.com/doi/10.1111/1745-9125.12236; Joseph L. Nedelec & Ian A. Silver, *Challenging Assumptions: A Genetically Sensitive Assessment of the Criminogenic Effect of Contact with the Criminal Justice System*, 35 J. Contemp. Crim. Just. 69, 73–75, 82 (2018) (analyzing data on a sample of pairs of same-sex twins in the United States; finding that within-pair differences in contact with the criminal justice institution had no general impact on the frequency of criminal behavior among twins after they reached their twentieth birthday and were in their twenties and thirties).

Compare Andrew D. Leipold, *The Puzzle of Clearance Rates, and What They Can Tell Us about Crime, Police Reform, and Criminal Justice*, 56 Wake Forest L. Rev. 47, 51–53, 55–57 & n.33, popular thinking, a concrete illustration may be helpful. Specifically, I look at the topic of creativity and the extent to which the occurrence of creativity responds to pertinent law. Put simply, research has found that the incidence of forms of creativity that are protectable by law has not been uniformly affected by the content of law.

Creativity is a social activity because it is dependent on social conditions.[136] Notably, it is a prized activity in, and hence important to, American society. Evidence of its societal importance is that a provision in the U.S. Constitution authorizes the federal government to protect creative works:[137] "The Congress shall have Power ... To promote the Progress of Science and useful Arts, by securing for limited Times to Authors and Inventors the exclusive Right to their respective Writings and Discoveries."[138] The foregoing provision, often named the

---

64–66, 89–90 (2021) (using yearly data on reported cases of violent crime (murder/nonnegligent manslaughter, rape, robbery, aggravated assault) and property crime (burglary, larceny/theft (excluding embezzlement/forgery), motor-vehicle theft, arson) in the United States for the period 1980 through 2019; examining the rates at which these cases were "cleared," i.e., resulted in an arrest or in a credible identification of the crime perpetrator(s); finding that yearly clearance rates did not exceed 50 percent for violent crime and 20 percent for property crime; describing the clearance-rate trend lines during 1980–2019 as being "relatively smooth" for violent crime and as "amazingly flat" for property crime; and suggesting that, under theory on the deterrence of crime, low clearance rates imply that punishment for crime is uncertain and hence that crime is undeterred by law and law-enforcement personnel), *with* Steven N. Durlauf & Daniel S. Nagin, *Imprisonment and Crime: Can Both Be Reduced?*, 10 CRIMINOLOGY & PUB. POL'Y 13, 17, 37 (2011) (reviewing empirical research; finding "relatively strong evidence" supporting the conclusion that the certainty of punishment deters crime, and finding "relatively little reliable evidence" for the conclusion that the severity of punishment deters crime), https://onlinelibrary.wiley.com/doi/full/10.1111/j.1745-9133.2010.00680.x, *and* Damon M. Petrich et al., *Custodial Sanctions and Reoffending: A Meta-Analytic Review*, 50 CRIME & JUST. 353 (2021) (including in a meta-analysis all studies available as of mid-2019 that quantitatively assessed the degree to which the rate of recidivism among individuals who were apprehended and prosecuted for criminal conduct was affected by a custodial punishment (e.g., a prison sentence, a juvenile detention, or a jail sentence) compared to a noncustodial punishment (e.g., probation, community service, or a suspended prison sentence); concluding that the recidivism rate responds about equally to each type of punishment, i.e., that deterrence of crime is unaffected by punishment severity).

See generally Alex Raskolnikov, *Criminal Deterrence: A Review of the Missing Literature*, 28 SUP. CT. ECON. REV. 1, 41–42, 46–47 (2020) (concluding that available research on crime does not provide answers to several important questions, including (i) whether law reduces the incidence of misdemeanors and (ii) whether efforts to curb crime produce benefits that outweigh the costs of the efforts).

[136] Jill E. Perry-Smith, *Social Yet Creative: The Role of Social Relationships in Facilitating Individual Creativity*, 49 ACAD. MGMT. J. 85, 96–97 (2006); Jill E. Perry-Smith & Christina E. Shalley, *The Social Side of Creativity: A Static and Dynamic Social Network Perspective*, 28 ACAD. MGMT. REV. 89, 102 (2003). *See also* Ruth Towse, *Copyright and Creativity: An Application of Cultural Economics*, 3 REV. ECON. RES. COPYRIGHT ISSUES 83, 87 (2006) (observing that evidence from the discipline of cultural economics indicates that the principal motivators prompting creativity by artists are typically nonfinancial incentives, especially social recognition and influence).

[137] *See generally* SAIL VOL. 1, *supra* note 4, at 15 (pointing out that social goals that are highly valued by Americans are expressed in the constitution of the United States).

[138] U.S. CONST. art. I, § 8, cl. 8.

"Intellectual Property Clause" of the Constitution, has been the basis for the enactment of federal legislation on copyrights and on patents, both of which are viewed as enhancing the welfare of society.[139] However, research has found that changes in U.S. copyright law have not brought about immediate, telling, or consistent effects on the number of authored works that are newly registered with the U.S. Copyright Office.[140] Nor have changes in copyright law been proven to benefit creativity over relatively long time intervals.[141] Similarly, patent law has not been shown in general to exert a material influence on the number of patents issued, and patents have not been shown to be a substantial determinant of economic productivity.[142]

Creativity, of course, is just a single illustration of a broader thesis, namely, that the content of law generally has no sizeable, long-term impact on the incidence of the society-significant social activities that it targets for regulation. However, if the thesis is correct and law does not bring about a material, lasting change in the frequency with which particular individual-level social behaviors occur, why is law a recurrent feature of structurally complex, democratically governed societies? One important sociological reason, I believe, is that law content on society-meaningful matters furnishes symbols that, by virtue of emanating from government, are salient to and socially influential in society.[143] Given that societies contain symbols and

---

[139]Eugene R. Quinn, Jr., *An Unconstitutional Patent in Disguise: Did Congress Overstep Its Constitutional Authority in Adopting the Circumvention Prevention Provisions of the Digital Millennium Copyright Act?*, 41 Brandeis L.J. 33, 37–43 (2002).

[140]Raymond Shih Ray Ku et al., *Does Copyright Law Promote Creativity? An Empirical Analysis of Copyright's Bounty*, 62 Vand. L. Rev. 1669, 1689, 1692, 1674, 1708 (2009) (using lags of one year, two years, and three years after change occurred in U.S. copyright law; deciding that one-year lags are the most appropriate for capturing the response of potential copyright registrants to change in copyright law and, hence, the number of new registrations that are due to such change; and concluding that predicting an impact on the frequency of a particular type of creative work from a modification of copyright law "is at best slightly better than a coin toss").

[141]Ivan Paak Liang Png & Qiu-Hong Wang, *Copyright Law and the Supply of Creative Work: Evidence from the Movies*, *in* Comparative Law and Economics 407, 409, 439 (Theodore Eisenberg & Giovanni B. Ramello eds., 2016) (studying (i) nineteen countries in the Organization for Economic Co-operation and Development that, during the period 1991–2005, changed their law in order to lengthen copyright protection for movies, and (ii) seventeen European countries that, during the period 1991–2005, changed their law in order to comply with the directive of a transnational body pertaining to copyright protection for music CDs and books; and finding that these changes in law did not increase the production of movies, music CDs, or books).

[142]Michele Boldrin & David K. Levine, *The Case Against Patents*, 27 J. Econ. Literature 3, 5–7 (2013) (reviewing empirical research). *See* Lisa Larrimore Ouellette & Andrew Tutt, *How Do Patent Incentives Affect University Researchers?*, 61 Int'l Rev. Law & Econ., March 2020, at 1, 15–16 (using data on universities in the United States; finding that the availability of royalties to researchers at these universities did not affect the frequency with which the researchers produced patented inventions).

[143]Rules for the behavior of individuals are adopted and applied not just by governments but also by non-government entities, e.g., business firms. The rules of non-government entities lack the imprimatur of government and are relevant to fewer people. As a result, they are less prominent and less influential as symbols in the society. Oren Perez, *Fuzzy Law: A Theory of Quasi-Legal Systems*, 28 Canadian J. L. & Jurisprudence 343, 356–57 (2015).

rarely die, most symbols evidently build, or at least preserve, societal cohesiveness and thereby work to counter societal stress. For the most part, then, the law content of a society acts symbolically to help the society combat destabilization[144]—in the words of one scholar, law acts "not so much to guide society, as to comfort it"[145]—and it undergoes revision in order to be in harmony with new social conditions, which conditions are manifested in substantially altered frequencies of society-important social activities in which individuals participate. In this regard, we should keep in mind that the revision of stress-inducing law may involve not only changes in the wording of statutes and administrative-agency rules, but also reinterpretations of, and refusals by government officers and/or employees to enforce, existing statutes and administrative-agency rules.[146] Whatever processes occur, they end in law that is different, in content or application, than before. Law content on key social activities, accordingly, is a response to and the result of alterations in how often the activities occur,[147] serves society by being a socially supportive symbol, and is understandable in terms of societal stress.

A concrete instance of the society-to-law sequence in the United States is provided by the federal Voting Rights Act of 1965 (on which I elaborate in Appendix 2 to the present chapter).[148] The Act aimed at providing equal access to voting for all U.S. citizens, regardless of race, and because the percentage of blacks in the U.S. South who were registered to vote was higher after the Act was adopted,[149] the Act has been portrayed as having "changed the face of this Nation"[150] and as having been "the most successful civil rights law in the history of the United States."[151] However, the percentage of blacks who were registered to vote in states of the South had been rising, and rising quickly, for more than a decade

---

[144] Explaining Law, *supra* note 18, at 11–12, 16; The Place of Law, *supra* note 49, at 59–61, 395–404.

[145] Thurman W. Arnold, The Symbols of Government 34 (1935), *available at* https://archive.org/details/in.ernet.dli.2015.34165/page/n3/mode/2up.

[146] Adam Shinar, *Dissenting from Within: Why and How Public Officials Resist the Law*, 40 Fla. St. U. L. Rev. 601, 606, 609–11 (2013). For a recent illustration of such resistance, see the following from the organization Fair and Just Prosecution: Press Release, With Roe v. Wade Overturned, 90 Elected Prosecutors Commit to Not Prosecute Abortions (June 29, 2022); *Joint Statement from Elected Prosecutors* (July 14, 2022). The Press Release and Joint Statement are available at https://fairandjustprosecution.org/news/fjp-releases.

[147] Explaining Law, *supra* note 18, at 47–52.

[148] Pub. L. No. 89-110, 79 Stat. 437 (1965) (codified at 52 U.S.C. § 10301 et seq. (2021). The United States Code, including title 52, is accessible at https://uscode.house.gov/download/download.shtml.

[149] Kevin J. Coleman, Cong. Res. Serv., The Voting Rights Act of 1965: Background and Overview 12–13 & tbl. 3 (2015).

[150] 152 Cong. Rec. H5161 (July 13, 2006) (statement of Rep. Eddie Bernice Johnson). *Accord*, Nat'l Archives Found., Voting Rights Act of 1965 (describing the Act as "a momentous achievement"), https://www.archivesfoundation.org/documents/voting-rights-act-1965.

[151] Jason Mazzone & Stephen Rushin, *From Selma to Ferguson: The Voting Rights Act as a Blueprint for Police Reform*, 105 Calif. L. Rev. 263, 294 (2017). *See* Justin Levitt, *Section 5 as*

prior to the Act.[152] This rise would logically have supplied a social foundation for new law—in the present case, the federal Voting Rights Act of 1965. Moreover, while the Act evidently accelerated the ongoing increase in voter registration among blacks in the South, the general absence of a material, long-term impact of law on social behavior means that the post-Act share of blacks in this region who were registered to vote was probably not much if any larger than the share that societal change would have eventually produced in the absence of the Act.[153] Despite the claims that have been made, therefore, the Act is unlikely to have sharply altered the social path of the country. Furthermore, blacks may not have received a substantial benefit from the Act in terms of their ability to influence government operation, government policy, and the content of law. Indeed, the Act may have reduced the political impact of blacks, as I explain in Appendix 2. Nonetheless, the Act symbolized fairness and equality,[154] and because these are fundamental ideals in the United States,[155] the Act would have promoted social cohesiveness in most segments of the American population even though it did little to change political outcomes.

Let me now summarize the above discussion and tie it to societal stress. The content of law on a matter that is important to a society is normally a society-wide symbol, but the social impact of the symbol is not necessarily uniform across the society, especially when the society is structurally complex. Consequently, although law content on a core social topic can be expected to lower the occurrence of societal stress in most segments of a society, it can still alienate a pronounced segment of the

---

Simulacrum, 123 YALE L.J. ONLINE 151, 151 (2013) (observing that the Act "is widely hailed as the most significant civil rights statute in American history").

152 James E. Alt, *The Impact of the Voting Rights Act on Black and White Voter Registration in the South*, *in* QUIET REVOLUTION IN THE SOUTH: THE IMPACT OF THE VOTING RIGHTS ACT, 1965-1990, at 351, 374 tbl. 12.1 (Chandler Davidson & Bernard Grofman eds., 1994); COLEMAN, *supra* note 149, at 13 tbl. 3.

153 EXPLAINING LAW, *supra* note 18, at 56.

154 S. Res. 232, 109th Cong., 151 CONG. REC. S9541 (2005) (sponsored by sixteen senators; describing the Act as "one of the most important civil rights victories in the history of the United States" and as a push for "fairness and equal access to the political process").

155 Ideals that are central to Americans are in statutes in the United States because they are in the federal Constitution; statutes in the United States must conform to the requirements of the Constitution. SAIL VOL. 1, *supra* note 4, at 14–15. The ideal of fairness is incorporated into the constitutional guarantee of due process, and the ideal of equality is incorporated into the constitutional guarantee of equal protection. Ross v. Moffitt, 417 U.S. 600, 609 (1974). The guarantees are in both the Fifth Amendment and the Fourteenth Amendment. See pt. 2.2 of *infra* Chap. 2.

society.[156] For example, the U.S. Supreme Court ruling[157] that in 1972 temporarily barred governments in the country from using capital punishment seems to have been responsible for a social reaction that led to an increase in the number of executions.[158] The reaction can be traced to societal stress: Being a prominent symbol, the 1972 Court decision activated certain segments of the American population and caused social stress that triggered the enactment of constitutionally permissible law authorizing executions. The use of capital punishment went up as a result—contrary to the goal of the opponents of the death penalty who brought the cases that yielded the decision.[159] The inability of law to alter substantially the long-term incidence of a societal activity (here, crime that warrants the death penalty[160]) does not mean, therefore, that law content has no impact on social life.

Of course, law content as a socially alienating symbol may be adopted or proposed on more than one topic during a particular period of time. Given the structural complexity of American society, a broad range of topics is and can be covered by the content of U.S. law during any one period. When new or proposed constitutional and/or statutory law on multiple topics estranges partly overlapping or entirely different groups in the U.S. population, this law can have a cumulative and widespread sociological impact. The affected groups, furthermore, may reinforce one another. Newly adopted or proposed law content on several society-significant social activities may, accordingly, have an effect that is greater than the arithmetic sum of the effects of new or proposed law content on the activities singly. The occurrence of a synergistic effect would be consistent with evidence that, in human groups having at least a minimum degree of complexity, the whole is typically more

---

[156] This hypothesis is compatible with the finding that rulings by the U.S. Supreme Court are generally in accord with the thinking of the American public. Christopher J. Casillas et al., *How Public Opinion Constrains the U.S. Supreme Court*, 55 Am. J. Pol. Sci. 74, 80 & tbl. 1 (2011). Some if not many federal-court rulings that hold a statute or government policy unconstitutional, despite their consistency with overall public opinion, may conflict with the beliefs of a not-insubstantial fraction of Americans. *E.g.*, Linda Greenhouse, *Public Opinion & the Supreme Court: The Puzzling Case of Abortion*, Daedalus, Fall 2012, at 69, 76.

[157] Furman v. Georgia, 408 U.S. 238 (1972). The ruling by the Court was grounded on the federal Constitution and specifically on the Eighth Amendment, which forbids government from, inter alia, using "cruel and unusual punishments." U.S. Const. amend. VIII. The Eighth Amendment, by its wording, applies to just the federal government, but the Court, using the Fourteenth Amendment, has extended the Eighth Amendment to state and local government. Gideon v. Wainright, 372 U.S. 335, 341 (1963).

[158] Explaining Law, *supra* note 18, at 20–25; Corinna Barrett Lain, *Furman Fundamentals*, 82 Wash. L. Rev. 1, 32–33, 47–49, 53–54, 63–66, 71 (2007).

[159] Daniel D. Polsby, *The Death of Capital Punishment? Furman v. Georgia*, 1972 Sup. Ct. Rev. 1, 2.

[160] Explaining Law, *supra* note 18, at 20–22 n.41 (reviewing quantitative social science studies that investigated the effect of the death penalty on the incidence of homicide). *Accord*, Patrick T. Brandt & Tomislav V. Kovandzic, *Messing Up Texas?: A Re-Analysis of the Effects of Executions on Homicides*, 10(9) PLoSOne, Sept. 23, 2015, at 1, 16–17.

than its separate parts.[161] In this way, new and proposed law content may push a society beyond a tipping point for societal stress and produce a society-level reaction.

1.7 The Plan of the Book

The prior Parts of this chapter set the stage for the quantitative studies that I undertake in the next three chapters and that will hopefully stimulate further scholarship on law and societal stress. While recognizing that law content can be a consequence of societal stress,[162] each of the studies examines law content as a *source* of such stress. The studies thus use the concept of society-level stress to understand what the institution of law does in social life. The studies unearth sociological differences between U.S. states—sociological differences that were (1) antecedents (and presumably causes) of state differences in tradition-embodying law that the U.S. Supreme Court held unconstitutional or (2) antecedents (and presumably causes) of state differences in reactions to a proposed change in the federal Constitution that was seen by segments of the public as undermining tradition. Societal stress is a logical byproduct of law when social traditions are believed to be at risk from a judicial ruling that invalidates existing law content or from a proposal that aims to bring about a society-significant change in law content. Chapters 2, 3, and 4 seek empirical evidence regarding the sociological forces and conditions that affect the occurrence of social stress in such situations; Chap. 5 uses the findings to develop theory on law-triggered social stress. Chapter 5 also discusses paths that might be followed in developing theory and conducting research on law-caused social stress.

I should mention here that none of the chapters in this book quantifies the amount of social stress. The reason is that, as discussed earlier,[163] the referent of a concept is not observable, and the observable (i.e., empirical) indicators of social stress have yet to be determined. Given the high degree of uncertainty that presently surrounds any operationalization of social stress, I avoid quantitative indicators of the concept in the following chapters and, instead, look for specific sociological forces and

---

[161] *See* Edgar Ennen & Ansgar Richter, *The Whole Is More Than the Sum of Its Parts – Or Is It? A Review of the Empirical Literature on Complimentarities in Organizations*, 36 J. Mgmt. 207, 208, 211, 223–25 (2010) (reviewing empirical research published in academic journals pertinent to the field of management; concluding that synergies are detectible in complex organizations that have several diverse elements when the organizations are examined as systems).

[162] *See* Comm. for Indus. Org. v Hague, 25 F. Supp. 127, 139 (D. N.J. 1938) ("Civil liberties derive their justification from a philosophy which tends to weaken or disappear in the face of passions and fears aroused by social stress and economic change"), *decree modified & aff'd*, 101 F.2d 774 (3d Cir.), *decree modified & aff'd*, 307 U.S. 496 (1939).

[163] See (i) the text accompanying *supra* note 82 and (ii) the paragraph accompanying *supra* notes 86 & 87.

conditions that plausibly affected whether change in law content was responsible for stressing American society. The social stress that arose from the process is deemed to be a latent phenomenon; as such, it is an acknowledged but unmeasured phenomenon, not a missing phenomenon. In analyzing data on sociological agents that potentially influenced the occurrence of social stress while positing social stress as a logical outcome of change and proposed change in law content, I take the same path as investigators who want to learn about individual-level stress and its sources, i.e., I employ the concept of stress to connect and make sense of observable phenomena.[164]

Chapters 2, 3, and 4 are each organized around an actual or proposed change in U.S. constitutional law whose substance is related to a social ideology that increased its footing among Americans during the last one-third of the twentieth century. Under this ideology, priority is given to individual rights rather than to social stability and established social patterns.[165] Law content that embodied this ideology, I hypothesize, triggered societal reactions that sought to protect traditional social arrangements. Because such reactions, when successful, bring about law content that approves traditional social forms and/or blocks proposed law content that disapproves traditional social forms, the next three chapters deal with sociological factors behind conservatism in the institution of law in the United States. In doing so, the chapters attempt to foster the recognition that adopted and advocated law that manifests a dominant social-political ideology can eventually create effects that are unanticipated and/or unwanted by the proponents and supporters of the law and its underlying ideology.[166] Societal stress is one such side effect, I argue, and the concept of societal stress thus helps to understand the role of law in a society.

Regrettably, law-linked social side effects, and the circumstances in which they occur, have received little scholarly consideration to date in macrosociology, a situation that is consistent with the rare mention of social side effects by the most salient court in the United States, viz., the U.S. Supreme Court.[167] However, law-created side effects merit attention, especially in societies where structural complexity and feedback loops can be expected to produce side effects, because there has long been reason to believe that side effects are often present in social

---

[164] Hinkle, *supra* note 25, at 561.

[165] Elisabeth Zoller, *Citizenship After the Conservative Movement*, 20 IND. J. GLOBAL LEG. STUD. 279, 283–84 (2013). *See also* EXPLAINING LAW, *supra* note 18, at 253–61 (using sample-survey data on the U.S. population; finding that, after the mid-1960s, an increase occurred in the prevalence of social values that favored personal interests and pursuits).

[166] EXPLAINING LAW, *supra* note 18, at 6; SAIL VOL. 1, *supra* note 4, at 42.

[167] In a search of U.S. Supreme Court cases, I found just two opinions that referred to social side effects of law. Cohen v. California, 403 U.S. 15, 24–25 (1971) (majority opinion); Paris Adult Theatre I v. Slaton, 413 U.S. 49, 73, 103 (1973) (Brennan, Stewart, & Marshall, JJ., dissenting). Both cases involved the protections afforded by the First Amendment to freedom from government action that is directed at restricting expression. See *supra* note 121 for the text of the First Amendment.

life.[168] Simply put, despite being on notice that the institution of law has unintended and unwanted effects, we have yet to investigate fully the social consequences that the institution of law has for society. We will be remiss if we continue to ignore them.

In prior scholarship, I identified macrosociological agents that helped to produce differences between the states of the United States in specific, socially salient law content.[169] Chapters 2, 3, and 4 in this book engage in not-dissimilar research, but with a particular focus: Using the law of and law-linked actions by states during the last half of the twentieth century, the chapters seek to locate macrosociological conditions and forces that were responsible for law content that was designed to maintain the social status quo in terms of marriage, race, and sex. Among Americans, marriage is sociologically important because it is a central feature of their culture and social life. The U.S. Supreme Court has thus observed that marriage "is a keystone of the Nation's social order" and "a building block of our national community."[170] Race and sex, although individual-level attributes, are important in social life since they have been and continue to be prominent bases on which American society is structured.[171] The Court acknowledged the importance of race when it pointed out that government-made distinctions involving race are suspect under the federal Constitution because they "reinforce the belief, held by too many for too much of our history, that individuals should be judged by the color of their skin."[172] The Court also acknowledged the importance of sex in American social life when it called attention to "the pervasive presumption that women are mothers first."[173] Although the Court has recognized that "[n]o longer is the female destined

---

168 Jon Elster, Explaining Social Behavior 303-05, 309-10, 440-41 (2007).

169 Explaining Law, *supra* note 18, at chs. 2, 3; SAIL vol. 1, *supra* note 4, at ch. 2 pt. 2.3; SAIL vol. 2, *supra* note 84, at chs. 2–6.

170 Obergefell v. Hodges, 135 S. Ct. 2584, 2601 (2015). The Court has made similar statements in other cases. *E.g.*, Loving v. Virginia, 388 U.S. 1, 12 (1967) ("Marriage is one of the 'basic civil rights of man,' fundamental to our very existence and survival" (internal citation omitted)).

171 Societal structure has been defined as the set of individual-level traits that mark social boundaries in the population of a society and that determine interpersonal relationships in the population. The structure of a society thus rests on the social differentiations that the society makes. Peter M. Blau, *A Macrosociological Theory of Social Structure*, 83 Am. J. Sociol. 26, 28 (1977).

172 Shaw v. Reno, 509 U.S. 630, 657 (1993) (majority opinion); Parents Involved in Community Schools v. Seattle School Dist. No. 1, 551 U.S. 701, 746 (2007) (plurality opinion). *Shaw* and *Parents Involved in Community Schools* were grounded on the Equal Protection Clause of the Fourteenth Amendment. See *infra* Chap. 2 pt. 2.2 for an explanation of the Clause. In a ruling based on the Fifteenth Amendment, the Court has said that "[o]ne of the principal reasons race is treated as a forbidden classification is that it demeans the dignity and worth of a person to be judged by ancestry instead of by his or her own merit and essential qualities." Rice v. Cayetano, 528 U.S. 495, 517 (2000). The Fifteenth Amendment provides that "The right of citizens of the United States to vote shall not be denied or abridged by the United States or by any State on account of race, color, or previous condition of servitude." U.S. Const. amend. XV, § 1.

173 Nevada Dept. of Human Resources v. Hibbs, 538 U.S. 721, 736 (2003) (quoting from the Parental and Medical Leave Act of 1986: Joint Hearing Before the Subcommittee on Labor–Management Relations and the Subcommittee on Labor Standards of the House Committee on

solely for the home and the rearing of the family,"[174] the change in sex roles that the United States has experienced over the past five or six decades did not radically transform American society. For example, about nine out of ten American women during the twentieth century married at some point in their lives (or, in the case of recent birth cohorts of women, are projected to do so);[175] at least three out of four American women in twentieth-century birth cohorts bore a child;[176] and even today the total fertility rate is about 4.0 children for a married, spouse-present woman in the United States.[177] Not surprisingly, the marriage institution in the United States incorporates established social biases that pertain to race[178] and embodies established social expectations that pertain to sex.[179]

In short, race and sex have long been mainstays of American social thinking and have long appeared in patterns of American marriage. Given the considerable inertia in American society, race and sex are attractive topics for a study of society-level properties that have led Americans to support law that recognizes traditional aspects of social life and to resist law that is thought to threaten these aspects. Although race and sex are not the only topics through which sources of resistance to law-pertinent social change can be identified—another obvious topic is religion—they have historically been cornerstones of the structure of American society and, for the purpose of the next three chapters, are conveniently tied together by the institution of marriage.

Structural-functionalism theory plays a role here. That theory, which is summarized in Sect. 1.2 of the present chapter, lends plausibility to the sociological

---

Education and Labor, 99th Cong. 99, 100 (1986) (statement of Women's Legal Defense Fund)), *available at* https://eric.ed.gov/?id=ED288599. *See also* Hoyt v. Florida, 368 U.S. 57, 62 (1961) (observing that women are "regarded as the center of home and family life" in America).

[174] Stanton v. Stanton, 421 U.S. 7, 14 (1975).

[175] Donald W. Hastings & J. Gregory Robinson, *A Re-Examination of Hernes' Model on the Process of Entry into First Marriage for United States Women, Cohorts 1891-1945*, 38 Am. Sociol. Rev. 138, 140 tbl. 1 (1973); Joshua R. Goldstein & Catherine T. Kenney, *Marriage Delayed or Marriage Forgone? New Cohort Forecasts of First Marriage for U.S. Women*, 66 Am. Sociol. Rev. 506, 510 tbl. 1, 512 tbl. 2, 513 fig. 1 (2001). *Cf.* SAIL vol. 1, *supra* note 4, at 24 fig. 1.2 (graphing percentages of men and of women in the United States who, in periods after the middle of the twentieth century, had not married by age 30 and by age 40).

[176] Donald T. Rowland, *Historical Trends in Childlessness*, 28 J. Fam. Issues 1311, 1314–15 tbl. 1, 1318 fig. 1, 1325 fig. 2 (2007).

[177] Lyman Stone, Inst. for Fam. Stud., *No Ring, No Baby: How Marriage Trends Impact Fertility* (2018), https://ifstudies.org/blog/no-ring-no-baby (last visited Nov. 15, 2022).

[178] In the United States during the period 1880–2000, less than 1.0 percent of all marriages involved a white whose spouse was a black, i.e., a white male and a black female or a white female and a black male. Roland G. Fryer, Jr., *Guess Who's Been Coming to Dinner? Trends in Interracial Marriage over the 20th Century*, 21 J. Econ. Persp. 71, 75, 76 fig. 1, 78, A2 tbl. A2 (2007) (displaying in graphs, for census years from 1880 to 2000, the percentages of all married couples in which the spouses were a white and a black).

[179] Mark Kotkin, *Sex Roles Among Married and Unmarried Couples*, 9 Sex Roles 975, 977, 982 (1983). *See also* the text accompanying note 14 in *infra* Chap. 4 (reporting that opposite-sex married-couple households were 99 percent of all married-couple households in 2019).

properties investigated in Chaps. 2, 3, and 4 as antecedents of and influences on the content of law addressing society-significant social patterns pertaining to race, sex, and marriage. In case studies in Chaps. 2, 3, and 4 (whose order is determined by the chronological sequence of applicable federal constitutional law), I use data on states to ascertain whether the properties are responsible for state differences in adopted law or reactions to proposed law. Given the nature of the sociological properties that are included in the studies and the social customs that have surrounded race, sex, and marriage in the United States, a relationship between a property and a between-state difference in adopted law or reaction to proposed law permits the inference that social stress was involved in the relationship. The inference gains credibility from empirical evidence that traditional social beliefs backed the state law considered in Chap. 2 (state law forbidding interracial marriage)[180] and Chap. 4 (state law forbidding same-sex marriage)[181] and that such beliefs were behind the hostility exhibited by some states to the proposed constitutional amendment considered in Chap. 3 (the Equal Rights Amendment).[182]

To help readers anticipate what the next three chapters are about, let me offer additional detail regarding the topics that are examined in these chapters. Chapter 2 concentrates on state law that prohibited marriage between persons defined by their race, while Chap. 4 focuses on state law that prohibited marriage between persons defined by their sex. Although the content of law differed between the two chapters, it shares a common attribute: In both chapters, the content of state law was held by the U.S. Supreme Court to offend the federal Constitution. While rulings by the Court typically manifest current social ideology,[183] what is important about the rulings with which Chaps. 2 and 4 are concerned is that they invalidated, on constitutional grounds, law content that reflected conventional social ideologies regarding marriage. Because each ruling was in conflict with tradition, it is presumed

[180] Ewa A. Golebiowska, *The Contours and Etiology of Whites' Attitudes Toward Black-White Interracial Marriage*, 38 J. Black Stud. 268, 271, 279, 280 tbl. 2, 284 (2007); Samuel L. Perry & Andrew L. Whitehead, *Christian Nationalism and White Racial Boundaries: Examining Whites' Opposition to Interracial Marriage*, 38 Ethnic & Racial Stud. 1671, 1676–78, 1680 tbl. 2, 1682 tbl. 3, 1683 tbl. 4 (2015).

[181] Amy B. Becker, *What's Marriage (and Family) Got to Do with It? Support for Same-Sex Marriage, Legal Unions, and Gay and Lesbian Couples Raising Children*, 93 Soc. Sci. Q. 1007, 1014–15, 1017 tbl. 1 (2012); Laura R. Olson et al., *Religion and Public Opinion about Same-Sex Marriage*, 87 Soc. Sci. Q. 340, 343–44, 348, 350 tbl. 2, 355 (2006). *See* Samuel L. Perry, *Bible Beliefs, Conservative Religious Identity, and Same-Sex Marriage Support: Examining Main and Moderating Effects*, 54 J. Sci. Study of Religion 792, 798–99, 802 tbl. 2 (model 2), 803 tbl. 3 (2015) (studying individual-level religious conservatism and its impact on the degree to which individuals opposed or endorsed law that allows same-sex couples to marry).

[182] Sandra K. Gill, *Attitudes toward the Equal Rights Amendment: Influence of Class and Status*, 28 Sociol. Persp. 441, 448–49, 455 tbl. 3, 457–58 & tbl. 5, 460 n.3 (1985).

[183] Kevin T. McGuire & James A. Simpson, *The Least Dangerous Branch Revisited: New Evidence on Supreme Court Responsiveness to Public Preferences*, 66 J. Pol. 1018, 1033 (2004). *See generally* SAIL vol. 1, *supra* note 4, at 14–15 (describing the sociological character of rulings by the U.S. Supreme Court that interpret the federal Constitution).

to have been a source of social stress in the states where the invalidated law existed. If the foregoing presumption is correct, whether social stress resulted from the rulings was determined in large part by the state-level sociological conditions and forces that supported the invalidated law. In other words, the state sociological attributes behind the state law that the Court struck down are taken to be important drivers of the occurrence of Court-generated social stress.

An additional aspect of the law content invalidated by the Court bears mentioning. The United States has, governmentally, a federal structure, and thus the states of the nation are, and have long been, encouraged to manage their own affairs and adopt law content of their own choosing.[184] Of course, when the U.S. Supreme Court concludes that the law of a state violates a provision of the federal Constitution, the ruling issued by the Court is applicable to every state and imposes a nationwide uniformity as to such law. The ruling is thus inconsistent with the practice of federalism. When the ruling touches on traditional American values regarding social life, the ruling is likely to cause disaffection among some segments of the population, thereby decreasing social cohesiveness and increasing the occurrence of social stress. This sociological impact receives a boost from the conflict that exists between the ruling and the belief in the inherent right of states to govern themselves.

Turning to the third case study—the subject of Chap. 3—we deal with a proposed amendment to the federal Constitution that explicitly sought to minimize government-made differentiations that involve the biological attribute of sex and the social attribute of gender. The states that opposed the amendment would have acted as they did because of traditional views of sex roles, views that were antithetical to the amendment. Social stress, accordingly, is a logical byproduct of the clash between the proposed amendment and such views. If social stress was a product of the advocated amendment, such stress is traceable to the state-level sociological conditions and forces that pushed states to oppose the amendment.

1.8 Logistic Regression and Its Role in the Book

The independent variables that are used in the studies reported in Chaps. 2, 3, and 4—the variables that potentially affected whether a change or advocated change in law engendered social stress in a state—were state-level sociological properties. Data on these properties were analyzed with logistic regression, a multivariate statistical technique that estimated whether each property was statistically related

[184] Elizabeth Ann Kronk Warner, *Justice Brandeis and Indian Country. Lessons from the Tribal Environmental Laboratory*, 47 ARIZ. ST. L.J. 857, 866–68 (2015).

In sample surveys of U.S. adults conducted since the 1980s, no less than two out of three respondents have said that the federal government should be confined to handling matters that state and local governments cannot handle. JOHN SAMPLES & EMILY EKINS, CATO INST., PUBLIC ATTITUDES TOWARD FEDERALISM: THE PUBLIC'S PREFERENCE FOR RENEWED FEDERALISM 29 fig. 30 (2014).

to, and could therefore be deemed to have had an impact on, the dependent variable, i.e., the content of state law governing eligibility to marry or the reaction by states to the proposed Equal Rights Amendment ("ERA"). Like other forms of regression, logistic regression gauges each relationship between an independent variable and a dependent variable holding constant every other independent variable in the set of independent variables being studied, i.e., in the regression model. For the independent-dependent relationships in the models in the next three chapters, I provide levels of statistical significance when the levels were at or below .10 since some readers will want this information, but I disregarded significance levels when deciding whether the independent variables in a model were related to the dependent variable. Significance levels were not considered because the data that I analyzed come from the entire universe of interest, not from a sample that was randomly drawn from this universe.[185] Instead, I evaluated models as a whole, with the evaluations based largely on how well the models fit the data and how many independent variables were employed by the models to achieve this fit. Preferred models were those that, regardless of levels of statistical significance, had the fewest independent variables that in combination were highly accurate predictors of what states said in their law on marriage or what states did with respect to the ERA.

Logistic regression was used, and least-squares regression was not used, in the chapters that follow because states were dichotomized and coded either 0 or 1 on the dependent variables.[186] Logistic regression was thus necessary for the studies in Chaps. 2, 3, and 4. However, logistic regression is also an intuitively appealing statistical technique for the studies because of the odds ratios that it estimates for the independent variables in a model. Odds ratios are intuitively meaningful: The odds ratio for an independent variable shows the degree to which change can be expected in the odds that a state was in the dependent-variable category that was coded 1 when the independent variable increased by a single measurement unit (e.g., percentage-point) in the state or when the state was a single measurement unit higher than another state on this independent variable. Of course, the independent variables in a model do not employ the same measurement unit and are unlikely to have the same standard deviation. As a result, standardized logistic-regression coefficients for the independent variables were computed, too, so that the impact of one independent

[185] SAIL VOL. 2, *supra* note 84, at 9–13.

[186] FRED C. PAMPEL, LOGISTIC REGRESSION: A PRIMER ch. 1 (2000). For another explanation of logistic regression and how logistic regression differs from least-squares regression, see Francis L. Huang & Tonya R. Moon, *What Are the Odds of That? A Primer on Understanding Logistic Regression*, 57 GIFTED CHILD Q. 197 (2013). During the past half-century, the limitations of least-squares regression have led to the greater use of logistic regression when the dependent variable is measured as a dichotomy. Chao-Ying Joanne Peng et al., *An Introduction to Logistic Regression Analysis and Reporting*, 96 J. EDUC. RES. 3, 3 (2002).

In analyzing the data with logistic regression, I employed Stata™ IC version 12.1; odds ratios were estimated using the LOGISTIC command, and regression coefficients were estimated using the LOGIT command. STATACORP, STATA BASE REFERENCE MANUAL: RELEASE 12, at 932, 970 (2011).

variable in a model could be compared to the impact of another independent variable.[187]

I should point out that, in coding the states on the dependent variables in Chap. 2 and Chap. 4, the number 1 was assigned to a state whose law on marriage manifested a tradition that the U.S. Supreme Court concluded could not, under provisions of the federal Constitution governing the rights of individuals, be embodied in law. All other states were assigned the number 0 on these dependent variables. An odds ratio calculated by logistic regression for an independent variable in Chap. 2 and Chap. 4 thus exceeds 1.000 when a measurement-unit increase or a measurement-unit advantage on the independent variable gave a state higher odds of having had such Court-invalidated law.[188] Because the states that were coded 1 presumably experienced social stress from the tradition-upending decision rendered by the Court, an independent variable whose odds ratio was above 1.000 is posited as an agent that raised the odds of occurrence of Court-induced social stress: An increase by a state of one measurement-unit on this independent variable presumptively raised the odds that the Court, by its ruling, brought about social stress in the state; a one measurement-unit advantage by a state on the independent variable presumptively raised the odds that the Court, by its ruling, brought about social stress in the state that had the additional measurement unit.

Similarly, in Chap. 3, the number 1 was assigned to states that reacted negatively to (i.e., opposed) the proposal to place the Equal Rights Amendment in the federal Constitution, and the number 0 was assigned to states that reacted positively to (i.e., favored) the proposal. Therefore, in a logistic-regression model for state responses to the proposed amendment, an independent variable whose odds ratio was above 1.000 gave a state higher odds of responding negatively to the proposed ERA when the state underwent a one measurement-unit increase in the independent

---

[187] In a model, coefficients were standardized only on the standard deviations of the indicators of the independent variables (i.e., the X variables). Coefficients were not standardized on the standard deviation of the indicator of the dependent variable (i.e., Y variable), because each dependent variable was measured as a dummy, i.e., as a dichotomy that was quantified with the numbers 0 and 1. Richard Williams, *Standardized Coefficients in Logistic Regression* 2–3 (2019), https://www3.nd.edu/~rwilliam/stats3/index.html (last visited Sept. 11, 2022).

Standardized coefficients were computed using the LISTCOEF command in Stata.

[188] Odds are related to, but differ from, probabilities. Odds are determined by the ratio of (i) the probability that a particular phenomenon will be observed and (ii) the probability that the phenomenon will not be observed. The ratio of (i) to (ii) is the odds that the phenomenon will be observed, e.g., the odds that a state will have law that forbids interracial marriage or law that forbids same-sex marriage. The probability of the phenomenon is the number of cases in which the phenomenon has been observed divided by the total number of cases, i.e., the number of cases in which the phenomenon has been observed plus the number of cases in which the phenomenon has not been observed. To illustrate, assume that a specific phenomenon has been found in thirty cases and has not been found in twenty cases. Since the total number of cases is 50, the probability that the phenomenon will be observed in a randomly-selected case is $30 \div (30 + 20) = 30 \div 50 = .60$, and the probability that the phenomenon will not be observed in a randomly chosen case is $20 \div (30 + 20) = 20 \div 50 = .40$. Therefore, the odds that the phenomenon will be found in a particular case are $.60/.40 = 1.5$ to one.

variable or when the state had, relative to another state, one more measurement unit of the independent variable than the other state. States that had a negative reaction to the proposal were assumed to be driven by tradition surrounding the sex attribute of individuals, tradition that a sizeable segment of the state population thought was endangered by the ERA. In Chap. 3, accordingly, an independent variable whose odds ratio was above 1.000 presumptively pushed up the odds that social stress was created in a state by the ERA and its advocacy.

Odds ratios less than 1.000 should be mentioned, too, because they appear in the studies that I report in the next three chapters. Given the premise in these chapters that the constitution-based Supreme Court decisions and the proposed ERA were able to cause social stress, an odds ratio that was below 1.000 for a given independent variable signals that a gain of one measurement unit on this independent variable decreased the odds that state-level social stress resulted from the Court rulings and the ERA; similarly, an odds ratio under 1.000 signals that social stress had lower odds of happening in states that, relative to other states, possessed one more measurement unit of the independent variable. Odds ratios below 1.000 are to be expected under structural-functionalism theory, which guides the present book and underlies the concept of societal stress, because structural-functionalism theory posits that social life generally limits the amount of internal conflict and normally does not move very far from being in a homeostatic condition.[189] Unsurprisingly, then, some societal agents will act to reduce the frequency of social stress from a Court decision or a proposed constitutional amendment.

Appendix 1. Research on the Impact of Law

Law and government policy are widely believed to have a substantial, lasting effect on the frequency with which society-significant social activities occur among individuals in a modern society. Acceptance of this view bolsters, in turn, the assumption that law and government policy are useful tools for improving the commonweal. But is the assumption warranted by social science evidence? In my view, it is not, because numerous shortcomings exist in the body of research that supports the assumption. Even though a single study cannot be expected to avoid every shortcoming—social scientists, after all, do not have access to everything they require to produce an unassailable study—the range of possible shortcomings must be kept in mind because even a single shortcoming has the potential to yield an erroneous, misleading, and/or incomplete picture of the societal impact of law and government policy. Put differently, consumers of social science research should understand that studies of the impact of law/policy on a particular social activity may suffer from one or more fatal deficiencies.

[189] See the text accompanying *supra* notes 48–53.

What types of problems do social scientists confront when they attempt to ascertain the effects of law and policy on society? For convenience, I look at two matters, which I label (1) research design and (2) data. In the instant Appendix, I discuss aspects of these matters that, in my experience, are often overlooked.[190] The discussion, I hope, will promote an awareness of the ease with which an ill-advised conclusion can be reached regarding whether, how, and the degree to which specific individual-level social behaviors respond to law/policy that aims to suppress or encourage them. In other words, considerable skepticism is merited when dealing with studies in which law/policy is found to have a substantial impact on the frequency of society-important social behaviors. I should add that such skepticism, in undermining support for the popular belief in the ability of law to solve social problems, can have a societal benefit. Specifically, the popular belief has been a source of social conflict over law/policy as different political groups have worked to change, while other political groups have worked to retain, current law/policy.[191] Sociology has an obligation to put readers on guard with respect to studies that buttress the belief in the ability of law/policy to bring about a large, lasting change in social life. Because sociology recognizes that societies require a high degree of internal cohesiveness and temporal consistency, sociologists need to encourage the readers of the studies to be on the lookout for problems in the studies.

Let me turn now to the two topics that I identified above—(1) research design and (2) data. I will use them to point out that many opportunities exist for defects and limitations in social science studies of the behavioral impact of law and government policy.

Research design. Every study of the impact of law/policy on the incidence of social behavior should be judged in terms of how well it is designed, i.e., how well its structure satisfies the principles of a sound study.[192] Ideally, such a study includes at least one jurisdiction ("treatment jurisdiction") in which change occurred in law/policy on a particular society-significant social activity and at least one jurisdiction ("control jurisdiction") in which such change did not occur but which is otherwise sociologically comparable to the treatment jurisdiction. A divergence after the law/policy change between the treatment jurisdiction(s) and the control jurisdiction(s) in the frequency of the dependent variable is a necessary condition for inferring that the new law/policy had an effect on the frequency. Notably, the degree to which a study adheres to the principles for sound research is inversely related to whether an effect is detected.[193] A study that fully embodies these principles, in

[190] In addition, see THE BIOSPHERE AND HUMAN Society, *supra* note 135, at ch. 3 pt. 3.1.

[191] James Davison Hunter, *The Culture War and the Sacred/Secular Divide: The Problem of Pluralism and Weak Hegemony*, 76 SOC. RES. 1307 (2009).

[192] For a well-designed study of whether a municipal gun-control law curtailed the incidence of homicides committed with a gun, see Chester L. Britt et al., *A Reassessment of the D.C. Gun Law: Some Cautionary Notes on the Use of Interrupted Time Series Designs for Policy Impact Assessment*, 30 LAW & SOC'Y REV. 361 (1996).

[193] FRANS L. LEEUW WITH HANS SCHMEETS, EMPIRICAL LEGAL RESEARCH: A GUIDANCE BOOK FOR LAWYERS, LEGISLATORS AND REGULATORS 122–25 (2016).

other words, is less likely to uncover an effect than a study that just partially embodies them.

Data. In addition to research design, attention must be paid to multiple aspects of the data that were employed to assess the impact that law and/or government policy had on the incidence of a given form of social behavior. I examine seven of these aspects.

1. The key independent variable in studies of the sociological effects of law and government policy is the content of law/policy that is pertinent to the dependent (i.e., outcome) variable, but mistakes can be made in determining this content.[194] While even a law-trained investigator can be wrong about the content of law/policy, an investigator who is not trained in law/policy seems more likely to make a mistake. Such mistakes, obviously, introduce error into the data being used for the key explanatory factor and pose a major risk to the accuracy of the findings that emerge from statistical analyses of the data.
2. The beginning and the ending points of the time period covered by the data must not be arbitrarily chosen. The selection of these time points must not be decided by, for example, the period for which data are available. Research on the effect of a change in law has shown that different post-change ending points can cause important differences in findings.[195] If the ending point can sway the results, the beginning point can, too.

   What, however, should supply the foundation for picking the start and end of the time interval covered by a study of the social impact of law/policy? Ideally, theory ought to play a role. With useful theory, credible time points can be chosen; without it, guesswork will be the basis for selecting time points. Unfortunately, theory in the macrosociology of law content is rudimentary at the moment and hence offers little if any guidance to researchers when they choose the beginning and ending time points for their data.
3. The length of the period before change occurs in the law/policy under study is critical. To gauge the impact of law/policy on the dependent variable, researchers must establish the pre-law/pre-policy baseline for the dependent variable. Their data for the dependent variable, therefore, must cover sufficient time to allow a reliable baseline to be accurately identified.

   A recently published study furnishes evidence of how an unreliable baseline (and data on an undifferentiated age range) may influence results. The dependent variable was the rate at which females aged 15–17 aborted pregnancies in the United States, and the central independent variable was whether U.S. states by statute mandated "parental involvement" in the decision-making process for such an abortion.[196] Employing data for the period 1985–2013, the study concluded

---

[194] See the paragraphs that accompany notes 34 to 36 in *infra* Chap. 3; in addition, see the text accompanying notes 78 and 79 in *infra* Chap. 4.

[195] Britt et al., *supra* note 192, at 370–71, 375, 377 tbl. 6.

[196] Theodore J. Joyce et al., *The Impact of Parental Involvement Laws on the Abortion Rate of Minors*, 57 DEMOGRAPHY 323 (2020).

that the rate at which pregnant minors aged 15–17 terminated pregnancies was unaltered by state parental-involvement statutes that were put in place after the middle of the 1990s, but was decreased 15 to 20 percent by state parental-involvement statutes that were put in place prior to the middle of the 1990s.[197] However, two features of the data used by the study merit attention. First, the data combined all females in the 15-to-17 age range, but by not separating 17-year-old females from 15- and 16-year-old females, the data probably exaggerated the effect of parental-involvement laws: In states that have a parental-involvement statute, some pregnant 17-year-old females who are nearing their eighteenth birthday when they conceive evidently postpone an abortion until they turn eighteen and are no longer subject to the statute.[198] Second, and directly related to the baseline for the study, the data analyzed did not begin until 1985. For the states that adopted parental-involvement laws prior to the mid-1990s, consequently, fewer than ten years of data could have been used to calculate the pre-law baseline, but a reliable baseline involving annual data is unlikely to be established without pre-law data that cover at least ten calendar years. The ten-year minimum, of course, would not have been met by the parental-involvement statutes that were adopted before the middle of the 1990s. As to these statutes, then, the study in all likelihood had an unreliable baseline, and its conclusion with respect to the impact of the statutes must be treated with caution.

4. The length of time over which the dependent variable is measured after a change in law/policy must be sufficient to ascertain whether post-change effects (assuming they occur) end quickly or continue for a lengthy period. The frequency of a society-significant social activity may be altered by law/policy in the short run but not in the long run. Unless the data that a study uses for the dependent variable cover a substantial post-law/post-policy period, the study will be unable to determine whether the effect of the law/policy disappears with the passage of time.
5. Data analyses examining the impact of law/policy on the incidence of social behavior (dependent variable) over a specific time interval must consider more than *whether* this incidence changed following the adoption of the law/policy. If such change occurred, the magnitude of the change is important: Was a rise or fall

[197] *Id.* at 326, 337-38 & fig. 2, 344. Females aged 15–17 accounted for approximately 9 percent of all induced abortions in the United States during the years 1985–1994. Computed from Centers for Disease Control & Prevention, *Trends in Pregnancies and Pregnancy Rates by Outcome: Estimates for the United States, 1976-96*, Vital & Health Stat., Series 21, No. 56, at 26 tbl. 2 (2000).

[198] Silvie Colman et al., *Misclassification Bias and the Estimated Effect of Parental Involvement Laws on Adolescents' Reproductive Outcomes*, 98 Am. J. Pub. Health 1881, 1882–83, 1884 (2008) (examining the response of the abortion rate in Texas to a state parental-involvement statute that was adopted in Texas in January 2000; comparing the abortion rate in Texas among 17 year-old females to the abortion rate in Texas among 18-year-old females during the twelve months from August 1, 1998 to July 31, 1999 and in 2000; concluding that prior studies of the effect of state parental-involvement law on the rate at which minor females abort pregnancies are likely to have yielded artificially high estimates of the effect because the studies did not distinguish 17-year-old females from younger females).

in the post-law/post-policy incidence of the behavior large, or was it small? A statistically significant change, in particular, is not necessarily a change that is sizeable in amount and of practical importance.

6. Research concerned with the social impact of law/policy must consider not just wanted types of outcomes; it must also investigate unwanted types of outcomes. Social-impact research is grounded on a concern with the public welfare, and socially undesirable consequences of law/policy thus ought not to be ignored by this research. If negative social outcomes occur, they must be found and taken into account because undesirable consequences may be at least as sociologically harmful as desirable consequences are sociologically beneficial.
7. Research focused on the impact of a statute must ascertain the date on which the statute was enforced. However, the enforcement date may not be easy to determine, and a belief that a researcher holds about the date may not be correct, or may be at least debatable. Obviously, an accurate assessment of the impact that the statute had on behavior is not possible unless, inter alia, the investigator pinpoints the date on which enforcement of the statute began.

    A handgun-control statute in the United States illustrates the problems that can arise in identifying the effective date of a statute and the consequences of such problems for quantitative social science studies of the impact of a statute. Accordingly, I examine the handgun-control statute at length.

    The legislation that produced the handgun-control statute, which is popularly known as the Brady Act, was passed by the U.S. Congress and signed by the U.S. President—i.e., was enacted—on November 30, 1993.[199] The Act instructed the U.S. Department of Justice to create a nationwide system of background checks on persons who seek to acquire (e.g., purchase) a handgun from "any licensed importer, licensed manufacturer, or licensed dealer."[200] However, the Act allowed five years after its enactment for the nationwide system to become operational, and until the federal system began to function, the Act required specified duties ("interim duties" or "interim requirements") to be performed by the "chief law-enforcement officer" in the geographic area where the potential handgun acquiror resides.[201] In particular, the chief law enforcement officer—an agent of the state or the state-created local government for the area of residence of the acquiror—was directed to ascertain within five business days whether the transfer of the weapon would be in breach of law. The Brady Act subjected the transfer to the five-day wait unless an official of the state of residence of the potential handgun acquiror, pursuant to the law of the state, issued a purchase permit in compliance with state law or unless the state of residence of the

[199] Brady Handgun Violence Prevention Act, Pub. L. 103-159, 107 Stat. 1536, 1546 (1993) (adding §§ (s)(1) & (s)(2) to 18 U.S.C. § 922) (codified as amended at 18 U.S.C. § 922(s)(1) (2022)). The Act defined a "handgun" as "a firearm which has a short stock and is designed to be held and fired by the use of a single hand." *Id.* at § 102(a)(2), 107 Stat. 1539.

[200] *Id.* at § 102(a)(1), 107 Stat. 1536 (adding § (s)(1) to 18 U.S.C. § 922).

[201] The "chief law enforcement officer" was defined as "the chief of police, the sheriff, or an equivalent officer or the designee of any such individual." *Id.* at § 102(a)(1), 107 Stat. 1539.

potential acquiror had a procedure through which transfer of the weapon to the acquiror was verified to be in compliance with state law.[202] Either condition exempted the transfer from the mandated five-day wait. At the time the legislation was enacted, twenty-three states—almost half of all states—evidently required background checks and hence qualified for the exemption.[203]

In the litigation that the above interim requirements triggered, the plaintiffs contended that the requirements conflicted with the structure of government in the United States as established by the Constitution of the nation. Several of the plaintiffs were successful: Enforcement of the background-check requirement was enjoined on May 16, 1994 by the federal district court in Montana;[204] on June 3, 1994 by a federal district court in Mississippi;[205] and on June 29, 1994 by the federal district court in Arizona.[206] During 1994, two other federal district courts—one in Vermont and one in Louisiana—also enjoined enforcement of the background-check requirement.[207]

By its terms, the Brady Act became effective 90 days after it was enacted,[208] i.e., became effective on the last day of February 1994. However, in four of the five states covered by the district courts that held the background-check duty to be unconstitutional, enforcement of the duty was halted by a court-issued injunction prior to the close of 1994. One of the five lower courts that invalidated the mandate—the federal district court in Louisiana—expressly put its ruling on hold while the ruling was appealed,[209] but none of the other four said that they were doing so. Since the four courts made no explicit statement that they were

---

[202] *Id.* at § 102(a)(1), 107 Stat. 1536, 1537.

[203] H.R. Rep. 103-344 (1993), 1993 U.S.C.C.A.N. 1984, 2000, *available at* 1993 WL 465097.

[204] Printz v. United States, 854 F. Supp. 1503 (D. Mont. 1994), *rev'd sub nom.*, Mack v. United States, 66 F.3d 1025 (9th Cir. 1995), *rev'd*, 521 U.S. 898 (1997). The U.S. Court of Appeals vacated the district-court injunction against enforcement of the Act on September 8, 1995. The U.-S. Supreme Court overturned the decision of the U.S. Court of Appeals on June 27, 1997.

[205] McGee v. United States, 863 F. Supp. 321 (S.D. Miss. 1994).

[206] Mack v. United States, 856 F. Supp. 1372 (D. Ariz. 1994), *rev'd*, 66 F.3d 1025 (9th Cir. 1995), *rev'd sub nom.*, Printz v. United States, 521 U.S. 898 (1997). The U.S. Court of Appeals vacated the district-court injunction against enforcement of the Act on September 8, 1995. The U.S. Supreme Court overturned the decision of the U.S. Court of Appeals on June 27, 1997.

[207] Frank v. United States, 860 F. Supp. 1030 (D. Vt. 1994) (injunction issued Aug. 2, 1994), *rev'd*, 78 F.3d 815 (2d Cir. 1995), *vacated & remanded*, 521 U.S. 1114 (1997); Romero v. United States, 883 F. Supp. 1076 (W.D. La. 1994) (injunction issued and stayed Dec. 8, 1994). In *Frank*, the U.S. Court of Appeals held, on March 14, 1996, that the background-check requirement was constitutional and reversed the decision of the district court; the U.S. Supreme Court overturned the ruling of the U.S. Court of Appeals on June 27, 1997.

[208] Pub. L. 103-159, § 102(a)(1), 107 Stat. 1536.

[209] Romero v. United States, 883 F. Supp. 1076, 1091 (W.D. La. 1994). *Romero* has no published appellate-court history.

granting stays of their injunctions, I will assume that they did not do so.[210] This assumption is key to the analysis that follows.

A few years later (on June 27, 1997), the U.S. Supreme Court agreed that the background-check mandate was unconstitutional, though it declined to rule on the waiting-period mandate because the latter mandate applied to handgun dealers and purchasers but no dealer or purchaser was a plaintiff in the case.[211] Under the Constitution, the Supreme Court wrote, the background-check mandate was inconsistent with the principle of federalism, a principle that is central to the organization of government in the United States.[212]

> The Federal Government may neither issue directives requiring the States to address particular problems, nor command the States' officers, or those of their political subdivisions, to administer or enforce a federal regulatory program.[213]

With the preceding history in mind, let us return to the matter of where and when the Brady was enforceable and enforced. The exemptions provided by the Act and the injunctions issued by the district courts reveal that the interim background-check duty established by the Act did not operate across all of the country for the entire period set by the Act. For instance, the duty was evidently applicable in just twenty-three states (i.e., $50 - 23$ exempted states $= 27 - 4$ court-enjoined states $= 23$). Furthermore, some governmental bodies in states that were obliged by the Act to conduct a background check are unlikely to have complied, or to have complied fully, while the district-court rulings that the required background check violated the Constitution made their way through the appellate process and to the Supreme Court. Although the precise extent of state noncompliance in the twenty-three states with the background-check duty prior to the Supreme Court decision is unknown, it is probably far from trivial. In mid-1997, of course, the Supreme Court eliminated the need for compliance.

The interim background-check requirement of the Brady Act, in short, was enforceable, though not necessarily enforced, in twenty-three states during part of 1994, during all of 1995 and 1996, and during part of 1997. Social science

---

[210]The filing of an appeal to contest a ruling of a federal district court does not automatically suspend an injunction issued by the district court; an application for a suspension must be submitted to the appellate court that has jurisdiction over the district court. Fed. R. App. P. 8(a)(2). I could find no indication in the opinions written in these cases by the Courts of Appeals or the U.S. Supreme Court that appellate-court suspensions of the injunctions were sought or, if sought, granted.

A conclusion that a court stayed an injunction without expressly saying so would be speculative and not tied to established law. Notably, the federal judiciary lacks a uniform test for deciding when to grant stays of final injunctions. Portia Pedro, *Stays*, 106 Calif. L. Rev. 869, 873 (2018) (observing that stays of final injunctions fall outside "the normal range of outcomes that we would expect from typical discretionary determinations. Instead, the factors that courts use [when making decisions on applications for stays] are arbitrary and vary unpredictably.").

[211]Printz v. United States, 521 U.S. 898, 935 (1997).

[212]Keith Werhan, *Checking Congress and Balancing Federalism: A Lesson from Separation-of-Powers Jurisprudence*, 57 Wash. & Lee L. Rev. 1213, 1218–19 (2000).

[213]521 U.S. at 935.

research must take this situation into account when it attempts to identify the degree to which the background-check requirement altered the frequency of violence. If the frequency of violence is measured with calendar-year data, the research can use data for just the two calendar years (namely, 1995 and 1996) during which the background-check requirement was in force.

The impact of the interim requirements of the Brady Act on the incidence of homicide has been addressed in several studies, each authored by different social scientists.[214] Of the studies, two concluded that the background-check requirement had either no impact or a negligible impact on homicide incidence, and one concluded that the requirement curtailed homicide incidence to a degree that, depending on the incidence measure, ranged from small to large.[215] The latest of the studies looked at both interim provisions. The interim waiting-period requirement was found to have moderately decreased—to be exact, decreased by 17 percent—the frequency of homicides committed with a handgun but to have had no influence on the frequency of homicides committed with a weapon other than a handgun. The interim requirement for a background check was found to have not changed the frequency of homicides committed with a handgun or with another type of weapon.[216] Because this study presumably improves on earlier research and reports more details about its data than earlier research, it merits further examination.

The interim period for the Brady Act began in February 1994 and ended in November 1998,[217] and the latest study gauged the impact of the interim-period provisions using calendar-year data for 1990 through 1998.[218] Unfortunately, the pre-Act baseline used by the study relied on just four points in time (i.e., 1990, 1991, 1992, and 1993), an interval that is too short to ensure a reliable baseline. The study design and data within the interim period are problematic, too. The U.S. Supreme Court invalidated the Act-mandated background check in June 1997, i.e., in the middle of the calendar year that preceded the ending calendar year for the data. Additionally, the study considered Mississippi, Montana, and Vermont to be states that required background checks during the entire interim

214 Jens Ludwig & Philip J. Cook, *Homicide and Suicide Rates Associated with Implementation of the Brady Handgun Violence Prevention Act*, 284 JAMA 585 (2000); Jeffrey D. Monroe, Homicide and Gun Control: The Brady Handgun Violence Prevention Act and Homicide Rates (2008); James M. La Valle, *"Gun Control" vs. "Self-Protection": A Case against the Ideological Divide*, 10 Just. Pol'y J. 1 (2013); Michael Luca et al., *Handgun Waiting Periods Reduce Gun Deaths*, 114(46) Proc. Nat'l Acad. Sci. 12162 (2017) [hereinafter *Handgun Waiting Periods*], https://www.pnas.org/doi/epdf/10.1073/pnas.1619896114, (last visited Aug. 30, 2022).

215 Andrew R. Morral, Rand Corp., *Effects of Background Checks on Violent Crime* [5] (2020), https://www.rand.org/research/gun-policy/analysis/background-checks/violent-crime.html.

216 *Handgun Waiting Periods*, *supra* note 214, at 12164 & tbl. 2.

217 See the text accompanying *supra* notes 199 to 201; Printz v. United States, 521 U.S. at 902.

218 *Handgun Waiting Periods*, *supra* note 214, at 12162; Table S3 in Luca et al., *Supporting Information*, a PDF file downloaded from https://www.pnas.org/doi/10.1073/pnas.1619896114#st04 (last visited June 5, 2022). The use of calendar-year data is shown by references to "state-year observations" and "state-years" in *Handgun Waiting Periods*, *supra* note 214, at 12163, 12164.

period, but injunctions issued by federal district courts in these states evidently stopped enforcement of the checks well before 1994 came to a close. Consequently, of the twenty-five states that the study believed were subject to the background-check mandate, three were not, and calendar-year data for 1997 and 1998 were used by the study even though during much of 1997 and all of 1998 the background-check requirement was unenforceable. The findings of the study, therefore, cannot be considered to be the last word on the question of whether and for how long the interim duties of the Brady Act affected or did not affect the incidence of homicides.

Appendix 2. The Voting Rights Act of 1965

The federal Voting Rights Act of 1965 in the United States sought to eliminate race-based obstacles to voting imposed by state and local governments.[219] In the words of the U.S. Supreme Court, "[t]he Voting Rights Act of 1965 reflects Congress' firm intention to rid the country of racial discrimination in voting[,] . . . an insidious and pervasive evil" that is present "in certain parts of our country through unremitting and ingenious defiance of the Constitution."[220] As recounted earlier,[221] the Act has garnered accolades because it is believed to have substantially moved the country toward this goal, but are the accolades warranted? Given the widespread assumption that regulatory law alters the social patterns that it targets and cures (or at least reduces) the social problems that it addresses, a positive answer to the question would be anticipated. A positive answer may be wrong, however, because credible evidence exists to conclude that the Act may have curtailed, not improved, the long-run ability of the black population living in southern U.S. states to employ the ballot to sway government.

The conclusion that the Voting Rights Act of 1965 was politically harmful to blacks stems from the findings of a study that examined the impact of the Act in North Carolina.[222] In this state, the Act evidently did more than remove

[219] Pub. L. No. 89-110, § 2, 79 Stat. 437, 437 (1965) ("No voting qualification or prerequisite to voting, or standard, practice, or procedure shall be imposed or applied by any State or political subdivision to deny or abridge the right of any citizen of the United States to vote on account of race or color") (codified as amended at 52 U.S.C. § 10301(a) (2022).

[220] South Carolina v. Katzenbach, 383 U.S. 301, 308–09 (1966). The Act is based on the Fifteenth Amendment to the Constitution. *Id.* at 308. The substantive section of the Fifteenth Amendment is reproduced in *supra* note 172. The Fifteenth Amendment became part of the Constitution in 1870. U.S. Gov't Printing Office, Amendments to the Constitution of the United States of America 33 ([1992]).

[221] *Supra* notes 150 & 151 and their accompanying text.

[222] Adriane Fresh, *The Effect of the Voting Rights Act on Enfranchisement: Evidence from North Carolina*, 80 J. Pol. 713 (2018). Section 5 of the Act was the focus of the study by Dr. Fresh and is considered to be "the heart" of the Act. Lani Guinier, *No Two Seats: The Elusive Quest for Political Equality*, 77 Va. L. Rev. 1413, 1419 (1991). *Accord*, Guy-Uriel E. Charles & Luis Fuentes-Rohwer,

government-created impediments to enfranchisement faced by blacks; it also seems to have generated social stress that galvanized whites to register to vote. In the mid-1960s, liberal political ideology was at a relative low point in North Carolina.[223] For whites in the state who disapproved the Act—a group that was undoubtedly a substantial share of all whites in the state[224]—the adoption of the Act would have been disquieting. Notably, the study (the "Fresh study") estimated that, over time, the Act produced an increase of 14 to 19 percentage points in voter registration

---

The Voting Rights Act in Winter: The Death of a Superstatute, 100 Iowa L. Rev. 1389, 1390, 1429 (2015) (observing that the Voting Rights Act is "widely regarded as the most successful civil rights statute ever enacted by Congress" and describing section 5 of the Act as "the most powerful tool in the VRA toolkit").

[223] Peter K. Enns & Julianna Koch, *Public Opinion in the U.S. States: 1956 to 2010*, 13 State Pol. & Pol'y Q. 349, 362 fig. 5(c) (2013) (BRFH Citizen Ideology scale). According to the authors of this study, the BRFH Citizen Ideology scale may be the best gauge of long-term change in political ideology at the state level. *Id.* at 361. *See generally*, Paul Burstein, *The Impact of Public Opinion on Public Policy: A Review and an Agenda*, 56 Pol. Res. Q. 29, 33 (2003) (concluding from a review of research that the content of law and government policy usually reflects the political ideology of the public).

[224] A national survey of the U.S. population conducted in May 1965 asked interviewees whether, "[i]n the recent showdown in Selma, Alabama over Negro voting rights," they "tended to side more with" the civil-rights advocates or with the "State of Alabama." Among whites, one out of five favored the State of Alabama; nearly half favored the civil-rights advocates. Andrew Kohut, Pew Res. Ctr., *From the Archives: 50 Years Ago: Mixed Views About Civil Rights But Support for Selma Demonstrators* [4] (2015, republished 2020). The fraction of whites who supported the State of Alabama, i.e., opposed voting rights for blacks, is likely to have been much larger in North Carolina than nationally because Americans who live in the South are in general more conservative than Americans who live in other geographic regions of the country. *See* David J. Harding & Christopher Jencks, *Changing Attitudes toward Premarital Sex: Cohort, Period, and Aging Effects*, 67 Pub. Opinion Q. 211, 223 tbl. 1 & n.8 (2003) (using data from the U.S. General Social Survey; controlling for age, sex, ethnicity, race, and decade in which age 18 was reached; finding that, with the foregoing controls, permissive attitudes toward premarital sex were less common among residents of the South than among residents of other regions); Allan Mazur, *Believers and Disbelievers in Evolution*, 23 Pol. & Life Sci. 55, 56, 59 & tbl. 4 (model 1) (2005) (using data from the U.S. General Social Survey; holding constant the educational attainment, age, race, and urban versus rural residence of respondents; finding that, with the foregoing controls, respondents in the South less often believed in evolution than respondents located outside the South).

In focusing on the "the recent showdown in Selma, Alabama," the survey question referenced the demonstrations in that city in February and March 1965; the purpose of the demonstrations was to protest actions by the state that kept blacks from voting. For a description of the demonstrations, see Nat'l Archives, Selma Marches (2020), https://www.archives.gov/research/african-americans/vote/selma-marches. The demonstrations have been characterized as the trigger for the passage of the Voting Rights Act. *Id.* On March 15, 1965, then-President Lyndon B. Johnson referenced the demonstrations in Selma in a speech to Congress urging approval of the Act. U.S. Ctr. for Legis. Aff., President Lyndon Johnson's Speech to Congress on Voting Rights, March 15, 1965, https://www.archives.gov/legislative/features/voting-rights-1965/johnson.html. On August 6, 1965, the Act was passed by Congress and signed into law by President Johnson. Pub. L. No. 89-110, 79 Stat. 437,446 (1965); LBJ Presidential Library, Voting Rights Act Media Kit (remarks on signing the Voting Rights Act), https://www.lbjlibrary.org/object/text/signing-voting-rights-act-08-06-1965.

Table 1.2 Racial composition of the voting-age population: North Carolina

Year	Whites (%)	Blacks (%)
1970	80.2	18.9
1980	78.1	20.3
1990	75.6	22.0

Source: see footnote 227

among blacks and an increase of 10 to 13 percentage points in voter registration among whites.[225] Although on its face the absolute difference between the former range and the latter range suggests that blacks politically gained from the Act, such a conclusion is premature. Let me explain.

Any assessment of the impact of the Act in North Carolina must take into account the racial composition of the population in that state, because among North Carolina residents who were eligible to vote by virtue of age, whites far outnumbered blacks. This can be seen in Table 1.2, which presents for each of three time points the percentage of the North Carolina voting-age population that was white and the percentage of the North Carolina voting-age population that was black.[226] The percentages were calculated from data obtained by the decennial censuses conducted in 1970, 1980, and 1990,[227] years that are within the time span covered by the study.[228] Readers should note that, for each year, the percentages in the rows do not sum to 100.0 because state residents who were not white or black are omitted.

The percentages in Table 1.2, however, do not end my analysis. Next, I estimate, for North Carolina, the number of whites who registered to vote because of the Act and the number of blacks who registered to vote because of the Act. The calculations were done using simple multiplication. Specifically, I multiplied each percentage for age-eligible whites in the table by .115, the decimal format for the midpoint of the 10-to-13 percentage-point range that the Fresh study estimated for whites. Similarly, I multiplied each percentage for age-eligible blacks in the table by 0.165, the decimal

[225] Fresh, *supra* note 222, at 714.

[226] The age at which a North Carolina resident became entitled to vote was not the same at all three time points. In 1971, the state lowered its minimum voting age from 21 years to 18 years. Act of July 21, 1971, ch. 1231, § 1, 1971 N.C. Sess. Laws 1794 (codified at N.C. Gen. Stat. § 163-55(a) (2022).

[227] The percentages were computed from:

- U.S. Bureau of the Census, 1970 Census of Population. 1 Characteristics of the Population. Part 35. North Carolina 57–62 tbl. 20 (1973) (persons aged 21 or older).
- U.S. Bureau of the Census, 1980 Census of Population. Vol. 1: Characteristics of the Population. Ch. B: General Population Characteristics. Part 35: North Carolina 28–33 tbl. 19 (1982) (persons aged 18 or older).
- U.S. Bureau of the Census, 1990 Census of Population. General Population Characteristics. North Carolina 97 tbl. 19 ([1992]) (persons aged 18 or older).

The cited Census Bureau publications are available at https://www.census.gov/programs-surveys/decennial-census/decade.html.

[228] Dr. Fresh analyzed voter-registration data for the period from 1958 to 1993. Fresh, *supra* note 222, at 715.

Table 1.3 Estimated number of Whites and Blacks who registered to vote per 100 adult residents: North Carolina

Year	Whites	Blacks	Difference
1970	9.2	3.1	6.1
1980	9.0	3.3	5.7
1990	8.7	3.6	5.1

format for the midpoint of the 14-to-19 percentage-point range that the Fresh study estimated for blacks. These arithmetic operations provide estimates of the number of whites and the number of blacks in North Carolina who, because of the Act, registered to vote per 100 adult residents of the state. The numbers for whites and for blacks accordingly represent Act-caused additions to voter registration in North Carolina for every 100 adults of the respective race in the state. Expressed another way, these North Carolina residents would not have registered to vote in the absence of the Act. Their numbers are reported in Table 1.3.

Table 1.3 is revealing. The second and third columns show that, over the course of the 1970–1990 period, the effect of the Act in North Carolina was the registration of approximately nine whites but fewer than four blacks in each set of 100 adult residents. The fourth (right-hand) column shows expressly what the second and third columns imply, viz., that for every 100 adults in North Carolina, the number of whites who registered to vote because of the Act was five or six larger than the number of blacks who registered to vote because of the Act. In North Carolina, consequently, the Act expanded, not contracted, the racial gap in registrations. Unless the Act induced dramatically larger proportions of registered blacks than registered whites to cast ballots in elections—a question that the Fresh study was unable to answer from the data available[229]—the Act is unlikely to have markedly improved the influence that blacks had on the political process and government in North Carolina. For at least some of the other states in the South (the geographic region at which the Act was principally directed[230]), the conclusion is probably the same; indeed, the presumption of generalizability of findings in social science

[229] Although the Act appreciably increased the frequency with which registered voters cast ballots in elections, the data did not allow a determination of whether the increase differed by race. Fresh, *supra* note 222, at 716–17 & tbl. 2.

[230] Peyton McCrary, *How the Voting Rights Act Works: Implementation of a Civil Rights Policy, 1965-2005*, 57 S.C. L. Rev. 785, 787–88 (2006). Although the Act was applied to some states outside the South, it was mainly enforced against states in the South. South Carolina v. Katzenbach, 383 U.S. 301, 318–19 (1966).

The states in the South, as designated by the U.S. Bureau of the Census, are Alabama, Arkansas, Delaware, Florida, Georgia, Kentucky, Louisiana, Maryland, Mississippi, North Carolina, Oklahoma, South Carolina, Tennessee, Texas, Virginia, and West Virginia. U.S. Bureau of the Census, Geographic Areas Reference Manual. Ch. 6: Statistical Grouping of States and Counties 24 tbl. 6-4 (1994), *available at* https://www.census.gov/programs-surveys/geography/guidance/geographic-areas-reference-manual.html.

supplies a basis for expecting that the conclusion would not be materially different across most of the South. Politically, in short, the Act seems not to have been of uniform help to Blacks in the South, and in many states in this region, it probably hurt them.

Chapter 2
The Constitution and State Law on Interracial Marriage

The social aspects of a society at a particular time are not disconnected from the social aspects of the society in the past. Unsurprisingly, therefore, the way in which American society treated interracial marriage in the middle of the twentieth century was built on an ideology that prevailed during the nineteenth century. Contemporaneous expressions of the ideology are revealing:[1]

- In 1871, the Supreme Court of Indiana wrote that for whites and blacks, "[t]he natural law which forbids their intermarriage . . . is as clearly divine as that which imparted to them different natures."
- In 1877, the Supreme Court of Alabama wrote that "Manifestly, it is for the peace and happiness of the black race, as well as of the white, that such laws [against black-white intermarriage] should exist. And surely there can not be any tyranny or injustice in requiring both alike, to form this union with those of their own race only, whom God hath joined together by indelible peculiarities, which declare that He has made the two races distinct."

These passages tell a story. That story is part of American social history and the foundation of Chapter 2.

2.1 The Federal Constitution and Personal Rights

Social activities that are significant in a structurally complex, democratically governed society become the subject of law in the society, but neither chance nor the idiosyncrasies of individuals are responsible, at least in the long run, for whether a particular significant activity is permitted or prohibited by law. Instead, the

[1] The following quoted passages are from: State v. Gibson, 36 Ind. 389, 404, 1871 WL 5021 (Ind. Sup. Ct. 1871); Green v. State, 58 Ala. 190, 195, 1877 WL 1291 (Ala. Sup. Ct. 1877).

L. D. Barnett, *Societal Stress and Law*,
https://doi.org/10.1007/978-3-031-30875-8_2

substance of lasting law on key social activities is the product of large-scale forces and conditions, and it changes within a jurisdiction, and differs between jurisdictions, in response to these forces and conditions.[2] Macrosociology, the discipline that focuses on the overarching social drivers of the structure and institutions of a society, can thus offer invaluable insight into why the constitutions and statutes of jurisdictions say what they do about key social activities.

In employing macrosociology, the present chapter and the next two chapters focus on law in the United States as that law expresses the rights of the individual with regard to certain core social activities. Specifically, the focus takes place within a framework under which state regulatory law on these rights would be determined by the structural and cultural aspects of social life in the state except for the constraint of the federal Constitution. State law (as well as the law of state subdivisions such as counties and cities) in the United States must comply with the rights-pertinent provisions of the Constitution,[3] including the Due Process Clause and Equal Protection Clause of the Fourteenth Amendment,[4] and state law is, therefore, less diverse nationally than it would be in the absence of these provisions. The Due Process Clause, the Equal Protection Clause, and similar provisions express ideals that lie at the heart of American society[5] and that establish a bottom below which the rights of individuals in the states of the United States cannot fall. By establishing for the country as a whole a lower limit for personal rights,[6] the provisions make state law less diverse than it could otherwise be, and while having a floor for the rights of individuals generally promotes social cohesion—a factor that is critical to avoiding disruptions in a society—the resulting homogeneity of law has not been without some adverse sociological consequences. These consequences merit attention because their tie to the Constitution is not obvious and they therefore go unacknowledged.

In this chapter and Chaps. 3 and 4, then, I do not view the rights-pertinent provisions of the Constitution in the manner that has been popular in court

[2]Larry D. Barnett, Explaining Law: Macrosociological Theory and Empirical Evidence 8–11, 15–16 (2015) [hereinafter Explaining Law].

[3] "This Constitution, and the Laws of the United States which shall be made in Pursuance thereof; and all Treaties made, or which shall be made, under the Authority of the United States, shall be the supreme Law of the Land; and the Judges in every State shall be bound thereby, any Thing in the Constitution or Laws of any State to the Contrary notwithstanding." U.S. Const. art. VI, cl. 2.

[4]U.S. Const. amend. XIV, § 1 ("All persons born or naturalized in the United States, and subject to the jurisdiction thereof, are citizens of the United States and of the State wherein they reside. No State shall make or enforce any law which shall abridge the privileges or immunities of citizens of the United States; nor shall any State deprive any person of life, liberty, or property, without due process of law; nor deny to any person within its jurisdiction the equal protection of the laws.").

[5]Larry D. Barnett, Societal Agents in Law: A Macrosociological Approach 15 (2019) [hereinafter SAIL vol. 1].

[6]Kansas v. Carr, 136 S. Ct. 633, 658 (2016) (Sotomayer, J., dissenting) ("The Federal Constitution guarantees only a minimum slate of protections; States can and do provide individual rights above that constitutional floor").

opinions—viz., as protectors of individuals.[7] Instead, I view these provisions as mechanisms that, in promoting the ideal of social justice, keep sociological differences between states from increasing state-to-state dissimilarities in rights-pertinent law. The distinction on which I proceed, though subtle, is central. Under the perspective adopted here, the Constitution acts as a metaphorical straightjacket that renders states unable to adopt law that fully reflects their own sociological conditions. The straightjacket will exist when, inter alia, Constitution-incorporated societal ideals clash with state-level social practices and the social beliefs that underlie these practices. The social practices that are of concern in the present book involve, inter alia, the biological attribute of race,[8] the subject of the present chapter. They involve, too, sex and gender, the subject of Chap. 3, and the sex composition of couples eligible to marry, the subject of Chap. 4.

The message of the present book stems from the straightjacket that the Constitution imposes. Put simply, the book argues that this straightjacket can generate sociological side-effects. In particular, the straightjacket is capable of fostering social stress and, in turn, social instability—impacts that must not be overlooked or neglected. While social stress can undoubtedly arise in numerous ways, I contend that one such way is from U.S. Supreme Court interpretations of the current text of the federal Constitution as well as from proposals to change the current text of the federal Constitution. American social life will be stressed when, ceteris paribus, sizeable population segments believe that a Court interpretation of or a proposed amendment to the Constitution jeopardizes a traditional social practice and the ideas on which the practice is based.

Societal stress is a mental formulation, of course, but I believe that it is a useful one. As a concept in macrosociology theory, societal stress is generic in character and can link seemingly disparate events that occur in social life. The events of relevance here are those that are socially disruptive and hence harmful to vital aspects of a society, especially social integration and/or system integration.[9] The former (social integration) involves the strength of inter-individual and inter-group ties in a society; the latter (system integration) involves the degree to which the

---

[7] *See, e.g.*, Shelley v. Kraemer, 334 U.S. 1, 22 (1948) (concluding that the rights to due process and equal protection specified in the Fourteenth Amendment are "guaranteed to the individual" and "are personal rights"); Palmore v. Sidoti, 466 U.S. 429, 434 (1984) (holding that government action that discriminates, or supports discrimination, on the basis of race cannot be justified on the ground that it "will promote the public peace by preventing race conflicts. Desirable as this is, and important as is the preservation of the public peace, this aim cannot be accomplished by laws or ordinances which deny rights created or protected by the Federal Constitution" (quoting Buchanan v. Warley, 245 U.S. 60, 81 (1917)).

[8] The U.S. Supreme Court has written, for example, that ("[d]istinctions between citizens solely because of their ancestry are by their very nature odious to a free people whose institutions are founded upon the doctrine of equality. For that reason, legislative classification or discrimination based on race alone has often been held to be a denial of equal protection." Hirabayashi v. United States, 320 U.S. 81, 100 (1943).

[9] David Lockwood, *Social Integration and System Integration*, *in* EXPLORATIONS IN SOCIAL CHANGE 244, 245–46, 249 n.6 (George K. Zollschan & Walter Hirsch eds., 1964).

structural components of a society fit together and work harmoniously with one another. Events that reduce social integration and events that reduce system integration, I maintain, are subsumable under the concept of societal stress. In the United States, such events may include some court interpretations of and proposed amendments to the federal Constitution.

Why is a judicial application of the U.S. Constitution and a proposal to change the text of the Constitution able to stress American society? Let me suggest the following answer. Even though law pertinent to society-significant forms of social behavior does not have a large, lasting influence on the frequency of that behavior in the United States (or, presumably, in any structurally complex, democratically governed nation),[10] the U.S. Constitution is a meaningful symbol to Americans, and symbols are important to how their society functions.[11] Therefore, an actual or proposed change in U.S. constitutional law will socially stress American society when (1) it alters, or is expected to alter, a society-significant social practice and (2) the alteration is perceived as imperiling a socially valued aspect of society. Importantly, social stress from one event in a set of events may fail to dissipate before another event in the set takes place, and when that happens, stress will accumulate. Eventually, accumulating social stress will push a society past a threshold and cause a reaction that aims to limit further change in constitutional law or restore constitutional law to its pre-change content. This reaction, if successful, reduces (or avoids a further rise in) the amount of societal stress, and allows law to fulfill its chief mission in social life, viz., protecting and promoting societal cohesiveness.

Even though the historical periods of a society are not independent of one another, a study of change in the society ought to be limited to a single period. Without a temporal limitation, the study can become unmanageable and/or its coverage can be superficial. In the instant book, accordingly, I concentrate on the period from and after the middle of the twentieth century. I do so not only because World War II constitutes a logical break in the history of the United States but also because I believe that society-level stress in the United States gradually built up during this period due to, inter alia, a series of actual changes in the interpretation of the Constitution and a proposed change in the text of the Constitution. All of these changes, furthermore, involved personal rights in prominent social practices and thus mark a law-defined age.[12]

Of course, designating the middle of the twentieth century as the start of the series of changes in law content is arbitrary in several respects. I begin with the point that the U.S. judiciary has engaged for more than 200 years in evaluating whether government action satisfies provisions of the national Constitution.[13] Moreover, in terms of race—the focus of the instant chapter—American society has long been

[10] See the sources cited in note 135 in *supra* Chap. 1.

[11] Explaining Law, *supra* note 2, at 11–12, 16.

[12] SAIL vol. 1, *supra* note 5, at ch. 4.

[13] Marbury v. Madison, which the U.S. Supreme Court decided in 1803, is popularly credited as initiating judicial review of the constitutionality of government action. Marbury v. Madison, 5 U.S.

fragmented by socio-economic differences between blacks and whites, and this fragmentation predates the twentieth century.[14] Similarly, American society since its inception has had a social role for women that is not the same as the social role it has had for men. Nonetheless, a work of scholarship must have boundaries, and the mid-twentieth century is a logical launching point for an inquiry into law-induced societal stress.

2.2 The Fourteenth Amendment and Race Distinctions

The present chapter revolves around two specific provisions of the Constitution of the United States. These provisions—the Due Process Clause of the Fourteenth Amendment and the Equal Protection Clause of the Fourteenth Amendment—are salient among the guarantees of personal rights that are expressed in the U.-S. Constitution, and they are, by their wording, applicable to the governments and agencies of states.[15] The Due Process Clause limits the ability of states to, inter alia, establish restrictions on the liberty of individuals, and the Equal Protection Clause limits the ability of states to create classifications of individuals.[16] The difference between the two provisions has been explained as follows:

> The Equal Protection and Due Process clauses protect distinctly different interests. On the one hand, the 'substantive component' of the Due Process Clause 'provides heightened protection against government interference with certain fundamental rights and liberty interests,' even when the challenged regulation affects all persons equally. In contrast, 'the essence of the equal protection requirement is that the state treat all those similarly situated similarly,' with its 'central purpose [being] the prevention of official conduct discriminating

---

(1 Cranch) 137 (1803). However, such review by the judiciary of government action predates *Marbury*. William Michael Treanor, *Against Textualism*, 103 Nw. U. L. Rev. 983, 985–88 (2009).

[14] John Iceland, *Racial and Ethnic Inequality in Poverty and Affluence, 1959–2015*, 38 Population Res. & Pol'y Rev. 615, 627 figs. 1 & 2 (2019). Evidence that American society has historically experienced such fragmentation is found in the U.S. Constitution. The Fourteenth Amendment was added to the Constitution in 1868. U.S. House of Representatives, The Constitution of the United States as Amended, H.R. Doc. 110–50, at 16–17 (2007). The chief goal of the equal protection guarantee in that Amendment was the protection of blacks against discrimination by states. Palmer v. Thompson, 403 U.S. 217, 220 (1971).

[15] *Supra* note 4.

[16] The Fifth Amendment, which applies to the federal government and its agencies, contains an explicit due process guarantee but not an explicit equal protection guarantee. U.S. Const. amend. V ("No person shall be . . . deprived of life, liberty or property, without due process of law"). In this respect, the Fifth Amendment is unlike the Fourteenth Amendment, which has both an explicit due process guarantee and an explicit equal protection guarantee. U.S. Const. amend. XIV, § 1, *supra* note 4. However, the due process guarantee in the Fifth Amendment has been held to include an equal protection guarantee that is equivalent to the state-applicable Equal Protection Clause of the Fourteenth Amendment. Weinberger v. Wiesenfeld, 420 U.S. 636, 638 n.2 (1975); Sessions v. Morales-Santana, 137 S. Ct. 1678, 1686 n.1 (2017).

on the basis of race [or other suspect classifications].' As such, equal protection only applies when the state treats two groups, or individuals, differently.[17]

Substantively, then, the guarantee of due process bars the State, when dealing with activities that American society treats as private, from suppressing "personal choices central to individual dignity and autonomy."[18] The guarantee of equal protection, on the other hand, aims to halt "intentional and arbitrary discrimination, whether occasioned by express terms of a statute or by its improper execution through duly constituted agents" of the State.[19] Both guarantees, accordingly, have the same underlying purpose, viz., to promote fairness.[20] Fairness, in turn, is essential to social integration.[21]

A matter that should perhaps be clarified here involves an aspect of the wording of the Fourteenth Amendment assurances of due process and equal protection. On their face, these assurances apply to actions by state governments and state-created agencies.[22] However, they also apply to actions by local governments such as cities, because local governments in a state are considered to be extensions of the state.[23] As a consequence, legislation enacted by a state government or a local government is subject to the Fourteenth Amendment guarantees of due process and equal protection. The foregoing point leads to a critical distinction under the Constitution between the legislative branch and the judicial branch of government in the United States. Specifically, legislatures set the standards for the behavior of individuals, but the federal courts have the final say as to the meaning of the Constitution, including the Fourteenth Amendment.[24] The result is that the federal judiciary can assess all

---

[17] Powers v. Harris, 379 F.3d 1208, 1215 (10th Cir. 2004) (internal citations omitted).

The due process guarantee includes both substantive due process and procedural due process. Substantive due process is concerned with "preventing governmental power from being used for purposes of oppression, regardless of the procedures used." Procedural due process, by contrast, requires that "an individual be given the opportunity to be heard in a meaningful manner." Thus, substantive due process deals with "the nature of the *right*" while procedural due process deals with "the *process* provided." Howard v. Grinage, 82 F.3d 1343, 1349–50 (6th Cir. 1996) (internal citations and quotation marks omitted).

[18] Obergefell v. Hodges, 135 S. Ct. 2584, 2597 (2015).

[19] Willowbrook v. Olech, 528 U.S. 562, 564 (2000). The quoted passage originally appeared in Sunday Lake Iron Co. v. Wakefield, 247 U.S. 350, 352 (1918).

[20] Bolling v. Sharp, 347 U.S. 497, 499 (1954) ("the concepts of equal protection and due process [] both stem[] from our American ideal of fairness"). *Bolling* involved a challenge to race segregation in Washington, D.C. public schools and was decided under the due process guarantee of the Fifth Amendment. *Supra* note 16. The Court concluded that "discrimination may be so unjustifiable as to be violative of due process." *Id.* at 499.

[21] Joel Brockner et al., *The Influence of Prior Commitment to an Institution on Reactions to Perceived Unfairness: The Higher They Are, the Harder They Fall*, 37 ADMIN. SCI. Q. 241 (1992).

[22] United Bhd. of Carpenters & Joiners, Local 610 v. Scott, 463 U.S. 825, 832 (1983); City of Cuyahoga Falls v. Buckeye Cmty. Hope Found., 538 U.S. 188, 194–96 (2003).

[23] Worcester v. Worcester Consol. St. Ry. Co., 196 U.S. 539, 549–50 (1905).

[24] Plaut v. Spendthrift Farm, 514 U.S. 211, 221–22 (1995) (concluding that legislatures and courts are assigned different governmental functions by the Constitution, writing that "this allocation of

legislation—federal, state, and local—to determine whether the legislation is in harmony with the Constitution. At the apex of the federal judiciary is, of course, the U.S. Supreme Court.[25]

2.2.1 *Brown v. Board of Education*

With the above in mind, let us turn to Brown v. Board of Education,[26] the first ruling in the series of socially pertinent and prominent cases decided by the U.S. Supreme Court that could have increased society-level stress in the United States after the midpoint of the twentieth century. *Brown*, which was announced by the Court on May 17, 1954, [27] dealt with the acceptability under the federal Constitution of provisions in state statutes and state constitutions that mandated race-based segregation of students in government-run (i.e., public) primary and secondary schools. The Court held that, even if the facilities and resources at the schools attended by black pupils were palpably the same as the facilities and resources at schools attended by white pupils, law that required public schools to serve students of just a single race was inconsistent with the ideals embodied in equal protection and hence unacceptable under the Fourteenth Amendment.[28]

Brown generated widespread public resistance,[29] a manifestation of social stress, but the scale of the resistance is unsurprising given that a large share of the American public at this time felt that the Court was wrong in deciding *Brown* as it did: Out of every ten adults in the United States during the remainder of the 1950s, no less than three—and often no less than four—disapproved of the ruling;[30] similarly, about

---

authority was a simple one. The Legislature would be possessed of power to 'prescrib[e] the rules by which the duties and rights of every citizen are to be regulated,' but the power of '[t]he interpretation of the laws' would be 'the proper and peculiar province of the courts.' " (citations omitted)).

[25] U.S. Const. art. III, § 1 ("The judicial Power of the United States, shall be vested in one supreme Court, and in such inferior Courts as the Congress may from time to time ordain and establish"); U.S. Const. art. VI, cl. 2 (Supremacy Clause), *supra* note 3.

[26] Brown v. Bd. of Educ., 347 U.S. 483 (1954).

[27] J. Sup. Ct. U.S., Oct. Term 1953, at 217.

[28] Brown v. Bd. of Educ., 347 U.S. 483, 495 (1954) ("in the field of public education the doctrine of 'separate but equal' has no place. Separate educational facilities are inherently unequal."). In a ruling a year later, the Court directed that race discrimination in public schools be ended with "all deliberate speed." Brown v. Bd. of Educ., 349 U.S. 294, 301 (1955). The 1954 ruling is commonly designated *Brown I*, and the 1955 ruling is commonly designated *Brown II*. My discussion of *Brown* in the text refers to just *Brown I* unless otherwise specified.

[29] Brent J. Aucoin, *The Southern Manifesto and Southern Opposition to Desegregation*, 55 Ark. Hist. Q. 173 (1996); Mark Golub, *Remembering Massive Resistance to School Desegregation*, 31 Law & Hist. Rev. 491, 504–07 (2013).

[30] Erica Frankenberg & Rebecca Jacobsen, *School Integration Polls*, 75 Pub. Opinion Q. 788, 807 tbl. 13 (2011).

half of all U.S. adults in 1956 believed that black students should not attend the same schools as white students.[31] A further indicator of societal stress from the ruling is found in the level of childbearing: In the South generally, the number of births per 1000 white women of childbearing age fell approximately 5% over the course of roughly 2 months about 9 or 10 months after *Brown* was decided.[32] Since fertility rates outside the South rose during the same 2-month period, *Brown* evidently disrupted, i.e., stressed, social life in the geographic region where racial segregation was most deeply ingrained.

The substantial social stress arising from *Brown* aids in understanding what happened in schools in the United States after the ruling. Under *Brown*, "[t]he transition to a unitary, nonracial system of public education was and is the ultimate end to be brought about."[33] Ensuing court-directed steps to reduce race discrimination in government-run schools (inside as well as outside the South) seem to have succeeded,[34] but only while they were in force. Once these steps ended, schools slowly became more segregated, especially in the South.[35] Moreover, the school integration that resulted from the court-directed steps was confined to students who attended public schools. The latter caveat is sociologically important: The prospect and occurrence of public-school desegregation prompted many white students to leave public schools and enroll in private schools, and their number may have grown over time.[36] The social experiment undertaken by the judiciary, accordingly, had unforeseen side-effects[37] and seems to have fallen well short of the ultimate goal that

In 1959, fifty-three out of every 100 U.S. adults believed that the *Brown* ruling "caused a lot more trouble than it was worth." Joseph Carroll, Gallup Inc., *Race and Education 50 Years After Brown v. Board of Education* (2004), https://news.gallup.com/poll/11686/race-education-years-after-brown-board-education.aspx (last visited Sept. 14, 2022).

[31] Frankenberg & Jacobsen, *supra* note 30, at 790 tbl. 1. This belief became less widespread after the 1950s. It declined to between one out of three and one out of four during the 1960s, and continued to decline during the 1970s and 1980s. *Id.*

[32] Ronald R. Rindfuss et al., *A Fertility Reaction to a Historical Event: Southern White Birthrates and the 1954 Desegregation Ruling*, 201 Sci. 178 (1978).

[33] Green v. County School Bd. of New Kent County, Va., 391 U.S. 430, 436 (1968). In *Green*, the Court applied both *Brown I* and *Brown II* (see *supra* note 28).

[34] Sean F. Reardon & Ann Owens, *60 Years After Brown: Trends and Consequences of School Segregation*, 40 Ann. Rev. Sociol. 199, 202–03, 205–06 (2014).

[35] Sean F. Reardon et al., *Brown Fades: The End of Court-Ordered School Desegregation and the Resegregation of American Public Schools*, 31 J. Pol'y Analysis & Mgmt. 876, 877, 897–900 (2012). The preceding article references appendixes that are in a December 2011 unpublished version of the article. The unpublished version, which has the same title as the published version, is available at https://cepa.stanford.edu/content/brown-fades-end-court-ordered-school-desegregation-and-resegregation-american-public-schools.

[36] Finis Welch, *A Reconsideration of the Impact of School Desegregation Programs on Public School Enrollment of White Students, 1968-76*, 60 Sociol. Educ. 215, 221 (1987).

[37] *See* Columbus Bd. of Educ. v. Penick, 443 U.S. 449, 483–86, 489 (1979) (Powell, J., dissenting) (identifying negative side-effects of public-school interventions by courts that focus solely "on racial balance in every school" and urging courts to "recognize limitations on judicial action inherent in our system and also the limits of effective judicial power").

the Court was pursuing, namely, a societal institution devoted to education that fully develops the potential of every student.[38] In this regard, it is notable that, while the racial integration of schools was likely responsible in the long run for more minority-white interaction and hence less prejudice among whites toward minorities,[39] the court-ordered steps failed to increase the number of years of education completed by blacks and did not improve the scores of black high-school seniors on standardized tests of skills in mathematics and reading.[40]

Brown is helpful as the starting point for this chapter, but it is not the basis for the study that *infra* Sect. 2.3 reports. In response to *Brown*, state and local governments in the South deployed multiple mechanisms for the purpose of maintaining racially segregated public schools.[41] Given their variety, the mechanisms differed in type even though they shared the same goal as law that explicitly required single-race public schools.[42] In turn, the differences between the types erect an obstacle to quantitative research on the sociological antecedents of law, because each mechanism would have been present in just a handful of jurisdictions. Since the dependent

[38] Dora W. Klein, *Beyond Brown v. Board of Education: The Need to Remedy the Achievement Gap*, 31 J.L. & Educ. 431, 436 (2002) (contending that *Brown* was concerned with bringing about "public schools that prepare all children to succeed in life"). *See* Milliken v. Bradley, 418 U.S. 717, 742 (1974) (underscoring, in the context of judicial remedies for de jure race segregation in public schools, the importance of focusing on the "quality of the educational process").

[39] Thomas F. Pettigrew & Linda R. Tropp, *A Meta-Analytic Test of Intergroup Contact Theory*, 90 J. Personality & Soc. Psychol. 751, 766 (2006).

[40] Steven G. Rivkin, *School Desegregation, Academic Attainment, and Earnings*, 35 J. Hum. Resources 333, 335, 337–38, 341–42 (2000).

[41] Forrest R. White, *Brown Revisited*, 76 Phi Delta Kappan 12 (1994) (listing as alternative mechanisms "gerrymandered school districts, liberal transfer policies, 'schools of choice,' staggered enrollment procedures, in-school segregation by tracking, and other quasi-legal devices").

[42] *E.g.*, Preston Valien, *The Status of Educational Desegregation, 1956: A Critical Summary*, 25 J. Negro Educ. 359, 359–61 (1956); Griffin v. County School Bd. of Prince Edward County, 377 U.S. 218, 222–23 (1964) (multi-year closure of all public schools by a county school board in Virginia during which period blacks in the county received no formal schooling); Green v. County School Bd., 391 U.S. 430, 432–33 (1968) (policy of a county school board in Virginia that allowed students to select the school they attend); United States v. Scotland Neck City Bd. of Educ., 407 U.S. 484, 486–87, 490 (1972) (creation, through a referendum in a North Carolina city, of a new school district within the city; and adoption of a student-transfer plan by the board of education in the new district); People Who Care v. Rockford Bd. of Educ., 111 F.3d 528, 535–36 (7th Cir. 1997) (policy of a local school board in Illinois that grouped students on the basis of their scholastic ability); United States v. School Dist. of Omaha, 521 F.2d 530, 539–44 (8th Cir. 1975), *vacated*, 433 U.S. 667 (1977) (policies of a municipal school board in Nebraska that established criteria allowing students to transfer to a school to which they had not been assigned; and that, in reducing nine-year elementary schools to seven years and establishing two-year junior high schools, permitted students to choose between school-attendance zones). *See also* Mary L. Dudziak, *The Little Rock Crisis and Foreign Affairs: Race, Resistance, and the Image of American Democracy*, 70 S. Cal. L. Rev. 1641, 1712–13 (1997) (describing a policy of a local school board in Arkansas that, pursuant to a race-neutral state statute, permitted a student upon request to be placed in a particular school after a hearing to ascertain, inter alia, whether the assignment of the student to the school might engender social strife).

variable in research on the sociological causes of law that differentiates on the basis of race should involve a single mechanism of law that some jurisdictions have adopted and others have not, quantitative research on the sociological antecedents of a particular mechanism directing students to race-specific schools would be unable to identify the antecedents reliably.

2.2.2 *Loving v. Virginia*

The above problem was avoided in my study. Specifically, I focused on a U.-S. Supreme Court decision—Loving v. Virginia—that invalidated a state statute, enacted in 1924, that prohibited marriage between a white and a nonwhite other than a descendant of Pocahontas.[43] In *Loving*, which was announced on June 12, 1967,[44] the Court held that the statute (1) was unacceptable under the Equal Protection Clause of the Fourteenth Amendment because its purpose was "to maintain White Supremacy" and (2) unacceptably infringed the liberty of individuals safeguarded by the Due Process Clause of the Fourteenth Amendment because "the freedom to marry" is "one of the vital personal rights essential to the orderly pursuit of happiness."[45] *Loving* is evidently an exception to the proposition that the substance of a Court ruling is usually in harmony with the views held by the majority of

[43] Loving v. Virginia, 388 U.S. 1, 5 n.4, 6 (1967). Two-and-a-half years before *Loving* was decided, the U.S. Supreme Court held unenforceable a state statute that criminalized nighttime cohabitation by a white and a black who were not married to one another. McLaughlin v. Florida, 379 U.S. 184, 187 (1964). In *McLaughlin*, the Court concluded that the statute, which was one of several statutes that sought to deter sexual intercourse outside of marriage, invidiously discriminated on the basis of race and hence violated the Equal Protection Clause of the Fourteenth Amendment. *Id.* at 191–94. "That a general evil will be partially corrected may at times, and without more, serve to justify the limited application of a criminal law; but legislative discretion to employ the piecemeal approach stops short of permitting a State to narrow statutory coverage to focus on a racial group." *Id.* at 194. Although the invalidated statute was tied to another statute of the state—a statute that forbid marriage between a white and a black—the Court declined to rule on the constitutionality of the latter (i.e., interracial marriage) statute. *Id.* at 187 n.6, 195–96.

[44] J. Sup. Ct. U.S., Oct. Term 1966, at 428.

[45] Loving v. Virginia, 388 U.S. 1, 11–12 (1967). *Loving* involved the prosecution, by the state of Virginia, of a white man and a black woman who resided in Virginia before and after they traveled to and were married in the District of Columbia. The defendants were convicted of violating (1) a Virginia-state statute that prohibited marriage between a "white person" and a "colored person" and (2) a Virginia-state statute that prohibited such persons from circumventing the statutory prohibition against interracial marriage by marrying outside Virginia if they intended to and did come back to Virginia and live there as a married couple. *Id.* at 2, 4. The case reached the U.S. Supreme Court through an appeal from the decision by the Supreme Court of Virginia, which held that state law on interracial marriage did not violate either the equal protection guarantee or the due process guarantee. Loving v. Commonwealth, 147 S.E.2d 78, 80, 82 (Va. 1966).

Americans at the time of the ruling.[46] According to sample surveys of the U.-S. population, more than nine out of ten white adults (and more than nine out of ten adults of all races) in 1958 disapproved of marriage between a black person and a white person, and although opposition subsequently declined, approximately three out of four adults still disapproved of such a marriage in 1968.[47] This sentiment is obviously inconsistent with the ruling of the Court in *Loving*, but it was manifested in the extent of interracial marriage among whites in the United States—simply put, the spouse of a married white was rarely a black.[48]

Loving, then, dealt with a social boundary that few members of the majority race wanted or were able to cross.[49] Of course, the decision of the U.S. Supreme Court in *Loving* did not require that the individuals in a marrying couple be of different races; the decision only allowed the individuals in a marrying couple to be of different races. *Loving*, therefore, could not alter individual-level choices of a spouse and could not change social practices regarding marriage. *Brown*, on the other hand, disrupted social life through judicial orders that sought to eliminate race segregation of students in public schools when a governmental actor was responsible for the segregation. Indeed, the U.S. Supreme Court, in deciding numerous cases after *Brown* that involved government-supported racial segregation of public-school students, expressly approved judicial intervention that had the goal of ending the segregation.[50] Such interventions, i.e., attempts to reshape existing patterns in social life, did not follow the ruling in *Loving*.[51]

But since *Loving* was less socially intrusive than *Brown*, did *Loving* create only minimal societal stress? I believe that the question should be answered in the

---

[46] Alan D. Monroe, *Public Opinion and Public Policy, 1980-1993*, 62 Pub. Opinion Q. 6, 14 tbl. 2 (1998); Christopher J. Casillas et al., *How Public Opinion Constrains the U.S. Supreme Court*, 55 Am. J. Pol. Sci. 74, 80 & tbl. 1 (2011).

[47] Joseph Carroll, Gallup Inc., *Most Americans Approve of Interracial Marriage* (2007), https://news.gallup.com/poll/28417/most-americans-approve-interracial-marriages.aspx (last visited Sept. 14, 2022). The extent of disapproval continued to diminish after 1968, but not until 1991 did opposition to black-white marriage fall below one-half of white adults and one-half of all adults. *Id.*

[48] See note 178 in *supra* Chap. 1 for a summary of Roland G. Fryer, Jr., *Guess Who's Been Coming to Dinner? Trends in Interracial Marriage over the 20th Century*, 21 J. Econ. Persp. 71 (2007).

[49] Throughout the twentieth century, whites comprised more than eighty percent of the U.-S. population. U.S. Census Bureau, Statistical Abstract of the United States: 2003. Mini-Historical Statistics, at 5 tbl. HS-2 (123rd ed.), https://www.census.gov/library/publications/2003/compendia/statab/123ed/hist.html (select "Population Characteristics: 1900 to 2002" hyperlink).

[50] Swann v. Charlotte-Mecklenburg Bd. of Educ., 402 U.S. 1, 15 (1971). For a list of the cases decided by the U.S. Supreme Court, see Martha Ann Peavy, U.S. Supreme Court Decisions and Desegregation in the South 102–05 app. A (May 2004) (unpublished Ed.D. dissertation, Univ. of Georgia).

[51] After *Loving*, the U.S. Supreme Court did not rule on another case involving the constitutionality of government action bearing on interracial marriage. I base this conclusion on a search that I conducted of the "U.S. Supreme Court Cases" database in Westlaw; the search was done on September 21, 2019 using the following search term: ("interracial marriage" or "cross-race marriage" or miscegenat!). Each post-*Loving* Court case identified by the search was checked for the issue of law it presented.

negative. *Loving*, I posit, added to the societal stress caused by *Brown* and the additional stress was sociologically important. I take this position because opposition to interracial marriage was long-standing, deep-seated, and prevalent in American society,[52] and was a key element, if not the most important element, in the support that existed for race-segregated public schools.[53] In the view of a large share of the majority race, same-race schools were a firewall that promoted same-race marriage and prevented cross-race marriage. Racial separation in schools was accordingly a device to attain what much of the American public considered to be a socially desired end, viz., racial homogeneity in marriage.[54]

By suppressing state law that banned cross-race marriage, then, *Loving* is likely to have generated not-insignificant societal stress. *Loving* would have built on the social stress that was created by *Brown* and subsequent judicial rulings on racially segregated public schools, and the social stress generated by *Loving* would not have been sociologically meaningless because the ruling nullified law that articulated the ultimate goal, viz., avoiding interracial marriage. Otherwise said, the amount of societal stress caused by *Brown* and ensuing judicial interventions in the social patterns of schooling was effectively a floor under the societal stress that *Loving* caused—stress that would necessarily have been sociologically consequential.

Of course, *Loving*-induced social stress would have been unevenly distributed in American society. As a result, state differences on macrosociological variables that promoted the presence of state law against interracial marriage logically reveal the macrosociological sources of the social stress caused by *Loving*. I attempt to identify these variables in Sect. 2.3.

[52] Randall Kennedy, *Interracial Intimacies: Sex, Marriage, Identity, Adoption*, 17 HARV. BLACKLETTER L.J. 57, 70–76 (2001); Randall Kennedy, *Marriage and the Struggle for Gay, Lesbian, and Black Liberation*, 2005 UTAH L. REV. 781, 782–84; text accompanying *supra* note 47.

[53] Anders Walker, Note, *Legislating Virtue: How Segregationists Disguised Racial Discrimination as Moral Reform Following Brown v. Board of Education*, 47 DUKE L.J. 399, 399–402 & n.7 (1997).

Whites in the South who disapproved of marriage between whites and nonwhites, besides opposing racially integrated schools, balked at making Hawaii a U.S. state. Among these whites, resistance to statehood for Hawaii was due largely to the concern that, if Hawaii became a state, the relatively high frequency of interracial marriage in Hawaii would serve as a model for the rest of the country and promote interracial marriage nationwide. Ann K. Ziker, *Segregationists Confront American Empire: The Conservative White South and the Question of Hawaiian Statehood, 1947-1959*, 76 PAC. HIST. REV. 439, 449–50 (2007). In Hawaii during the 1950s, approximately one marriage out of every three involved an interracial couple. Robert C. Schmitt, *Demographic Correlates of Interracial Marriage in Hawaii*, 2 DEMOGRAPHY 463, 465–66 & tbl. 1 (1965). Hawaii achieved statehood in 1959. Proclamation No. 3309, 24 Fed. Reg. 6868–69 (Aug. 25, 1959).

[54] *Compare* the text accompanying *supra* notes 30 & 31 *with* the text accompanying *supra* note 47.

2.3 A Study of State Bans on Interracial Marriage

Before describing the dependent variable and the independent variables in my study, I consider a question that must be answered by every investigator who undertakes research on the societal agents that drive law content in the states of the United States: Should the research be limited to the 48 coterminous states, or should it include all 50 states? Although the number of cases would be larger if Alaska and Hawaii were in the data, Alaska and Hawaii differ culturally from the continental states in ways that are directly pertinent to my study,[55] creating the possibility that state law in Alaska and Hawaii during the period on which I focus was the result, at least in part, of sociological agents that are unique to these states and that I have not measured. Accordingly, the 48 states in the continental United States serve as the universe for my study.[56]

2.3.1 Variables and Their Measurement

Investigators can improve their ability to unearth cause-effect relationships when their independent variables are measured at a point in time that precedes the point in time at which their dependent variable is measured. This temporal sequence, however, may not exist in the data that I employ here. The independent variables in my study are measured as of 1960, and although the dependent variable—whether a state had law that banned interracial marriage—is measured as of December 1966 (see *infra* Sect. 2.3.1.1), the states where such law was present had adopted it long

---

[55] David W. S. Wong, *Spatial Patterns of Ethnic Integration in the United States*, 50 PROF. GEOGRAPHER 13, 17–18 & tbl. 1, 30 app. 1 (1998) (using data from the 1990 U.S. census; finding that the percentage of multi-race, multi-ethnic households was generally much higher in Alaska and Hawaii than in the continental states). *Compare* Schmitt, *supra* note 53, at 465–66 & tbl. 1 (reporting that interracial marriages represented about one-third of all marriages in Hawaii during the 1950s), *with* Thomas P. Monahan, *Interracial Marriage in a Southern Area: Maryland, Virginia, and the District of Columbia*, 8 J. COMP. FAM. STUD. 217, 223 tbl. 2 (1977) (reporting that mixed-race marriages were slightly less than one percent of all marriages in the District of Columbia during 1950-59), *and* Larry D. Barnett, *Interracial Marriage in California*, 25 MARRIAGE & FAM. LIVING 424, 425 (1963) (reporting that interracial marriages were less than 1.5 percent of all marriages in California during the last half of the 1950s). Interracial couples have been able to marry lawfully in the District of Columbia since at least the late nineteenth century. M. Annella, *Some Aspects of Interracial Marriage in Washington, D.C.*, 25 J. NEGRO EDUC. 380, 384–85 (1956). Interracial couples could lawfully marry in California after the supreme court of that state, in October 1948, invalidated the California statutes that barred such marriages; the court held, inter alia, that the statutes violated the equal protection guarantee of the Fourteenth Amendment to the federal Constitution. Perez v. Lippold, 198 P.2d 17, 18, 29 (Cal. 1948).

[56] *See generally* LARRY D. BARNETT, SOCIETAL AGENTS IN LAW: QUANTITATIVE RESEARCH 28 n.35 (2019) [hereinafter SAIL VOL. 2] (listing three reasons that a macrosociological study of state law might want to omit Alaska and Hawaii).

before 1960.[57] Are the independent variables and the dependent variable in the wrong temporal order in my study? My answer is that they are not. As democracies, states have the ability to alter their law at any time. Consequently, the states whose law banned interracial marriage both before 1960 and in 1966 had essentially chosen in 1966 to retain the bans. Under this line of reasoning, the time at which the dependent variable in my study was measured can be deemed to have been *after* the time at which the independent variables were measured, and the independent variables that are statistically related to the dependent variable can be viewed as causal agents that determined whether states continued their bans on interracial marriage.

2.3.1.1 Dependent Variable

The dependent variable in the present study was whether a state, as of the date on which the U.S. Supreme Court agreed to consider the case of Loving v. Virginia, had law in force that prohibited cross-race marriage. In states where such a prohibition existed, the case presumably caused social stress, and a search for the sociological forces that generated the prohibitions can reveal the societal agents responsible for this stress. My study thus assembles and tests data on states of the United States for the purpose of uncovering the sociological variables that are statistically related to whether states by law banned interracial marriage when the U.S. Supreme Court accepted the *Loving* case. At that time, such law existed in 17 states,[58] and all of these states were coded 1 on the dependent variable; the remaining thirty-one states were coded 0 on the dependent variable. The Appendix at the end of the instant chapter reproduces the text of the relevant prohibitions in each of the states that were coded 1. However, the Appendix does not reproduce all provisions of law bearing on interracial marriage in a state that had such law. Among the latter provisions are statutes in states (including Virginia) that prohibited a state resident from traveling to another state for the purpose of evading the ban on interracial marriage in the state of residence.[59] A further illustration is a statute in Mississippi that criminalized the production or dissemination of any "printed, typewritten or written" material that is "in favor of social equality or of intermarriage between whites and negroes"; an individual or entity convicted of violating the statute was subject to imprisonment for up to 6 months and/or a fine up to $500.[60]

[57] Peggy Pascoe, What Comes Naturally: Miscegenation Law and the Making of Race in America 63, 81, 99 (2009).

[58] The opinion of the Court in *Loving* lists sixteen states that had law proscribing interracial marriage. Loving v. Virginia, 388 U.S. 1, 6 n. 5. As I explain in the text below, I have added Maryland to the list.

[59] *E.g.*, *supra* note 45.

[60] Miss. Code Ann. § 2339 (1942, recompiled 1956). Section 2339 was left out of the next (i.e., 1972) Mississippi Code, because the section was deemed to be unconstitutional. E-mail from Christopher Noe, Assistant Director, Grisham Law Library, Univ. of Mississippi, to Margaret

In the coding of the states on the dependent variable, one state—Maryland—warrants discussion. To begin with a brief history, the U.S. Supreme Court received the *Loving* case through an appeal filed by the defendants (Richard Loving and his wife Mildred Jeter) who had been convicted of violating Virginia law banning interracial marriage.[61] The appeal to the U.S. Supreme Court resulted from a decision, which had been rendered by the highest court of the Commonwealth of Virginia, that held the interracial-marriage ban to be valid under both the federal constitution and the state constitution.[62] The U.S. Supreme Court gave notice of its likely jurisdiction over the case on December 12, 1966,[63] an action that, under the rules of the Court, resulted in oral argument before the Court over the issues of constitutional law that were presented by the case.[64] Oral argument took place on April 10, 1967.[65] As the Court points out in its opinion holding that the Fourteenth Amendment guarantees of due process and equal protection are violated by law that prohibits cross-race marriage,[66] the Maryland statute that forbade such a marriage had been rescinded when the Court announced its ruling on June 12, 1967.[67] However, the repeal was the subject of an act that was passed by the Maryland legislature on March 24, 1967 and that fixed June 1, 1967 as its effective date.[68] The sequence and timing of these five events is shown in Fig. 2.1.

As the diagram makes clear, the Maryland statute that prohibited interracial marriage was still in force when the Court took jurisdiction of the *Loving* case in

Stewart, Delaware Law School Library, Widener Univ. (Oct. 8, 2019, 11:39 AM CDST) (on file with author). However, section 2339 has not been repealed. *Id.* Consequently, the section remains law. It is, nonetheless, unenforceable under the First Amendment which supports, inter alia, the freedom to communicate ideas in a safe manner in public places and forbids government from unnecessarily interfering with such communication. Thornhill v. Alabama, 310 U.S. 88, 101–02 (1940) ("The freedom of speech and of the press guaranteed by the Constitution embraces at the least the liberty to discuss publicly and truthfully all matters of public concern without previous restraint or fear of subsequent punishment. . . . Freedom of discussion, if it would fulfill its historic function in this nation, must embrace all issues about which information is needed or appropriate to enable the members of society to cope with the exigencies of their period."). The text of the First Amendment is reproduced in note 121 in *supra* Chap. 1.

[61] *Supra* note 45.

[62] Loving v. Commonwealth, 147 S.E.2d 78 (Va. 1966).

[63] Loving v. Virginia, 385 U.S. 986 (1966) ("probable jurisdiction noted").

[64] Sup. Ct. R. 16(4) (adopted April 12, 1954 as amended through June 1964) and Sup. Ct. R. 16 (6) (adopted June 12, 1967, effective Oct. 2, 1967), https://www.supremecourt.gov/ctrules/scannedrules.aspx. The wording of Rule 16 was not altered during the designated period. Rules of the Supreme Court of the United States 1, 15 (1964); Rules of the Supreme Court of the United States 1, 14 (1967).

[65] Loving v. Virginia, 388 U.S. 1 (1967).

[66] *Id.* at 12.

[67] In its opinion in Loving v. Virginia, the Court lists fourteen states (including Maryland) that had abrogated their prohibitions on cross-race marriage during "the past 15 years." 388 U.S. at 6 n.5. Among the fourteen states, Maryland acted last. The prohibitions in the other thirteen states were repealed between 1951 and 1965. Pascoe, *supra* note 57, at 242–43.

[68] Ch. 6, §§ 1, 3, 1967 Md. Laws 15.

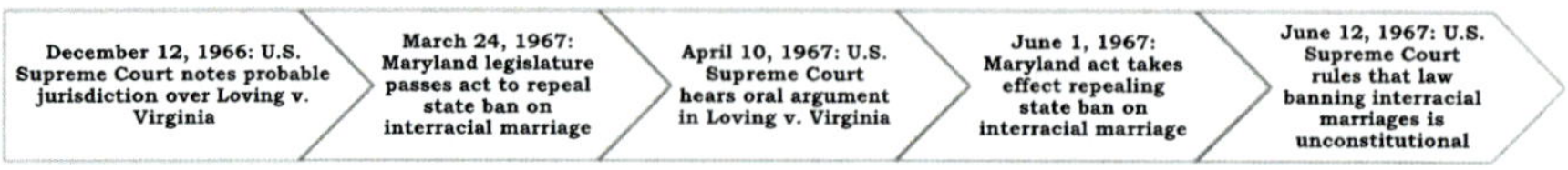

Fig. 2.1 Timeline: Loving v. Virginia and the Maryland ban on interracial marriage

December 1966, and it was also in force when, in April 1967, the Court heard oral argument on the issues of constitutional law involved in the case. In December 1966, the legislation to repeal the Maryland statute that banned interracial marriage had not been passed—indeed, the bill that produced the legislation had not even been introduced in the Maryland General Assembly[69]—and in April 1967, it had been passed but had not yet taken effect. Repeal took place while the Court was mulling the case, and less than 2 weeks before the Court ruled on the case.

Of what relevance is the timeline for the Maryland statute on interracial marriage? The appearance as well as the disappearance of law on a topic is not a single-stage event; rather, the adoption of law involves a series of events,[70] as does the repeal of law. The above-described timeline for Maryland illustrates how the choice of a particular event and date can affect whether, when logistic regression is used to analyze data, a state is coded 1 or 0 on the dependent variable. Choosing one of the first three dates in the timeline for Maryland requires that Maryland be coded 1 (i.e., designated as having law that prohibits interracial marriage); choosing either of the last two dates requires that Maryland be coded 0 (i.e., designated as not having law that prohibits interracial marriage). Therefore, picking a specific spot on the timeline will affect the coding of Maryland on the dependent variable. This coding decision can, in turn, have an impact on the results of the data analysis.

Unfortunately, the coding decision from the timeline is complicated by the rationale that the U.S. Supreme Court used to decide McLaughlin v. Florida.[71] *McLaughlin*, on which the Court ruled 2 years before it accepted Loving v. Virginia for review, arose from convictions under a state criminal statute that proscribed overnight cohabitation by a white and a black of opposite sex.[72] The Court, employing a rationale that foretold the main rationale that it employed in *Loving*, held that the statute violated the equal protection guarantee of the Fourteenth

[69] The General Assembly of Maryland passed the legislation during its 1967 session, which began on January 18, 1967. LAWS OF THE STATE OF MARYLAND: SESSION OF THE GENERAL ASSEMBLY JAN. 18, 1967 TO MARCH 28, 1967 (1967).

[70] Any one of nine law-related events may be used when assessing the impact of a change in law on the frequency of an activity. Chester L. Britt et al., *A Reassessment of the D.C. Gun Law: Some Cautionary Notes on the Use of Interrupted Time Series Designs for Policy Impact Assessment*, 30 LAW & SOC'Y REV. 361, 368–69 (1996).

[71] McLaughlin v. Florida, 379 U.S. 184 (1964). See the discussion of *McLaughlin* in *supra* note 43.

[72] *Id.* at 184, 185 n.1. The statute provided that both members of the cohabiting couple were subject to imprisonment or a monetary fine for "habitually liv[ing] in and occupy[ing] in the nighttime the same room." Evidence of sexual intercourse between the members of the couple was not necessary to prove that the statute had been violated. *Id.* at 186. The Court announced its decision in *McLaughlin* on December 7, 1964. J. SUP. CT. U.S., Oct. Term 1964, at 106.

Amendment.[73] Specifically, the Court concluded in *McLaughlin* that the state statute "treats the interracial couple made up of a white person and a Negro differently than it does any other couple" and hence "trenches upon the constitutionally protected freedom from invidious official discrimination based on race."[74] When the justices of the Court decided to rule on whether the Virginia state law at issue in *Loving* complied with the requirements of the Fourteenth Amendment, they therefore had an unmistakable signpost that directed them to the destination they would reach.[75] Since the rationale in *McLaughlin* led to the outcome in *Loving*, the date on which the Court announced its likely jurisdiction over the *Loving* appeal—i.e., the December 1966 event in the timeline—offers a logical basis for fixing the classification of Maryland on the dependent variable. Maryland is thus coded 1 on the dependent variable.[76]

2.3.1.2 Independent Variables

In the present study, I investigate a set of independent variables and attempt to ascertain which, if any, of them affected whether states had law that forbid interracial marriage. I posit that the U.S. Supreme Court, by accepting the case of Loving v. Virginia and hence signaling that law prohibiting interracial marriage might soon be voided, generated social stress in states that possessed such prohibitions and that each independent variable having a statistical link to the dependent variable influenced whether the Court added stress in these states. However, independent variables cannot supply insight into the causes of increases and decreases in social

[73] In *Loving*, unlike in *McLaughlin*, the Court based its ruling on the due process guarantee as well as on the equal protection guarantee. See text accompanying *supra* note 45. However, less than one page of the opinion of the Court in *Loving* is devoted to the due process guarantee while roughly five full pages are spent on the equal protection guarantee.

[74] McLaughlin v. Florida, 379 U.S. 184, 188, 196 (1964).

[75] Ariela R. Dubler, *From McLaughlin v. Florida to Lawrence v. Texas: Sexual Freedom and the Road to Marriage*, 106 Colum. L. Rev. 1165, 1179, 1187 (2006) (arguing that the interpretation of the Constitution by the Court in *McLaughlin* was the foundation for, and the "stepping stone to," the ruling by the Court in *Loving*); Andrew Koppelman, *Defending the Sex Discrimination Argument for Lesbian and Gay Rights: A Reply to Edward Stein*, 49 UCLA L. Rev. 519, 522 (2001) (pointing out that the Court in *McLaughlin* and in *Loving* rejected the defense that the statutes at issue were constitutional because they applied equally to each race covered by the statutes; and contending that the key case rebuffing this defense was *McLaughlin* rather than *Loving*); Jeffrey A. Williams, *The Equal Application Defense: The Equal Application Defense*, 9 U. Pa. J. Const. L. 1207, 1211 (2007) (writing that *McLaughlin* was the critical opinion disapproving race-based classifications in legislation addressing sexual intimacy, and that "*Loving* merely followed suit, however resoundingly").

[76] The selection of December 1966 in the timeline affects the coding of just Maryland among the states that the Court names in its *Loving* opinion as having repealed their law against interracial marriage "over the past 15 years." Loving v. Virginia, 388 U.S. 1, 6 n.5 (1967). All of the other states on the list repealed their law before 1966. *Supra* note 67.

stress unless they are chosen. The choice of an independent variable requires that its empirical indicator be designated, too.

The selection of independent variables and their indicators is among the critical decisions that an investigator makes when designing a study, and perhaps because the selection occurs early in the design process, it has an outsized impact on whether the study produces worthwhile results. With this in mind, I started my choice of independent variables for the present study with an earlier work of mine that attempted to devise evidence-based formal theory on macrosociological agents that determine the content of law on society-significant social patterns.[77] The foregoing work led me to include five independent variables in the present study—culture, cultural heterogeneity, social disorder, societal fragmentation, and societal rationality. The data for the empirical indicator of each independent variable came from the decennial census of the population of the United States that was conducted in 1960.[78]

Culture refers to the assumptions that the members of a society make, for the most part implicitly and subconsciously, about the physical and social settings in which they live.[79] The assumptions that comprise the culture of a society are important sociologically because, inter alia, they express governing social values and hence guide the social behavior of the members of the society. Inasmuch as culture shapes social life and social life produces the content of law, culture is able to influence whether a particular proscription or prescription is brought into the law of a society and remains in that law. In prior research, I have employed the geographic regions of the United States (as designated by the U.S. Census Bureau) to capture differences in culture and ascertain whether the differences molded the content of law. A different measure is necessary in the present study, however, because just one of the 17 states that was coded 1 on the dependent variable is located outside the South and every state in the South was coded 1. Each region of the United States, therefore, was virtually homogeneous in terms of whether interracial marriage was prohibited by law, and an alternative measure of culture had to be found.

---

[77] SAIL VOL. 1, *supra* note 5, at ch. 2 pt. 2.3.

[78] State-level data on the indicators of all of the independent variables except cultural heterogeneity were obtained from one of the following sources: (1) U.S. Census Bureau, Census of Population and Housing, https://www.census.gov/prod/www/decennial.html. To locate the state reports that are available on this web page, select "Census of Population and Housing, 1960"; under "1960 Census of Population," select "Vol. 1. Characteristics of the Population". (2) U.S. CENSUS BUREAU, CENSUS OF POPULATION: 1960. VOL. I. CHARACTERISTICS OF THE POPULATION. PART 34: NEW YORK (1963). This publication is available online at the U.S. Census Bureau Library, https://archive.org/details/1960censusofpopu134unse. (3) U.S. CENSUS BUREAU, CENSUS OF POPULATION: 1960. VOL. I. CHARACTERISTICS OF THE POPULATION. PART 49: WASHINGTON (1963). This publication is available online at the U.S. Census Bureau Library, https://www.census.gov/library/publications/1961/dec/population-vol-01.html.

State data for the indicator of cultural heterogeneity were obtained from the source cited in *infra* note 86.

[79] For further explanations of culture, see SAIL VOL. 2, *supra* note 56, at 44–45, 107, 163, 198–99.

In the instant study, I measured culture by the extent of adherence in each state to the then-dominant cultural ideal for the family and for women, an ideal that extolled the nuclear family and the "stay-at-home mom."[80] The measure was thus based on currently married, husband-present females (white and nonwhite) who had one or more children of their own below the age of six;[81] specifically, the indicator of culture was the percentage of these females aged 14 and older in each state who were labor force participants in 1960.[82] The percentage appears to be an accurate gauge of the cultural ideal that existed in 1960 for family life and gender roles, because at this time relatively few married mothers of young children left the home to take paying positions in the economy: In the U.S. population as a whole in 1960, only about one out of every five currently married, husband-present females who had a child of her own younger than age six was in the labor force.[83] States, of course, will differ on this fraction, and the extent of adherence to tradition in family life and sex roles will

---

[80] David Popenoe, *Can the Nuclear Family Be Revived?*, Society, July-Aug. 1999, at 28, 29.

[81] An "own" child was defined as a "single (never-married) son, daughter, stepchild, or adopted child of the family head or subfamily head." U.S. Bureau of the Census, Census of Population: 1960. Volume I: Characteristics of the Population. Part 1: United States Summary, at LVIII (1964) [hereinafter U.S. Summary]. A "family" was defined as "two or more persons living in the same household who are related to each other by blood, marriage, or adoption; all persons living in one household who are related to each other are regarded as one family." *Id.* A "subfamily" was "a married couple with or without own children, or one parent with one or more own children under 18 years old, living in a housing unit and related to the head of the household or his wife." *Id.* For the definition of "household," see *id.* at LV.

[82] The percentage in each state was obtained from table 116 in the state reports for the 1960 census. *Supra* note 78. The "labor force" is composed of employed individuals, unemployed individuals, and active-duty U.S. military personnel. Individuals are classified as unemployed if they are "looking for work" or are "waiting to be called back to a job from which they had been laid off or furloughed." U.S. Summary, *supra* note 81, at LXI–LXII. Individuals are unemployed, therefore, if they "had no employment during the reference week, were available for work at that time, and had made specific efforts to find employment sometime during the 4-week period ending with the reference week. *Note:* People who were waiting to be recalled to a job from which they had been laid off need not be looking for work to be classified as unemployed." U.S. Bureau of Labor Statistics, Glossary (definition of "unemployed"), https://www.bls.gov/bls/glossary.htm.

[83] U.S. Summary, *supra* note 81, at 1-501 tbl. 196.

Unfortunately, attitudes toward whether women who have young children should be employed outside the home were not measured in public opinion surveys conducted in the United States during the 1950s or during the first half of the 1960s. Hazel Erskine, *The Polls: Women's Role*, 35 Pub. Opinion Q. 275, 282–86 (1971). In two surveys conducted during the last half of the 1960s, these attitudes were measured using the question whether "[w]orking career women with young children" are "more helpful or more harmful to American life." The belief that such women were "more harmful" was held by exactly half of all respondents in 1965 and by nearly half (46 percent) in 1969. *Id.* at 286. However, public opinion surveys may materially underestimate the extent to which Americans oppose gender equality. *See* Matthew J. Streb et al., *Social Desirability Effects and Support for a Female American President*, 72 Pub. Opinion Q. 76, 80–83, 86 (2008) (using a "list experiment" in interviews during 2006 with a probability-selected national sample of U.-S. residents; concluding that then-current gender ideals artificially increase by ten to twenty percentage points the share of Americans in public opinion surveys who express support for having a woman as president of the country).

vary inversely with the size of the fraction, with a larger fraction representing less adherence in a state to tradition in marriage and family life. Since less adherence signals weaker support for such tradition, a higher percentage in the measure of culture is expected to be associated with lower odds that state law barred between-race marriage. If, as expected, an inverse relationship is found, the indicator presumably captures more than just conventionalism in family form and the role of women. Instead, the indicator can be assumed to capture traditionalism in culture as a whole and to be useful for identifying the effects of culture on numerous topics of law, not just law addressing marriage.

Cultural heterogeneity has the potential to shape law on a topic because it involves the range of value-anchored viewpoints that are widely shared in a society. Logically, an increase in cultural diversity brings into the population of a society more value-linked viewpoints, and it also diminishes the number of widely endorsed viewpoints, some of which will be viewpoints on family life and sex roles. Importantly, value dissimilarity raises the incidence of activities that involve overt or covert conflict,[84] and thereby destabilizes social life. Since a society resists destabilization, value dissimilarity puts pressure on the society to change so that social conflict is lessened. When the society responds to the pressure, its conflict-reducing change can be expected to occur in the form of, inter alia, (1) social tolerance for, if not the acceptance of, value-grounded viewpoints that deviate from tradition and (2) law that is restricted to the value-grounded viewpoints, including the precepts of morality, that the members of the society hold in common. Morality, we should keep in mind, is at the heart of what law says and does not say about society-significant social activities; as the U.S. Supreme Court has pointed out, "law . . . is constantly based on notions of morality."[85] Therefore, greater cultural heterogeneity, by narrowing the range of value-grounded viewpoints embraced by society as a whole, leads to the removal from law of prohibitions and prescriptions that do not reflect common values and that in turn become a source of social conflict. Under this reasoning, more cultural heterogeneity is likely to leave law against interracial marriage with less social support, and the extent of cultural heterogeneity is thus expected to be inversely related, ceteris paribus, to the odds of such law.

In the instant study, cultural heterogeneity was measured as of 1960 by the percentage of the residents of each state who were "foreign born", i.e., by the percentage of persons in each state who were born outside the United States and

[84] *E.g.*, Mark T. Berg et al., *Neighborhood Cultural Heterogeneity and Adolescent Violence*, 28 J. Quantitative Criminology 411, 419–21, 427 fig. 1, 429 (2012) (finding that cultural heterogeneity increases the incidence of violent crime committed by adolescents).

[85] Bowers v. Hardwick, 478 U.S. 186, 196 (1986). Although the U.S. Supreme Court subsequently reversed its ruling in *Bowers*, the reversal does not undermine the observation by the Court that law arises from morality. Larry D. Barnett, The Place of Law: The Role and Limits of Law in Society 243 n.126 (2011).

whose parents were not U.S. citizens.[86] The percentage is for the total state population, and hence includes state residents of all ages, every race, and both sexes. A higher percentage is assumed to represent less commitment to the traditional form of the family institution in the United States. An inverse relationship, accordingly, can be anticipated between the measure employed here for the extent of cultural heterogeneity in a state and the odds that the state had law banning interracial marriage.

Social disorder, too, is an agent that may mold law content on marriage (as well as on other forms of social behavior). Social disorder, obviously, is a matter of degree that runs from complete order to total disorder, but no society—certainly no society that is structurally complex, technologically advanced, and democratically governed—will be at either end of the continuum. A society that is characterized by perfect order will lack the flexibility required to respond effectively to sharp changes in its physical environment and compete, socially or economically, with other societies. At the same time, a society that is characterized entirely by disorder, i.e., a complete absence of patterned social behavior, is by definition impossible. A fully disordered society cannot exist because a prerequisite to social life is that its participants be able to make generally accurate predictions regarding the behavior of other participants. In the absence of social patterns, correct predictions will be a matter of luck, and their frequency in the long run will not exceed chance.

In short, societies will be somewhere between the two ends of the disorder-to-order continuum and spread along the continuum. Whether the content of law in a society stays the same or changes can be affected by the amount of social disorder in the society because this amount is logically a determinant of, and ceteris paribus directly proportional to, the amount of social pressure that exists for societal change, including change in law content. Law that prohibits interracial marriage, therefore, is considered to be more likely in states that are characterized by relatively small amounts of social disorder than in states that are characterized by relatively large amounts of social disorder.

In the present study, the measure of social disorder in each state is the percentage of all resident women aged 30–34 years old who, in 1960, had been married at least once but were currently unmarried due to divorce, i.e., whose (only or last) marriage resulted in divorce.[87] Since the data were for the age range 30–34, the marriages and divorces would have occurred no more than a decade-and-a-half in the past. In Census Bureau publications, the percentages are reported for women as well as for men in each state, but the amount of social disorder is more likely to be captured by the marital status of women than of men. Marriage and divorce are posited to have sex-differentiated social impacts in the United States for three reasons. First, conformity to dominant social practices regarding entry into marriage has been greater

---

[86] The percentages were drawn from Campbell Gibson & Kay Jung, U.S. Census Bureau, *Historical Census Statistics on the Foreign-Born Population of the United States: 1850 to 2000*, at [62] tbl. 14 (Working Paper No. 81, 2006). In 1960, 5.4 percent of the total population of the United States was classified as foreign-born. *Id.* The definition of "foreign born" is in *id.* at 5.

[87] The percentages were obtained from table 105 in the state reports for the 1960 census. *Supra* note 78.

among women than among men.[88] Second, entry into marriage has evidently affected the social position of women more than it has affected the social position of men.[89] Third, exit from marriage through divorce has unsurprising sex-linked effects—women more than men are likely to experience a long-term reduction in income, a higher incidence of poverty, and a greater frequency of single parenthood.[90] The foregoing sex differences suggest that, in the U.S. population, divorce disrupts the social situation of women to a greater degree and for a longer time than it disrupts the social situation of men. Consequently, the measure of social disorder in each state as of 1960 was the prevalence in the state of previously married, divorced women rather than the prevalence of previously married, divorced men.

Societal fragmentation may be a double-edged sword as a factor in the content of law. On the one hand, fragmentation in a society—the degree to which the population of a society is divided into socially distinct groups—may push the society to accommodate at least some of the groups that are the basis of the fragmentation. On the other hand, such fragmentation may act as a wedge between the groups (or some of the groups) and produce resistance to accommodation. Notably, both of the foregoing alternatives (accommodation and resistance to accommodation) seem to be compatible with current theory in macrosociology, and both, therefore, require attention in scholarship on the macrosociology of law content. Whether a society through its law accommodates (or resists accommodation) is undoubtedly not random and is likely determined by large-scale social forces affecting the society and by macro-level social conditions in the society. If so, the types of social circumstances in which one alternative occurs differ from the types of social circumstances in which the other alternative occurs. Research on these circumstances will allow the formulation of theory that predicts when societal fragmentation is followed by societal accommodation and when it is not, i.e., when, in the face of societal fragmentation, the content of pertinent law changes and when it stays the same.

---

[88] For example, the median age at first marriage in the United States has been lower for women than for men. Catherine A. Fitch & Steven Ruggles, *Historical Trends in Marriage Formation, United States 1850 – 1990, in* THE TIES THAT BIND: PERSPECTIVES ON MARRIAGE AND COHABITATION 59, 64 fig. 4.1, 66 fig. 4.2 (Linda J. Waite et al. eds., 2000). *See also* SAIL VOL. 1, *supra* note 5, at 24 fig. 1.2 (presenting data on the United States from the middle of the twentieth century onward; showing that women have been more likely than men to marry by age 30 and by age 40).

In the United States, women are more likely than men to be strongly attached to religion. SAIL VOL. 1, *supra* note 5, at 39 fig. 1.4 (bottom graph). The greater religiousness of women bolsters the contention that tradition is more often observed in the behavior of women than in the behavior of men.

[89] EXPLAINING LAW, *supra* note 2, at 120–21 n.58 (discussing sex differences in the frequency of post-marriage adoptions of the surname of the other spouse as evidence that, in the United States, marriage has an impact on the social status of women more than it has an impact on the social status of men).

[90] Thomas Leopold, *Gender Differences in the Consequences of Divorce: A Study of Multiple Outcomes*, 55 DEMOGRAPHY 769, 786 figs. 1a & 1b, 791 fig. 4b, 792 (2018).

In the instant study, the empirical indicator of societal fragmentation is the percentage in 1960 of the overall population of each state that was nonwhite. The percentage aggregates all residents in a state regardless of their age, sex, and nation of birth.[91] In the coterminous United States as a whole, blacks were 94.3% of all nonwhites in 1960.[92]

Although *societal rationality* has a counterpart in individual human beings, it is an attribute of a social system and, as such, is a society-level phenomenon. The rationality of a society is assumed to vary directly with the amount of knowledge being used by the society and is thus posited to represent the ability of the society to adopt plausible solutions to its problems. As a society becomes more rational, in other words, the society is more likely, ceteris paribus, to respond to a problem with the approach that holds the greatest promise for effectively dealing with the problem. Effective solutions for problems in a structurally complex society will include, unsurprisingly, the removal of societal rigidities and practices that inhibit social change. In the instant study, the empirical indicator of societal rationality—which I hypothesize will be inversely related to the presence of a prohibition on interracial marriage—is the median number of years of schooling completed in each state as of 1960 by persons aged 25 and older.[93] The indicator combines both sexes and all races, i.e., includes men and women as well as whites and nonwhites.

To aid the reader, Table 2.1 provides a synopsis of the preceding discussion. The first two columns of the table list the variables in the study and show their mnemonic labels. The third (right-hand) column describes the indicator of each variable, i.e., the manner in which each variable was quantified.

2.3.2 *Data Analysis*

Because states were coded either 0 or 1 on the dependent variable, maximum-likelihood logistic regression was used to probe the data for relationships between the independent variables and MARRLAW. However, regression in any form raises the question whether the intercept should be left out or left in when estimating the relationships of the independent variables to the dependent variable. For reasons explained elsewhere, I believe that omission of the intercept is generally preferable in macrosociological research on law content,[94] but because the question does not yet have a definitive answer, I report the results of regressing MARRLAW on the independent variables with the intercept as well as without it.

---

[91] The percentages were computed from data in table 94 of the state reports for the 1960 census. *Supra* note 78.

[92] Computed from U.S. SUMMARY, *supra* note 81, at 1-145 tbl. 44.

[93] The data were obtained from table 103 in the state reports for the 1960 census. *Supra* note 78.

[94] SAIL VOL. 2, *supra* note 56, at 4–9.

Table 2.1 Variables and their empirical indicators

Variable	Mnemonic label	Empirical indicator (state-level measure)
Dependent variable		
Whether, as of December 12, 1966, state law proscribed interracial marriage	MARRLAW	States whose law banned interracial marriage were coded 1; states whose law did not ban interracial marriage were coded 0.
Independent variables		
Culture	LABORFORCE	The rate of labor force participation in 1960 among women who were married, were living with their husband, and had a child of their own under the age of six. The rate is expressed as a percentage.
	NOTINLABOR	The rate of *non*participation in the labor force in 1960 among women who were married, were living with their husband, and had a child of their own under the age of six. The rate is expressed as a percentage. NOTINLABOR = 100.0 − LABORFORCE.
Cultural heterogeneity	FOREIGNBN	The percentage of persons in 1960 who had been born outside the United States and whose parents were not U.S. citizens.
Social disorder	DIVORCED	The percentage in 1960 of females aged 30–34 who had been married at least once and were currently unmarried because their (only or last) marriage ended in divorce.
Societal fragmentation	NONWHITE	The percentage of the population in 1960 that was nonwhite.
	WHITE	The percentage of the population in 1960 that was white. WHITE = 100.0 − NONWHITE.
Societal rationality	EDUCATION	The median number of years of education that had been completed as of 1960 by persons who were in the age range 25 and older.

Table 2.2 Summary statistics for the indicators of the independent variables

Indicator	Mean	Standard deviation	Minimum, Maximum
LABORFORCE	19.9%	3.92 pct. pts.	12.5%, 32.1%
FOREIGNBN	4.1%	3.26 pct. pts.	0.4%, 13.6%
DIVORCED	3.0%	0.96 pct. pts.	1.3%, 6.5%
NONWHITE	10.1%	10.17 pct. pts.	0.2%, 42.3%
EDUCATION	10.5 years	1.08 years	8.7 years, 12.2 years

pct. pts. percentage points

2.3.2.1 Regression Models

Summary statistics for the independent variables aid in considering the results of the regression analysis. Table 2.2 provides, for the 48 coterminous states, the mean, the

Table 2.3 Regression models for MARRLAW

	Model 1A	Model 1B	Model 2A	Model 2B	Model 3A	Model 3B
Odds ratio for						
LABORFORCE	1.150[c]	1.360	0.716[c]	0.790	–	–
FOREIGNBN	0.320[c]	0.322[c]	–	–	0.342[c]	0.322[c]
DIVORCED	–	–	–	–	2.145[c]	1.426
NONWHITE	–	–	1.802[c]	1.764[c]	–	–
EDUCATION	–	–	–	–	–	–
INTERCEPT	–	0.037	–	0.203	–	4.713
Number of states	48	48	48	48	48	48
Number of states wrongly predicted	8	8	6	5	8	9
Accuracy rate (%) for predictions of						
States coded 1	76.5	80.0	86.7	92.9	76.5	72.2
States coded 0	87.1	84.9	87.9	88.2	87.1	86.7
All states	83.3	83.3	87.5	89.6	83.3	81.3

– denotes that the variable/intercept was omitted
The superscripts of a, b, and c denote levels of statistical significance: [a] ≤0.10; [b] ≤0.05; [c] ≤0.01

standard deviation, and the highest as well as the lowest numerical value of the indicator of each independent variable.

Table 2.3 reports the results of the regression estimations for models that consist of two independent variables. Models with two independent variables are appealing because of their simplicity relative to models with more than two. The ultimate goal of science is theory, and everything else being equal, a theory concerned with a particular phenomenon becomes more attractive as the number of causal agents in the theory diminishes. Notably, models having more than two independent variables did not markedly improve model fit in the instant study, and they often generated extreme odds ratios and/or determined perfectly (i.e., with a probability of 0.0 or 1.0) where numerous if not all states would be on the dependent variable.[95] Extreme parameter estimates and perfect determinations of units of observations (here, states) are evidence that the estimates obtained are invalid.[96] One or both of these problems were also encountered with some models that had two independent variables.

[95] STATACORP, STATA BASE REFERENCE MANUAL RELEASE 12, at 976 (2011). Reports by Stata of one or more perfect determinations were checked with and verified by the PREDICT command. *Id.*

[96] *See* Paul D. Allison, *Convergence Failures in Logistic Regression* 1, 7 (SAS Global Forum, Paper 360, 2008) (recommending an examination of coefficients that have been estimated in maximum-likelihood logistic regression because "[v]ariables with non-existent coefficients will invariably have large parameter estimates, typically greater than 5.0"); DAVID W. HOSMER & STANLEY LEMESHOW, APPLIED LOGISTIC REGRESSION 138 (2d ed. 2000) (pointing out that perfect determinations in a model mean that maximum-likelihood parameter estimates "do not exist" for the independent variables in the model).

Models that had two independent variables and that exhibited either problem are not included in Table 2.3.

The results in Table 2.3 are for three models, each presented in two forms—one (designated A) that is estimated without the intercept and one (designated B) that is estimated with the intercept. For these models, the table provides the following information: the odds ratio for each independent variable and the level of statistical significance of the odds ratio; the number of states used by the model for its estimates; the number of states that were not in the category of MARRLAW (1 or 0) where the model predicted that they would be; the percentage of all states that the model forecast would be coded 1 on MARRLAW and that were in fact coded 1; the percentage of all states that the model forecast would be coded 0 on MARRLAW and that were in fact coded 0; and the percentage of all states whose coding on MARRLAW (whether 1 or 0) was correctly anticipated by the model.[97] I should point out that levels of statistical significance, although reported, were *not* a criterion for evaluating the independent variables, individually or collectively, that comprised the models in Table 2.3; significance levels are shown solely for the reader who wishes to consider them. The degree to which the models fit the data, especially the rates at which the models correctly assigned states to the categories of MARRLAW, was thus central to choosing the most attractive model.[98]

Before looking at the accuracy of the models in Table 2.3, we need to consider whether the odds ratios estimated for any model in the table suffered from either excessive collinearity or an influential outlier. The possibility of the former was tested with the Variance Inflation Factor ("VIF") score. The independent variables in the models, however, had VIF scores well below the threshold (10.0) at which concern arises that collinearity is unacceptable.[99] The possibility of the latter—whether one or more states might have unduly affected the odds ratios—was examined by computing, for every state in each of the models, Cook's Statistic and the probability that the state would be in the category of MARRLAW that it was in.[100] Concern that a state may be an influential outlier exists when (1) the numerical value of Cook's Statistic for the state is at least 1.00 or is noticeably higher than the numerical values of Cook's Statistic for other states and/or (2) the state has a very

[97] The ESTAT CLASSIFICATION command in Stata was used to determine the number and percentage of states that were correctly and incorrectly assigned by a model to the categories of the dependent variable. STATACORP, *supra* note 95, at 957–58.

[98] My disregard of statistical significance and my reliance on model fit is explained in SAIL VOL. 2, *supra* note 56, at 9–13, 17–18.

[99] DAMODAR N. GUJARATI & DAWN C. PORTER, BASIC ECONOMETRICS 340 (5th ed. 2009). Variance Inflation Factor scores were computed in the present study using the VIF, UNCENTERED command for each logistic-regression model that omitted the intercept. For a logistic-regression model that included the intercept, a linear-regression model was estimated using the REGRESS command, and the Variance Inflation Factor scores were obtained using the VIF command. As to the procedure for models with the intercept, see RICHARD WILLIAMS, MULTICOLLINEARITY 11 (2015), https://www3.nd.edu/~rwilliam/stats2/l11.pdf.

[100] J. SCOTT LONG & JEREMY FREESE, REGRESSION MODELS FOR CATEGORICAL DEPENDENT VARIABLES USING STATA 151–53 (2d ed. 2006); HOSMER & LEMESHOW, *supra* note 96, at 173, 180.

low probability of being in the category of the dependent variable where it is. When criterion (1) and/or criterion (2) is met by a model, odds ratios for the independent variables in the model may have been inordinately affected by one or more particular states, and I thus re-estimated the model without each suspect state, i.e., with 47 states rather than 48. Under these criteria, re-estimation was necessary for all models except Model 2A, but in the case of Models 1A, 1B, 3A, and 3B, the odds ratios obtained from re-estimation for the independent variables were similar to the odds ratios that had been obtained when these models were estimated using 48 states. In the case of Model 2B, re-estimation was necessary because one state (West Virginia) was suspect under both of the above criteria. Although re-estimation yielded odds ratios for an independent variable and the intercept that differed noticeably from their counterparts in the original estimation, i.e., in the estimation with 48 states, two states in the re-estimation were perfectly predicted. Accordingly, the output from the re-estimation was of dubious validity,[101] and I did not treat West Virginia as an outlier, i.e., I based the results for Model 2B on all 48 states. Nonetheless, some skepticism regarding the results for Model 2B, as reported in Table 2.3, may be justified.

Which model offers the most appealing account of the dependent variable? Since all of the models in Table 2.3 consist of two independent variables, the models are equal in terms of simplicity and must be differentiated in terms of their fit to the data. Under this criterion, Models 2A and 2B have an edge. For example, Model 2A yielded two fewer wrong predictions than either Model 1A or Model 3A, and Model 2B yielded three fewer wrong predictions than Model 1B and four fewer wrong predictions than Model 3B. Furthermore, when compared to the other models in Table 2.3, Models 2A and 2B were clearly the best at predicting the states that were in the MARRLAW category that was coded 1, i.e., the states having law that proscribed interracial marriage. Table 2.3 also shows that the presence or absence of the intercept was neither advantageous nor disadvantageous to the fit of a model: As seen in the bottom row of Table 2.3, inclusion or omission of the intercept made no difference for states as a whole under one set of independent variables (Models 1A, 1B), and while making a difference for states as a whole in the other sets (Models 2A, 2B and 3A, 3B), the differences are small in magnitude and opposite in direction.

2.3.2.2 Model 2A and Model 2C

The acceptance by the U.S. Supreme Court of Loving v. Virginia in December 1966 signaled the forthcoming end of the enforceability in the United States of law that prohibited interracial marriage.[102] If this acceptance generated societal stress in the states that had law banning interracial marriage, the Court-triggered increase in stress

[101] *Supra* note 96.

[102] See text accompanying *supra* notes 71 to 75.

can be explained by the sociological factors that were responsible for the presence of such law. Model 2A, which is my preferred model in light of the above-noted uncertainty involving Model 2B, suggests that state-to-state differences in interracial-marriage law as of December 1966 are largely explainable by two sociological variables in 1960, viz., culture and societal fragmentation. These variables obviously represented powerful sociological forces, because they predicted the existence or nonexistence of law banning interracial marriage in fully 42 of the 48 coterminous states. To be more precise, Model 2A tells us that when labor-force participation went up one percentage-point among married, husband-present women who have a child of their own younger than age six, the odds that a state would ban interracial marriage went down by 28.4%. When the share of nonwhites in a state population rose by one percentage-point, the odds that the state would ban interracial marriage increased by 80.2%. The standardized coefficients[103] revealed that the odds of a state prohibiting interracial marriage were affected by NONWHITE far more than they were affected by LABORFORCE: For a one standard-deviation increase in NONWHITE, the factor change in the odds was 397.31; for a one standard-deviation increase in LABORFORCE, the factor change in the odds was 0.27. A factor change above 1.00 is compared to a factor change below 1.00 by taking the *inverse* of either the former or the latter;[104] for example, the inverse of 0.27 for LABORFORCE is $1.00 \div 0.27 = 3.70$, which is much less than the 397.31 for NONWHITE. The foregoing relationships of independent variables to the dependent variable, readers should not forget, are net of each other, i.e., the effect of each independent variable occurred while the other was held constant.

A further point warrants mention. Although culture may not be as influential as societal fragmentation in shaping state law on interracial marriage, culture not-infrequently attracts attention in scholarship on the institution of law.[105] Since culture is a topic of more than minimal interest in the macrosociology of law, I extend my examination of its impact on state interracial-marriage law. The negative relationship between LABORFORCE and MARRLAW in Model 2A means that the odds that a state will by law ban interracial marriage rise when adherence to the nuclear-family ideal increases in the state, i.e., when *nonparticipation* in the labor force grows by one percentage-point among married, husband-present women who have an own child younger than age six. To ascertain the magnitude of the effect of greater conformity to the ideal of the nuclear family, I created two new variables for the coterminous states. One variable (labeled NOTINLABOR) was formed by subtracting the LABORFORCE percentage for each state from 100.0; the other variable (labeled WHITE) was formed by subtracting the NONWHITE percentage for each state from 100.0. The results of regressing MARRLAW on NOTINLABOR and WHITE are shown as Model 2C in Table 2.4, which also reproduces the results for Model 2A to help in seeing the differences between the two models and their results.

---

[103] See note 187 and its accompanying text in *supra* Chap. 1.

[104] LONG & FREESE, *supra* note 100, at 179.

[105] Roger Cotterrell, *Law in Culture*, 17 RATIO JURIS 1, 6 (2004).

Table 2.4 Regression Models 2A and 2C for MARRLAW

	Model 2A	Model 2C
Odds ratio for		
LABORFORCE	0.716[c]	–
NOTINLABOR	–	1.790[c]
NONWHITE	1.802[c]	–
WHITE	–	0.588[c]
INTERCEPT	–	–
Number of states	48	48
Number of states wrongly predicted	6	7
Accuracy rate (%) for predictions of		
States coded 1	86.7	77.8
States coded 0	87.9	90.0
All states	87.5	85.4

Superscripts are used to denote levels of statistical significance: [a] ≤0.10; [b] ≤0.05; [c] ≤0.01
– denotes that the variable/intercept was omitted

Under Model 2C, the odds ratio for NOTINLABOR was 1.790.[106] Accordingly, the odds that a state would forbid interracial marriage were 79% higher when married women in the state who reside with their husband and have an own child below age six experienced a one percentage-point increase in the extent to which they are *outside* the labor force (while the share of the population that is white remains the same). Under Model 2C, as under Model 2A, the odds of a state ban on interracial marriage were affected much less by the extent of commitment to the conventional commandments of culture than by the degree of societal fragmentation. For a one standard-deviation increase in NOTINLABOR, the odds changed by a factor of 9.78; for a one standard-deviation increase in WHITE, the odds changed by a factor of 0.005. The inverse of the latter is 1.00 ÷ 0.005 = 200.00, which far exceeds the 9.78 obtained for NOTINLABOR.

The consequences of between-state differences in culture and in societal fragmentation for whether interracial marriage is prohibited by law can be visualized by graphing the probability that a state has such a prohibition (i.e., is coded 1 on MARRLAW) at the various levels of the empirical indicator of each independent variable when the empirical indicator of the other independent variable remains at a designated numerical value. Figure 2.2 shows the probabilities that are predicted by Model 2A. The vertical axis for each graph in the figure designates the probabilities from 0 to 1.0, and the horizontal axis for each graph shows the numerical values of the indicator that is generating the probabilities. The predicted probabilities in the top graph are thus for the different levels of LABORFORCE when NONWHITE was held at

[106] Cook's Statistic was computed for Model 2C, but did not exceed 0.25 for any state. The state having the smallest likelihood of being coded as it was on MARRLAW had a probability of 0.23 of being so coded. The foregoing measures led me to conclude that, under Model 2C, no state skewed the results and was an influential outlier.

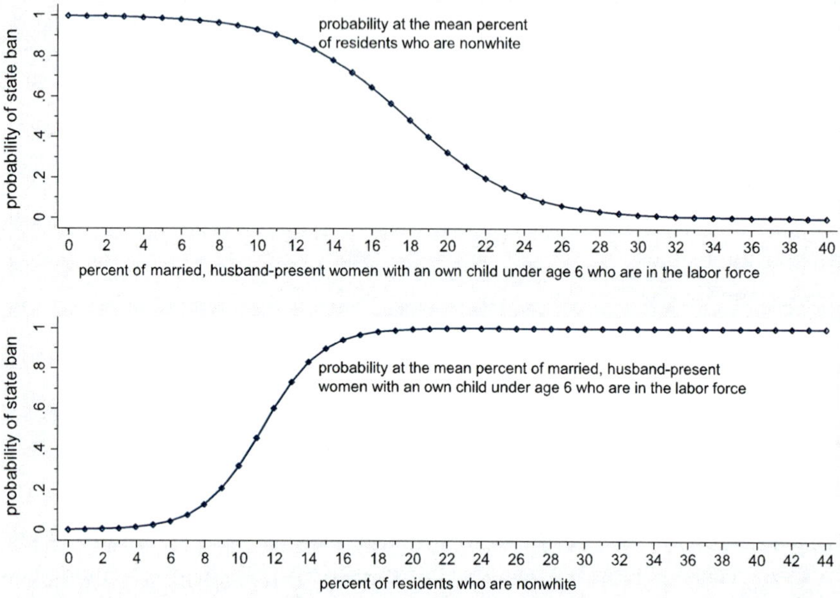

Fig. 2.2 Probability of state ban on interracial marriage: predictions by Model 2A

its mean, and the predicted probabilities in the bottom graph are for the different levels of NONWHITE when LABORFORCE was kept at its mean.[107] The mean, minimum, and maximum numerical value of the indicator of each independent variable in Model 2A can be found in Table 2.2.

What conclusions can be drawn from Fig. 2.2? I begin by noting the dissimilarity between the slope of the line for the probabilities in the top graph and the slope of the line for the probabilities in the bottom graph. Specifically, differences in culture brought about gradual movement in the probability that a state had law prohibiting interracial marriage, but differences in race-grounded societal fragmentation brought about rapid movement and the effect was confined to just a portion of the range of fragmentation. The slope of the line for societal fragmentation is striking: Law against interracial marriage grew much more likely as the nonwhite share of a state population rose from about 5% or 6% to about 17% or 18%, after which the likelihood of such law plateaued.

Extending the analysis, the graphs in Fig. 2.2 are also useful because they reveal where societal thresholds can be expected for the presence or absence of law against interracial marriage. Since an increase in LABORFORCE reduced the odds that a state would have law against interracial marriage, the focus should be on the numerical

---

[107]The predicted probabilities and the graphs for them were obtained with the MARGINS and MARGINSPLOT commands in Stata. STATACORP, *supra* note 95, at 1027, 1034, 1038–39, 1099–1106.

values of LABORFORCE above which (with NONWHITE at its mean) the probability of a state being coded 1 on MARRLAW was less than 50.0%. This probability—i.e., the probability at which a state had a less-than-even chance of possessing law barring interracial marriage—was reached when LABORFORCE was 18%. (The probability was then 0.48.) When LABORFORCE was four percentage-points higher, i.e., when LABORFORCE was 22%, the probability of a state being coded 1 on MARRLAW was just 0.20.

Let us turn to NONWHITE (with LABORFORCE at its mean). The analysis is informed by the nature of the relationship between NONWHITE and MARRLAW—an increase in NONWHITE raised the odds that a state had law prohibiting interracial marriage. Here, then, the focus should be on the numerical values of NONWHITE above which a state had a better-than-even chance of possessing law against interracial marriage. When NONWHITE was 12%, the probability of a ban on interracial marriage was 0.60; when NONWHITE was just three percentage-points higher, i.e., when NONWHITE was 15%, the probability of a ban on interracial marriage was fully 0.90.

2.4 Conclusion

In the enterprise of science, data are essential; without data, scientists cannot identify the causes of a phenomenon such as the content of law. The data analyzed in *supra* Sect. 2.3 add to the evidence that jurisdictions do not decide spontaneously whether they will or will not ban particular social activities.[108] What law says when it seeks to regulate social behavior, in other words, is not random but, instead, is the result of macro-level agents. Notably, this finding and the evidence for it are contrary to a position taken in some law-review scholarship. According to this scholarship, substantive law on social matters is unpredictable and/or due to conditions within the institution of law.[109] The foregoing position, however, is at variance with the evidence from data analyses that proscriptions and prescriptions of law aimed at core social matters are ordinarily adopted by jurisdictions, as well as jettisoned by jurisdictions, in response to measurable, jurisdiction-level sociological agents.[110] Because such agents can vary in type and magnitude, law content that addresses social life differs across time and space. The present book seeks to locate these agents in order to shed light on and bolster the case for the concept of societal stress. The book contends that societal stress is generated when the content of tradition-backed law in the jurisdiction is altered or threatened, and that the sociological

[108] Further evidence is in SAIL VOL. 1, *supra* note 5, at ch. 2 pts. 2.3, 2.4.

[109] *See* Oona A. Hathaway, *Path Dependence in the Law: The Course and Pattern of Legal Change in a Common Law System*, 86 IOWA L. REV. 601, 650–51 & n.191 (2001).

[110] SAIL VOL. 1, *supra* note 5, at ch. 2 pts. 2.3, 2.4; Sect. 3.2 in *infra* Chap. 3; Sect. 4.2 in *infra* Chap. 4.

determinants of the presence/absence of this content are agents that affect whether such stress occurs.

The instant chapter has concentrated on law that disallowed marriage between two individuals who are not of the same race but otherwise legally eligible to marry, and the data analysis led to the conclusion that culture and race-based societal fragmentation largely accounted for whether such law existed in a state: The odds that a state had law against interracial marriage went down as the population of the state diverged more from the American cultural ideal for the family institution, and the odds went up as the population of the state experienced more fragmentation along racial lines. Since the U.S. Supreme Court in Loving v. Virginia invalidated such law in the states that had it, social stress was plausibly created by the ruling, and the odds of the occurrence of such stress were decreased by nonconformity with the tradition-endorsed family form and increased by race-based fragmentation. As the standardized regression coefficients show,[111] however, deviation from the traditional family ideal lowered the odds that societal stress would occur much less than race-based fragmentation raised them.

In sum, societal stress is a promising concept for advancing macrosociological scholarship that seeks to understand the institution of law. Importantly, the concept can be accommodated comfortably within structural-functionalism theory. Because the concept not only offers a way to interpret empirical links between macrosociological agents and law content but also has a home in theory, it is an implement that macrosociologists who study law should consider for inclusion in their tool kit.

Appendix: State Law That as of December 12, 1966

Prohibited Interracial Marriage

State	Law
Alabama	"The legislature shall never pass any law to authorize or legalize any marriage between any white person and a negro, or descendant of a negro." ALA. CONST., art. 4, § 102 (1940).
	"If any white person and any negro, or descendant of any negro intermarry, or live in adultery or fornication with each other, each of them shall, on conviction, be imprisoned in the penitentiary for not less than two nor more than seven years." ALA. CODE § 14-360 (1959).
Arkansas	"All marriages of white persons with negroes or mulattoes are declared to be illegal and void." ARK. STAT. § 55-104 (1947).
	"Whoever shall contract marriage in fact, contrary to the prohibitions of the third and fourth [§§ 55-103, 55-104] sections of this act, and whoever shall knowingly

(continued)

[111] See note 187 and its accompanying text in *supra* Chap. 1.

State	Law
	solemnize the same, shall be deemed guilty of a misdemeanor, and shall upon conviction be fined or imprisoned, or both, at the discretion of the jury who shall pass on the case, or if the conviction shall be by confession, or on demurrer, then at the discretion of the court." ARK. STAT. § 55-105 (1947).
Delaware	"A marriage is prohibited and void between — . . . (2) A white person and a negro or mulatto." DEL. CODE ANN. tit. 13, § 101(a) (1953).
Florida	"All marriages between a white person and a negro, or between a white person and a person of negro descent to the fourth generation, inclusive, are hereby forever prohibited." FLA. CONST. art, 16, § 24 (1963).
	"It is unlawful for any white male person residing or being in this state to intermarry with any negro female person; and it is in like manner unlawful for any white female person residing or being in this state to intermarry with any negro male person; and every marriage formed or solemnized in contravention of the provisions of this section shall be utterly null and void, and the issue, if any, of such surreptitious marriage shall be regarded as bastard and incapable of having or receiving any estate, real, personal or mixed, by inheritance." FLA. STAT. § 741.11 (1964).
Georgia	"It shall be unlawful for a white person to marry anyone except a white person. Any marriage in violation of this section shall be void." GA. CODE ANN. § 53-106 (1961).
	"Any person, white or colored, who shall marry or go through a marriage ceremony in violation of the provision of section 53-106 shall be guilty of a felony, and shall be punished by imprisonment in the penitentiary for not less than one year and not more than two years." GA. CODE ANN. § 53-9903 (1961).
Kentucky	"Marriage is prohibited and void: . . . (2) Between a white person and a Negro or mulatto; . . . ." KY. REV. STAT. ANN. § 402.020 (1963).
Louisiana	"Miscegenation is the marriage or habitual cohabitation with knowledge of their difference in race, between a person of the Caucasian or white race and a person of the colored or negro race. Whoever commits the crime of miscegenation shall be imprisoned, with or without hard labor, for not more than five years." LA. REV. STAT. ANN. § 14:79 (1950).
Maryland	"All marriages between a white person and a negro, or between a white person and a person of negro descent, to the third generation, inclusive, or between a white person and a member of the Malay race or between a negro and a member of the Malay race, or between a person of negro descent, to the third generation, inclusive, and a member of the Malay race, are forever prohibited, and shall be void; and any person violating the provisions of this section shall be deemed guilty of an infamous crime, and punished by imprisonment in the penitentiary not less than eighteen months nor more than ten years; provided, however, that the provisions of this section shall not apply to marriages between white persons and members of the Malay race, or between negroes and members of the Malay race,

(continued)

State	Law
	or between persons of negro descent, to the third generation, inclusive, and members of the Malay race, existing prior to June 1, 1935." MD. CODE ANN., CRIMES & PUNISHMENTS, § 398 (Michie 1957).[112]
Mississippi	"The marriage of a white person with a negro or mulatto, or person who shall have one-eighth or more of negro blood, shall be unlawful and void." MISS. CONST. art. 14, § 263 (1956).
	"The marriage of a white person and a negro or mulatto or person who shall have one-eighth or more of negro blood, or with a Mongolian or a person who shall have one-eighth or more of Mongolian blood, shall be unlawful, and such marriage shall be unlawful and void; and any party thereto, on conviction, shall be punished as for marriage within the degrees prohibited by the last two sections; and any attempt to evade this and the two preceding sections by marrying out of this state and returning to it shall be within them." MISS. CODE ANN. § 459 (1956).[113]
	"Persons being within the degrees within which marriages are declared by law to be incestuous and void, or persons whose marriage is prohibited by law by reason or [sic.] race or blood and which marriage is declared to be incestuous and void, who shall cohabit, or live together as husband and wife, or be guilty of a single act of adultery or fornication, upon conviction shall be punished by imprisonment in the penitentiary for a term not exceeding ten (10) years." MISS. CODE ANN. § 2000 (1956).
Missouri	"All marriages between . . . white persons and negroes or white persons and Mongolians . . . are prohibited and declared absolutely void . . . ." MO. ANN. STAT. § 451.020 (Vernon 1952).
	"No person having one-eighth part or more of negro blood shall be permitted to marry any white person, nor shall any white person be permitted to marry any negro or person having one-eighth part or more of negro blood; and every person who shall knowingly marry in violation of the provisions of this section shall, upon conviction, be punished by imprisonment in the penitentiary for two years, or by fine not less than one hundred dollars, or by imprisonment in the county jail not less than three months, or by both such fine and imprisonment; and the jury trying any such case may determine the proportion of negro blood in any party to such marriage from the appearance of such person." MO. REV. STAT. § 563.240 (1949).
North Carolina	"All marriages between a white person and a negro, or between a white person and a person of negro descent to the third generation, inclusive, are hereby forever prohibited." N.C. CONST. art. XIV, § 8 (1944).
	"All marriages between a white person and a negro, or between a white person and a person of negro descent to the third generation inclusive, are forever prohibited, and shall be void. Any person violating this section shall be guilty of an infamous crime, and shall be punished by imprisonment in the county jail or State's prison

(continued)

[112]The statutory phrase "Malay race" evidently referred to a person whose skin color is "yellow" or who had a parent with "yellow" skin. United States v. Dow, 25 F. Cas. 901, 903 (Cir. Ct., D. Md., 1840) (No. 14990).

[113]In section 459, the phrases "last two sections" and "two preceding sections" refer to sections 457 and 458. Section 457 prohibits marriage between certain types of blood-related kin; section 458 defines the word "incestuous" with regard to marriage and provides that a marriage covered by section 457 or section 458 is "incestuous and void." MISS. CODE ANN. §§ 457, 458 (1956).

State	Law
	for not less than four months nor more than ten years, and may also be fined, in the discretion of the court." N.C. GEN. STAT. § 14-181 (1953).
Oklahoma	"The marriage of any person of African descent, as defined by the Constitution of this State, to any person not of African descent, or the marriage of any person not of African descent to any person of African descent, shall be unlawful and is hereby prohibited within this State." OKLA. STAT. ANN. tit. 43, § 12 (West 1954).[114]
	"Any person who shall marry in violation of the preceding section, shall be deemed guilty of felony, and upon conviction thereof shall be fined in any sum not exceeding five hundred dollars, and imprisonment in the penitentiary not less than one nor more than five years." OKLA. STAT. ANN. tit. 43, § 13 (West 1954).
South Carolina	"The marriage of a white person with a negro or mulatto, or person who shall have one-eighth or more of negro blood, shall be unlawful and void. . . ." S.C. CONST. art. 3, § 33 (1962).
	"It shall be unlawful (a) for any white man to intermarry with any woman of either the Indian or negro races or any mulatto, mestizo or half-breed, (b) for any white woman to intermarry with any person other than a white man[,] or (c) for any mulatto, half-breed, Indian, negro or mestizo to intermarry with a white woman; and any such marriage or attempted marriage shall be utterly null and void and of no effect. Any person who shall violate any provision of this section shall be guilty of a misdemeanor and, on conviction thereof, shall be punished by a fine of not less than five hundred dollars or imprisonment for not less than twelve months or both in the discretion of the court. . . ." S.C. CODE ANN. § 20-7 (1962). Section 20-7 included an exception for "white persons" and "Catawba Indians." Under the exception, marriage between a White and a Catawba Indian was lawful after March 11, 1960; the exception also provided that a White and a Catawba Indian who were cohabiting as spouses before March 11, 1960 were to be considered lawfully married. Act of March 11, 1960, No. 597, 1960 S.C. Acts 1539 (codified at S.C. CODE ANN. § 20-7) (1962).
Tennessee	"The intermarriage of white persons with negroes, mulattoes, or persons of mixed blood, descended from a negro to the third generation inclusive or their living together as man and wife in this State is prohibited. The legislature shall enforce this section by appropriate legislation." TENN. CONST. art. 11, § 14 (1955).
	"The intermarriage of white persons with negroes, mulattoes, or persons of mixed blood descended from a negro, to the third generation inclusive, or their living together as man and wife in this state, is prohibited." TENN. CODE ANN. § 36-402 (1955).
	"The person knowingly violating the provisions of § 36-402 shall be guilty of a felony, and undergo imprisonment in the penitentiary not less than one (1) nor more than five (5) years; and the court may, on the recommendation of the jury, substitute, in lieu of punishment in the penitentiary, fine and imprisonment in the county jail." TENN. CODE ANN. § 36-403 (1955).

(continued)

[114] The Constitution of Oklahoma provided: "Wherever in this Constitution and laws of this State, the word or words, 'colored' or 'colored race,' 'negro' or 'negro race,' are used, the same shall be construed to mean or apply to all persons of African descent. The term 'white race' shall include all other persons." OKLA. CONST. art. 23, § 11 (reproduced in Marquez v. Lorenzen, 441 P.2d 986, 988 (Okla. 1965)), repealed 1978. Under this provision, native-American Indians were considered to be members of the "white race" and not to be of "African descent." Blake v. Sessions, 220 P. 876, 878 (Okla. 1923).

State	Law
Texas	"If any white person and negro shall knowingly intermarry with each other in this State, or having so intermarried in or out of the State shall continue to live together as man and wife within this State, they shall be confined in the penitentiary not less than two nor more than five years." TEX. PENAL CODE ANN., art. 492 (Vernon 1952).
	"It shall not be lawful for any person of Caucasian blood or their descendants to intermarry with Africans or the descendants of Africans. If any person shall violate any provision of this article, such marriage shall be null and void." TEX. REV. CIV. STAT. ANN., art. 4607 (Vernon 1951).
Virginia	"It shall hereafter be unlawful for any white person in this State to marry any save a white person, or a person with no other admixture of blood than white and American Indian. . . ." VA. CODE ANN. § 20-54 (1950, 1960 repl. vol.).
	"All marriages between a white person and a colored person shall be absolutely void without any decree of divorce or other legal process." VA. CODE ANN. § 20-57 (1950, 1960 repl. vol.).
	"If any white person intermarry with a colored person, or any colored person intermarry with a white person, he shall be guilty of a felony and shall be punished by confinement in the penitentiary for not less than one nor more than five years." VA. CODE ANN. § 20-59 (1950, 1960 repl. vol.).
West Virginia	"Any white person who shall intermarry with a negro shall be guilty of a misdemeanor, and, upon conviction thereof, shall be fined not exceeding one hundred dollars, and confined in jail not more than one year. . . ." W. VA. CODE § 4697 (1961).
	"All marriages between a white person and a negro . . . shall be void from the time they are so declared by a decree of nullity." W. VA. CODE § 4701 (1961).

Source: see *supra* Sect. 2.3.1.1

Abbreviations used: *Ann.* annotated; *art.* article; *Civ.* civil; *Const.* constitution; *Gen.* general; *Rev.* revised; *Stat.* statutes; *tit.* title

Chapter 3
Sex and the Equal Rights Amendment

3.1 Introduction

> The overall implication of the equal rights amendment is nothing less than the sharp reduction in importance of the family unit, [with] the eventual elimination of that unit by no means improbable.[1]

> The ERA will ensure all citizens have the opportunity to reach their full potential. Women and men must have equal rights for a democracy to thrive.[2]

---

[1] 132 Cong. Rec. 23,317 (1986) (memorandum dated May 4, 1970; authored by William H. Rehnquist, Ass't. Att'y Gen., U.S. Dep't of Justice). Mr. Rehnquist became an associate justice of the U.S. Supreme Court in January 1972 and chief justice in September 1986; he remained chief justice until his death in September 2005. Supreme Court Historical Society, *William H. Rehnquist, 1986-2005*, https://supremecourthistory.org (open "Teaching Center" drop-down menu).

A statement similar to that of Mr. Rehnquist was made by then-retired U.S. Senator Sam J. Ervin, Jr., *The Question of Ratification of the Equal Rights Amendment*, 56 Cong. Dig. 171, 171, 177 (1977) ("The Equal Rights Amendment . . . constitutes an effort to convert men and women into identical legal beings . . . . In so doing, the Amendment emulates Procrustes, the fabled robber of ancient Greece, who stretched or mutilated his victims to make them conform to the length of his bed. It is the height of folly to command legislative bodies to ignore sex in making laws. . . . As a consequence, the Amendment imperils the welfare of wives and mothers and their children and the highest interests of society itself.")

[2] 161 Cong. Rec. E705 (2015) (statement of Rep. Carolyn B. Maloney). A similar statement is in: 163 Cong. Rec. S2044, S2045 (2017) (statement of Sen. Ben Cardin) (arguing the Equal Rights Amendment should be added to the Constitution because "how a nation treats its women is a good barometer of that nation's potential for success as a whole").

In addition, see Ruth Bader Ginsburg, *Ratification of the Equal Rights Amendment: A Question of Time*, 57 Tex. L. Rev. 919, 945 (1979) (contending that the Equal Rights Amendment is necessary both to maintain the pace of "the trend toward opening opportunities to women" and "to spark overdue change in laws and in the perspective of public officials—judges, legislators, and administrators"). When the foregoing article was published, Ms. Ginsburg was a professor at the Columbia University law school; she was an associate justice of the U.S. Supreme Court from 1993 until her death in 2020. Supreme Court Historical Society, *Ruth Bader Ginsburg, 1993-2020*, https://supremecourthistory.org (open "Teaching Center" drop-down menu).

L. D. Barnett, *Societal Stress and Law*,
https://doi.org/10.1007/978-3-031-30875-8_3

The Equal Rights Amendment ("ERA") that the U.S. Congress proposed in 1972 for possible addition to the Constitution of the nation provides that "Equality of rights under the law shall not be denied or abridged by the United States or by any State on account of sex."[3] However, during the congressionally specified ratification period—March 1972 through June 1982—the number of states that assented to the ERA was not sufficient to satisfy the requirement that the Constitution imposes for the adoption of an amendment. To be precise, during 1972–1982 thirty-five states assented,[4] but under article V of the Constitution,[5] thirty-eight had to do so. Nonetheless, the ERA may yet be placed in the Constitution, because three states assented to it after 1982—one in 2017, one in 2018, and one in 2020. [6] There is uncertainty, however, whether the action by the three states will count and whether the action taken by five ratifying states for the purpose of retracting their ratification will be effective.[7] Both sets of states (the post-1982 assenters and the retractors) will be considered further in *infra* Sect. 3.2.1.

Although the text of the United States Constitution would be altered by the addition of the ERA, dispute exists over the degree and substance of change in American society that the ERA would bring about. As illustrated by the passages that introduced the first paragraph of this chapter, both opponents and proponents predict that the ERA will have major ramifications for social life in America if it becomes part of the Constitution: Opponents expect that the social fabric will be seriously damaged; proponents, by contrast, anticipate significant social benefits. However, participants in a political debate are not impartial observers and hence the predictions they make about the effect of a proposed change in law may well be wrong. To deal with the matter, I consider, inter alia, empirical social science research on the impact of ERA-pertinent law.

[3] *Proposed Amendment to the Constitution of the United* States, H.R.J. Res. 208, 92d Cong., § 1, 86 Stat. 1523 (1972) [hereinafter H.R.J. Res. 208].

[4] Thomas H. Neale, Cong. Res. Serv., R42979, The Proposed Equal Rights Amendment: Contemporary Ratification Issues 12–16 (2018), https://fas.org/sgp/crs/misc/R42979.pdf.

[5] "The Congress, whenever two thirds of both houses shall deem it necessary, shall propose amendments to this Constitution, or, on the application of the legislatures of two thirds of the several states, shall call a convention for proposing amendments, which, in either case, shall be valid to all intents and purposes, as part of this Constitution, when ratified by the legislatures of three fourths of the several states, or by conventions in three fourths thereof, as the one or the other mode of ratification may be proposed by the Congress . . . ." U.S. Const. art. V.

[6] Neale, *supra* note 4, at 5–6 (Nevada and Illinois); Virginia Legislative Information System, 2020 Sess., HJ1 and SJ1, https://virginiageneralassembly.gov. (under "Search Legislation with LIS," enter bill number and then select "Go").

[7] A definitive answer to these questions has not been provided by litigation to date. *See* Equal Means Equal v. Ferriero, 3 F.4th 24 (1st Cir. 2021); Virginia v. Ferriero, 525 F.Supp.3d 36 (D. D.C. 2021), *dismissing Virginia as a party*, 2022 WL 605733 (D.C. Cir. 2022).

3.1.1 The Likely Social Effect of the ERA

Before turning to quantitative social-science studies whose findings offer evidence of the likely impact of the ERA on American society, let me provide a statistical picture of the frequency with which women in the United States have over time deviated from societally endorsed ideals. A judgment regarding whether the ERA will alter patterns of social behavior requires consideration of behavioral changes that have already occurred among women, i.e., that have occurred without the ERA in the Constitution. The statistical picture helps in another way, too. By supplying the historical context of the 1972–1982 political battle over ratification of the ERA, it offers an understanding of the resistance that the ERA has encountered.

To begin with the obvious, American ideals traditionally have instructed women to marry and bear children. In this regard, the years around 1960 are notable because American life was then characterized by social convention. Thus the U.S. Supreme Court observed in 1961 that "[d]espite the enlightened emancipation of women from the restrictions and protections of bygone years, and their entry into many parts of community life formerly considered to be reserved to men, [the] woman is still regarded as the center of home and family life" in American society.[8] Since social conditions at a particular time do not, in general, change abruptly and their impact does not dissipate quickly, the nature of social life shortly before and after 1960 would have influenced Americans in subsequent years. During 1972–1982, accordingly, traditional ideals were capable of fueling political opposition to the ERA.

What statistical evidence backs the claim that, in the decades immediately following World War II, the social behavior of American women was in line with traditional ideals?

- Since 1890, the lowest median ages for first marriages by American women occurred during the years 1949–1962.[9]
- Women who reached their 25th birthday during the 1950s and 1960s were in the birth cohorts of 1925–1934 and 1935–1944. Of every 100 women in the United States who were members of these cohorts, more than 80 married by their 25th birthday.[10]

---

[8] Hoyt v. Florida, 368 U.S. 57, 58, 61–62, 65 (1961) (deciding that the equal protection guarantee of the Fourteenth Amendment to the Constitution allowed a statute to make jury service optional for women even though such service was obligatory for men).

[9] U.S. Census Bureau, Historical Marital Status Tables – Table MS-2, Estimated Median Age at First Marriage: 1890 to present (2020), https://www.census.gov/data/tables/time-series/demo/families/marital.html. During 1949-1962, the median age at first marriage among U.S. women was 20.1 to 20.3. *Id.*

[10] Rose M. Kreider & Jason M. Fields, U.S. Census Bureau, *Number, Timing, and Duration of Marriages and Divorces: 1996*, CURRENT POPULATION REP., Feb. 2002 (P70-80), at 4 tbl. 1.

- More than 80 out of every 100 U.S. women who married for the first time between 1945 and 1954 were in these marriages 15 years later, i.e., in the 1960s.[11]
- U.S. total fertility rates, which were first estimated in 1917, reached a high during 1956–1960. In 1960, for example, the total fertility rate in the United States was 3.61 children per woman among women of all races and 3.51 children per woman among White women. Among White women in that year, fewer than one out of five had not borne a child by age 30.[12]

The preceding statistics make clear that, in the United States around the year 1960, women who never married, women who were unmarried due to divorce, and women who did not ever bear a child were out of line with social norms and, by implication, with what their society expected. Trends in the exact extent of the deviation during the twentieth century and early twenty-first century can be seen in Fig. 3.1. The figure uses data on females in the United States across this period and shows trends in (1) the percentage of females aged 15 and older who had never been married, (2) the percentage of females aged 15 and older who had been married but were currently unmarried due to divorce, and (3) the percentage of women aged 45–49 who had not given birth to a child.[13] The plots of (1), (2), and (3) in the inner region of Fig. 3.1 are designated in the legend for the figure as "never married," "unmarried-

[11] *Id.* at 5 tbl. 2. More than seventy out of every 100 of these women were still in their first marriages twenty-five years later, i.e., in the 1970s. *Id.*

[12] Selma Taffel, Nat'l Ctr. for Health Statistics, Trends in Fertility in the United States 14 fig. 7, 38 tbl. 13 (DHEW Pub. No. (HRA) 78-1906) (1977). See Sect. 1.4.3 in *supra* Chap. 1 for an explanation of the total fertility rate.

From 1936 to 1961, no less than ninety percent of White women in the United States thought that a married couple should have at least one child; the mean number of children that White women in these years believed was optimal ranged from 2.8 to 3.6. Judith Blake, *Ideal Family Size Among White Americans: A Quarter of a Century's Evidence*, 3 Demography 154, 164 tbl. 5, 166 (1966).

[13] The percentages for (1) and for (2) were obtained from the following sources: (a) U.S. Census Bureau, 2003 Statistical Abstract: Mini-Historical Statistics – Table HS-11. Marital Status of the Population by Sex: 1900 to 2002 [hereinafter Table HS-11], https://www.census.gov/library/publications/2003/compendia/statab/123ed/hist.html. This source provides percentages from decennial census data for 1900-1960 and from Current Population Survey data for 1970-2000. (b) U.S. Census Bureau, Historical Marital Status Tables, Table MS-1 (2021) https://www.census.gov/data/tables/time-series/demo/families/marital.html. This source supplied just raw numbers; the percentages appearing in Figure 3.1 were calculated by me from the raw numbers for the years 2005, 2010, 2015, and 2020.

The percentages for (3) were obtained from the following sources: (a) Robert L. Heuser, Nat'l Ctr. for Health Stat., Fertility Tables for Birth Cohorts by Color: United States, 1917-73, at 229 tbl. 7A (1976) (reporting data for 1917-1974), *available at* https://www.cdc.gov/nchs/nvss/cohort_fertility_tables.htm. A "birth" is defined as a live birth. *Id.* at 1. (b) B. E. Hamilton & C. M. Cosgrove, Nat'l Ctr. for Health Stat., Cohort Fertility Tables, https://www.cdc.gov/nchs/nvss/cohort_fertility_tables.htm (last visited Sept. 24, 2022). On this web page, the following tables provided data used in Figure 3.1: Table 7 under "Detailed Cohort Fertility Tables and Files" (reporting data for 1961-2006); and Table 7 under "Updated Detailed Cohort Fertility Tables and Files" (data for 2007-2010).

Percentages for (3) have not been published for years after 2010.

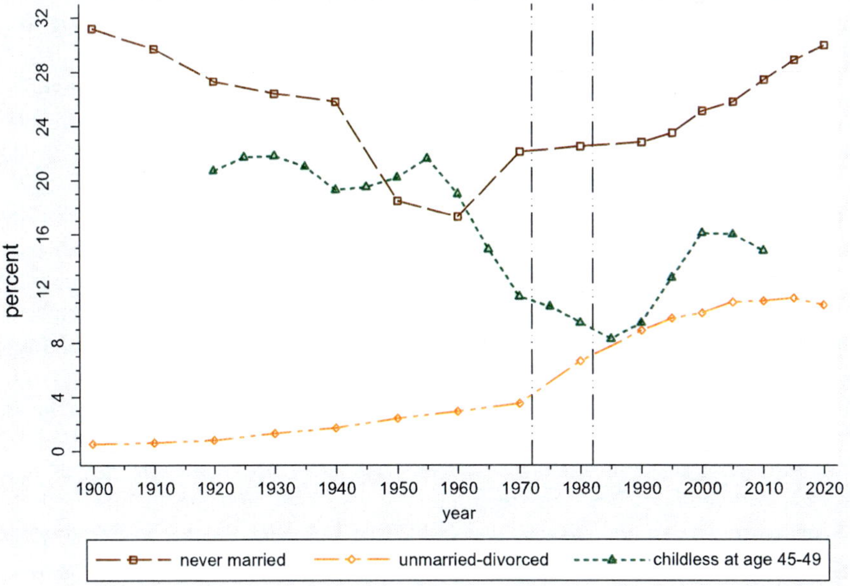

Fig. 3.1 Nonconformity by women to societal norms for marriage and childbearing: United States since 1900 (Source: see note 13)

divorced," and "childless at age 45–49," respectively. The last year on the horizontal axis of the figure is 2020, but plot (3), i.e., the percentage of women aged 45–49 who were childless, ends in 2010 because data for subsequent years are unavailable.

Figure 3.1 reveals the degree to which, and the movement that has occurred over time in the degree to which, women in the United States diverged from the social norms of their society regarding marriage and childbearing.[14] In doing so, the figure portrays the social context of the ERA at the time of the congressionally designated ERA-ratification period, and provides a backdrop to the studies, discussed *infra*, that

[14]The percentages in plots (1) and (2) are a function of, inter alia, year-specific distributions of age within the female population aged 15 and older. Unsurprisingly, the age distribution of the female population in the United States has not remained constant over time. Frank Hobbs & Nicole Stoops, U.S. Census Bureau, Demographic Trends in the 20th Century 54 fig. 2-2 (CENSR-4) (2002). Although each percentage in plot (1) and plot (2) is tied to the age distribution of females in a specific year, the percentages in the figure are not adjusted for the cross-time variation in age distribution, and hence are not standardized on the age distribution in a particular year, because the percentages in these plots are affected by changes in other factors, too. One such additional factor affecting the percentages is the sex ratio in the population, especially the sex ratio in particular age ranges. *See* Larry D. Barnett, Societal Agents in Law: Quantitative Research 47, 85 nn.63–64 (citations to and summaries of studies) (2019) [hereinafter SAIL vol. 2]. The actual, i.e., unadjusted, percentages that are used in the figure keep each percentage in its own social setting and allow the percentages from the social setting in circa 1960 to be compared to the percentages from the social settings in other years.

are pertinent to whether U.S. social life would be altered by the ERA. The years that bound the ratification period (1972–1982) are marked by the vertical lines (comprised of long dashes and dots) in the inner region of the figure.

Let us begin with the share of females aged 15+ who had never been married. Figure 3.1 shows that, between 1900 and 1960, the share underwent a sizeable decline (from 31.2% to 17.3%). The direction of change in the share then reversed, and the share expanded by nearly five percentage points between 1960 and 1970 (from 17.3% to 22.1%). Over the next 20 years, however, the share barely moved. Specifically, the share went from 22.1% in 1970 to 22.5% in 1980 and to 22.8% in 1990. The decade of interest here, of course, is 1970–1980, because it is the decade closest to the ratification period. During this time, the figure reveals, never-married females aged 15+ were less common than they had been during the initial four decades of the twentieth century. To express the point in another way, marriage attracted American females during 1970–1980 much more than it did in prior decades of the twentieth century.

Turning next to the prevalence of females aged 15+ who had been married but were currently unmarried because their marriage (or, if married more than once, their last marriage) ended in divorce, we see that a different course was followed: Figure 3.1 informs us that, from 1900 onward, these females enlarged their presence among all females aged 15+. However, while their share grew during the years that are relevant to the present discussion, the share was small at this time—3.5% in 1970 and 6.6% in 1980. Notably, most of these women were likely to remarry.[15] For an American woman in 1970–1980, therefore, being a wife had considerably greater appeal than being a divorcée.

Lastly, let us look at the share of women who reached the end of their reproductive years without having borne a child. Figure 3.1 shows that, during the time period covered, childlessness among women who were 45–49 years of age was at its lowest levels from 1970 to 1985—11.4% were childless in 1970 and 8.3% were childless in 1985. However, two matters should be kept in mind when considering childlessness. One deals with voluntary childlessness; the other deals with involuntary childlessness. Both affect the interpretation of the percentages in the figure for women who did not become mothers, and readers may want to think about each matter when examining the figure.

---

[15] Robert Schoen et al., *Marriage and Divorce in Twentieth Century American Cohorts*, 22 DEMOGRAPHY 101, 105 tbl. 2, 111 (1985) (using data on the United States; estimating, for divorced women in 1975 and divorced women in 1980, that 83 percent and 78 percent, respectively, would remarry). *See also* Larry Bumpass et al., *Changing Patterns of Remarriage*, 52 J. MARRIAGE & FAM. 747, 749, 753–54 & tbl. 3 (1990) (using data for the years 1975-1984 in the United States; projecting that 72 percent of all U.S. women who separated from their husbands would remarry within twenty years after separating). Among divorced women in the United States who remarried during the period 1970 to 1983, the mean length of time from divorce to remarriage was never more than 3.3 years, with a rise in the mean taking place between 1975 and 1983. Barbara Foley Wilson, Nat'l Ctr. for Health Stat., *Remarriages and Subsequent Divorces: United States*, VITAL & HEALTH STAT. 12 tbl. K (Series 21, No. 45, DHHS Pub. No. (PHS) 89-1923) (1989).

As to voluntary childlessness, the social-economic conditions that lead a woman to decide against bearing even one child stem from social-economic conditions that she experienced at ages younger than 45–49. The lows in voluntary childlessness in the United States during 1970–1985 are thus the result of social-economic conditions that existed before 1970–1985. Given that the mean age of childbearing among American females was roughly 26 years during the 1972–1982 period,[16] the relevant conditions would have existed in and around 1946–1956.

As to involuntary childlessness, i.e., infertility, one study has estimated that, in a wealthy nation, approximately 1.5–2.0% of all childless women 20–44 years old who are in a union and attempting to conceive cannot become pregnant and bear a child.[17] However, the prevalence of infertility among females varies across time periods because it is subject to social, demographic, and medical factors; when these factors increase or decrease in magnitude, the extent of infertility is affected.[18] For example, because infertility increases quickly among women after their 35th birthday,[19] the rate of involuntary childlessness will rise in a female population, ceteris paribus, as women in the population delay attempts at conception until they are in their thirties[20] and as women who have not married by age 40 become a larger fraction of all females in the population.[21] In addition, infertility results from excessive body fat as well as from inadequate body fat.[22] Since obesity grew in frequency among American women (and men) during the last half of the twentieth century[23]—the result of changes in social practices involving nutrition and physical exercise—obesity would have been responsible for more female infertility during this period. Because the portion of infertility due to medical conditions and the portion due to social-economic conditions will vary in size across time, the United

---

[16] Robert Schoen, *Timing Effects and the Interpretation of Period Fertility*, 41 Demography 801, 815-16 tbl. 1 (2004). The mean age is for all births, not just first births. *Id.* at 811.

[17] Maya N. Mascarenhas et al., *National, Regional, and Global Trends in Infertility Prevalence Since 1990: A Systematic Analysis of 277 Health Surveys*, 9(12) PLOS Med., Dec. 2012, at [1], [6] & fig. 2.

[18] Felice Petraglia et al., *The Changing Prevalence of Infertility*, 123 Int'l J. Gynecology & Obstetrics 54 (2013) (summarizing research); S. Philip Morgan, *Late Nineteenth- and Early Twentieth-Century Childlessness*, 97 Am. J. Sociol. 779, 781–84 & fig. 2, 799–801 (1991) (providing time-period and birth-cohort data on childlessness among married women in the United States during the late nineteenth century and early twentieth century; concluding that childlessness was materially affected by practices that caused women to put off marriage and childbearing).

[19] Petraglia et al., *supra* note 18, at 54–56; William L. Ledger, *Demographics of Infertility*, 18(Supp. 2) Reprod. Med. Online S11, S12 (2009).

[20] Petraglia et al., *supra* note 18, at 55–56.

[21] Sarah R. Hayford, *Marriage (Still) Matters: The Contribution of Demographic Change to Trends in Childlessness in the United States*, 50 Demography 1641, 1645, 1654–66 & tbl. 4 (2013).

[22] Brooke V. Rossi et al., *Modifiable Risk Factors and Infertility: What Are the Connections?*, 10 Am. J. Lifestyle Med. 220, 224–25 (2016).

[23] Cheryl D. Fryar et al., Nat'l Ctr. for Health Stat., *Prevalence of Overweight, Obesity, and Extreme Obesity Among Adults Aged 20 and Over: United States, 1960-1962 Through 2013-2014*, Health E-Stats, July 2016, at [1], [3], [4] tbl. 1.

States is unlikely to have had a female involuntary-childlessness rate within the range of 1.5–2.0% throughout the period covered by Fig. 3.1

With the preceding background, we consider what Fig. 3.1 tells us about the character of American social life when the ERA could have been placed in the Constitution. Once we know this, we have a basis for determining whether American society would have been materially altered by the ERA.[24] That determination is of more than academic interest because, as pointed out in the first paragraph of the present chapter, the ERA may still become part of the Constitution.

If the ERA would have freed many women from their traditional societal role, it would presumably have increased (1) the percentage of women who never married, (2) the percentage of women who were unmarried due to divorce, and (3) the percentage of women who did not bear a child during their lifetime. However, as we see in Fig. 3.1, the percentages for (1) and (2) began to rise before the 1972–1982 ratification period, and their growth after 1982 took place even though the ERA was not in the Constitution. The percentages for (3) had fallen prior to, and fell during, the ratification period, and while they subsequently reversed direction and increased, their post-period upward movement occurred without the ERA in the Constitution. Figure 3.1, accordingly, suggests that the ERA would not have materially altered the social paths taken by women in the United States. This conclusion, however, carries a qualification. Specifically, because the percentages in (1) and (2) combine *all* ages above age 14, they do not rapidly embody alterations in the percentages that occur only at certain ages. For never-married females and unmarried-divorced females, the trends seen in Fig. 3.1 are likely to have originated among younger adult females. With the passage of time, aging brought younger people (and their social patterns) into older age brackets, and mortality removed older people from the population. These processes eventually altered the social character of the adult population as a whole, but they did so gradually. In other words, the gender-pertinent social patterns of the full population necessarily changed at a slow pace. Unfortunately, the age-specific data required to measure such alterations from the beginning of the twentieth century are apparently unavailable.

In summary, Fig. 3.1 supplies no persuasive reason to believe that the ERA would have substantially affected the course of American society.[25] The figure also lends credence to the contention that the 10 years surrounding 1960 were a period in U.S. history when, relative to prior and/or subsequent 10-year intervals, sex roles and marriage as a societal form were largely conventional.[26] Conventionalism was a

---

[24] Application of the ERA would have begun two years after its ratification by the required number of states. H.R.J. Res. 208, *supra* note 3, at § 3.

[25] This conclusion is consistent, too, with the trend in labor-force participation among married, husband-present U.S. women who have an own child younger than age six. See Figure 3.4 and the discussion in *infra* Sect. 3.3.

[26] Claudia Goldin, *The Quiet Revolution That Transformed Women's Employment, Education, and Family*, 96(2) AEA PAPERS & PROC. 1, 8 (May 2006) (concluding from a variety of time-series and birth-cohort data that sex roles for American women "began to change in the late 1960s and

major source of opposition to the ERA,[27] and given the inertia that exists in social life, the conventionalism of America in 1960 would have persisted among adults, especially adults who were not young, and would have thereby contributed to the fate of the ERA during 1972–1982.

Figure 3.1, we should keep in mind, offers only suggestive evidence that the ERA would have produced negligible societal change if it had been ratified by a sufficient number of states and placed in the Constitution.[28] Definitive evidence requires data analyses in which one or more other potential causes of gender-relevant social change are statistically held constant. Is such evidence available in social science research on the effects of ERA-comparable provisions in state constitutions ("state ERAs")? Whatever social impact these state provisions had is probably similar to the social impact that the federal ERA would have had. Unfortunately, however, just a single study applying a multivariate statistical technique to numeric data has been published on the socio-economic consequences of state ERAs,[29] and two aspects of the study (the "Medoff study") limit confidence in its conclusion that state ERAs produce "mixed" economic results for women.[30] I begin by discussing each of the two aspects.

1970s"). *Accord*, Larry D. Barnett, Societal Agents in Law: A Macrosociological Approach 23–26 (2019) [hereinafter SAIL vol. 1].

[27] *See* Sarah A. Soule & Brayden G. King, *The Stages of the Policy Process and the Equal Rights Amendment, 1972-1982*, 111 Am. J. Sociol. 1871, 1884, 1895 tbl. 3 (2006) (finding that greater support in a state for gender-role equality raised the odds that an ERA-ratifying bill, once introduced in a state legislature, would be approved by both chambers of the legislature); David C. Nice, *State Opposition to the Equal Rights Amendment: Protectionism, Subordination, or Privatization?*, 67 Soc. Sci. Q. 315, 323, 326–27 (1986) (concluding from state-level data on several variables that "considerable support" exists for the thesis that states opposed the ERA in order to keep women in "a relatively disadvantaged position" rather than to safeguard social advantages enjoyed by women or to restrict the involvement of government in social life). *Accord*, Louis Bolce et al., *ERA and the Abortion Controversy: A Case of Dissonance Reduction*, 67 Soc. Sci. Q. 299, 301, 303–05 (1986) (finding that traditional personal beliefs generated resistance to the ERA); Jeffrey Ling & Tom W. Rice, *Voting in Iowa's 1980 and 1992 ERA Referendums*, 20 Women & Pol. 59, 61, 62, 63 tbl. 1 (1999); Ernest H. Wohlenberg, *Correlates of Equal Rights Amendment Ratification*, 60 Soc. Sci. Q. 676, 679–81 (1980).

[28] A descriptive review of court decisions concluded that state ERAs did not clearly improve the status that women had under law. Paul Benjamin Linton, *State Equal Rights Amendments: Making a Difference or Making a Statement?*, 70 Temp. L. Rev. 907, 941 (1997). Such a review does not supply the type of evidence that is needed to ascertain the impact of law on the frequency or level of a social phenomenon. See Appendix 1 in *supra* Chap. 1.

[29] Marshall H. Medoff, *The Effect of the Equal Rights Amendment on the Economic Status of Women*, 13 Atlantic Econ. J. 60 (1985) [hereinafter *State ERAs*]. The study by Professor Medoff appears to be unique; I was unable to locate any other research on the socio-economic effects of state ERAs that analyzed quantitative data with a multivariate statistical technique. I exclude a study of the socio-economic effects of state statutes that are worded similarly to the ERA. The latter study is by Charles A. Register & Donald R. Williams, *Some Evidence on the Impact of State-Level Equal Rights Legislation*, 67 Soc. Sci. Q. 869 (1986).

[30] *State ERAs*, *supra* note 29, at 67. The results are detailed in the paragraph in the text that accompanies *infra* notes 37–41.

First, a study of the impact of law on the frequency of a particular phenomenon (the dependent variable in the study) obviously requires data on the frequency of that phenomenon. An optimally designed study includes, inter alia, data on this frequency over a lengthy time span before as well as after the law was adopted and enforced.[31] The data for the pre-law period constitute the baseline to which the data for the post-law period are compared, and without data that allow a reliable estimate of the baseline, the degree to which the law altered the frequency of the phenomenon is unknowable. A decision as to whether the law exerted an effect on the phenomenon requires that the post-law frequency of the phenomenon diverge from the pre-law, i.e., baseline, frequency. In the absence of such a divergence, the necessary conclusion is that the law was ineffective.

The Medoff study made a pre-law to post-law comparison of the dependent variable, but the comparison was limited. The dependent variable was the ratio, in the United States, of the mean annual earnings of females who were employed full-time to the mean annual earnings of males who were employed full-time. The sole comparison of before-after data on the dependent variable, however, involved only 2 calendar years, viz., a calendar year (1969) when no state had an ERA-equivalent provision in its constitution and a calendar year (1976) when some states did.[32] As a result, the dependent variable was not measured across multiple years before, and across multiple years after, an ERA-equivalent provision was present in the constitution of states. Obviously, a reliable estimate of the pre-law baseline of the dependent variable is likely to require data for many pre-law years, and a reliable gauge of the post-law frequency of the dependent variable is likely to need data for many post-law years. The pre-law to post-law comparison of states on the dependent variable in the Medoff study thus yielded a finding that may well be inaccurate.[33]

Let me turn to the second aspect of the Medoff study that undermines the defensibility of its conclusion. The aspect is a potential problem in any investigation of the effect(s) of state law, but social science investigations may be especially prone to it. Social scientists who are untrained in law will probably be unfamiliar with all sources of information regarding the content of state law (including session laws) and be unable to judge the credibility of each source. As a result, social scientists can inadvertently rely on an inaccurate or incomplete list that classifies each state in terms of whether it has or does not have law of a particular content, e.g., an ERA in its constitution. Where more than one list exists and the lists are inconsistent as to the presence/absence of such law, the classification of states in a study will be contingent upon the list used, and investigators who rely on different lists will not classify states identically.[34] Clearly, the results of a multivariate statistical analysis concerned with

---

[31] See Appendix 1 in *supra* Chap. 1.

[32] *State ERAs*, *supra* note 29, at 62–63.

[33] The study found that the adoption of a state ERA was associated with a 5.5 percent reduction in the earnings of women relative to men. *Id.* at 63.

[34] *Compare* Linda J. Wharton, *State Equal Rights Amendments Revisited: Evaluating Their Effectiveness in Advancing Protection against Sex Discrimination*, 36 Rutgers L.J. 1201, 1288–93

the impact of state law can depend on the classification of the states in terms of the content of their law. The categorization of the states on whether their state constitutions contained an ERA-comparable provision, in other words, may determine whether socio-economic dissimilarities between U.S. states are found to result from such a provision.

The Medoff study is illustrative. The study was interested in states that placed an ERA-equivalent provision into their constitution prior to 1976 (though the study was apparently not interested in states that did so during the nineteenth century).[35] In its list of these states, however, the study omits two states that have been identified elsewhere as adopters of a state ERA during the years on which the study evidently concentrated.[36]

Despite its omission of the two states, the Medoff study merits consideration. Notably, its results are not encouraging to ERA proponents. For example, the addition of an ERA to a state constitution was found to have reduced by 5.5% the female-to-male ratio of monetary wages among full-time, full-year workers.[37] In other words, the relative earnings of women who worked were harmed rather than helped by a state ERA. Furthermore, in terms of the distribution of women relative to men across occupations as a whole in 1976, no difference was uncovered between states whose state constitution had an ERA and states whose state constitution did

---

(2005), *with* Leslie W. Gladstone, Cong. Res. Serv., Equal Rights Amendments: State Provisions 3–6 (2004), https://digital.library.unt.edu/ark:/67531/metacrs7397. Wharton, but not Gladstone, includes New Jersey and Rhode Island as states having a state ERA. The New Jersey ERA-equivalent provision is in the New Jersey constitution of 1947 and was in force as of January 1, 1948. N.J. Const. art. 1, ¶ 1, & art. X, ¶ 4; Robert F. Williams, *The New Jersey Equal Rights Amendment: A Documentary Sourcebook*, 16 Women's Rts. L. Rep. 69, 70, 71, 120 (1994). The Rhode Island ERA-equivalent provision is in the Rhode Island constitution of 1986 and was in force upon its approval by a majority of voters in an election held on November 4, 1986. R.I. Const. art. I, § 2, & art. XIV, § 2; Rhode Island Secretary of State, Constitution of the State of Rhode Island and Providence Plantations viii–ix, 1–2, 4, 35 (annotated ed. 1988), *available at* https://helindigitalcommons.org/lawarchive/26.

[35] *State ERAs*, *supra* note 29, at 61 n.3. No source is cited by Professor Medoff for the states that he named as having an ERA-equivalent provision in their constitution. *Id.* at 61 n.3.

In his study, Professor Medoff focused on ERA-comparable provisions that were placed in state constitutions during the twentieth century but before 1976. *Id.* at 61 & n.3. According to Professor Medoff, no state adopted an ERA-comparable provision during the twentieth century until after 1969. *Id.* at 63. His study was thus confined to state ERAs adopted in 1970-1975. *Id.* at 61 & n.3.

During the nineteenth century, ERA-equivalent provisions were added to the state constitution of California (1879), Montana (1899), Utah (1896), and Wyoming (1890). Wharton, *supra* note 34, at 1288–93.

[36] The omitted states were Louisiana and New Jersey. Wharton, *supra* note 34, at 1290, 1291. According to Gladstone, *supra* note 34, at 4-5, Louisiana has a state ERA, while New Jersey does not. Louisiana, however, had a state ERA as of 1974. La. Const. art. I, §§ 3, 12; Lee Hargrave, *The Declaration of Rights of the Louisiana Constitution of 1974*, 35 La. L. Rev. 1, 6, 9, 37, 40 (1974). New Jersey added an ERA-comparable provision to its state constitution during the last half of the 1940s. *Supra* note 34. The text of these state ERAs is reproduced in Wharton, *supra* note 34.

[37] *State ERAs*, *supra* note 29, at 62–63.

not have an ERA.[38] However, differences were found for certain occupations,[39] and these differences were hypothesized to be the reason for the female-male earnings differential in states that possessed an ERA,[40] leading the investigator to conclude that women in a state derive an overall, albeit "small," benefit from an ERA in the constitution of their state.[41] The findings of the study and their interpretation are, of course, open to challenge because the design of the study was not optimal and because the study classified two states as lacking an ERA in their respective constitutions when the constitutions of these states evidently included an ERA.

Before discussing the sociological implications of the above study, mention should be made of another study by the same investigator. The latter study compared states that ratified the proposed ERA for the federal Constitution to states that did not, and found that the socio-economic position of women was not generally better in the ratifying states than in the non-ratifying states; indeed, in some respects, it was worse.[42] The social forces that drove states to favor ratification of the federal ERA, accordingly, did not seem to have broadly helped women.

Both of the foregoing studies, I should point out, relied heavily on cross-sectional data. As was common in social science research that was completed at the time these studies were done (and that even today is not uncommon), neither of the two studies measured its variables with time-series data, i.e., data for numerous points in time. The absence of time-series data in these studies must be taken into account because time-series data are less likely than cross-sectional data and variants of cross-sectional data to produce the conclusion that a given independent variable is related to and has an effect on the dependent variable.[43] Since the type of data utilized by the two studies supplied no clear evidence that women gained large, across-the-board social or economic advantages from state constitutional provisions equivalent to the federal ERA or from state support for the federal ERA, time-series data are unlikely to yield a different conclusion.

---

[38] *Id.* at 62, 63–64, 66–67.

[39] The study investigated whether state ERAs changed the sex distribution of employees in three occupational categories. State ERAs were found to have improved the distribution of women relative to men in two of the categories, viz., (i) non-farm managers and administrators, and (ii) sales workers, but they worsened the distribution of women relative to men in the third category, viz., professional and technical workers. *Id.* at 64–65.

[40] *Id.* at 66.

[41] *Id.* at 67.

[42] Marshall H. Medoff, *The Equal Rights Amendment: An Empirical Analysis of Sexual Discrimination*, 18 Econ. Inquiry 367, 378 (1980). The states that were designated by Professor Medoff as having ratified the ERA included states that, after ratifying the ERA, adopted measures to rescind their ratification. *Compare id.* at 367 n.3 *with infra* Table 3.1. Whether the Constitution permits a state to withdraw its ratification of the ERA is uncertain. Brendon Troy Ishikawa, *Everything You Always Wanted to Know About How Amendments are Made, But Were Afraid to Ask*, 24 Hastings Const. L.Q. 545, 546–47, 557–58 (1997). If it does, rescinding states should be counted as non-ratifying states.

[43] Frans L. Leeuw with Hans Schmeets, Empirical Legal Research: A Guidance Book for Lawyers, Legislators and Regulators 122–25 (2016).

Table 3.1 Non-ratification, ratification, and rescission of ratification of the Equal Rights Amendment by U.S. States during the congressionally specified ratification period (March 1972–June 1982); coding on NONRAT and NONRATRES

State	States not ratifying ERA; year ERA was ratified by ratifying states	Year that ratification was rescinded by rescinding states	NONRAT	NONRATRES
Alabama	Non-ratifying state		1	1
Alaska	1972		0	0
Arizona	Non-ratifying state		1	1
Arkansas	Non-ratifying state		1	1
California	1972		0	0
Colorado	1972		0	0
Connecticut	1973		0	0
Delaware	1972		0	0
Florida	Non-ratifying state		1	1
Georgia	Non-ratifying state		1	1
Hawaii	1972		0	0
Idaho	1972	1977	0	1
Illinois	2018		1	1
Indiana	1977		0	0
Iowa	1972		0	0
Kansas	1972		0	0
Kentucky	1972	1978	0	1
Louisiana	Non-ratifying state		1	1
Maine	1974		0	0
Maryland	1972		0	0
Massachusetts	1972		0	0
Michigan	1972		0	0
Minnesota	1973		0	0
Mississippi	Non-ratifying state		1	1
Missouri	Non-ratifying state		1	1
Montana	1974		0	0
Nebraska	1972	1973	0	1
Nevada	2017		1	1
New Hampshire	1972		0	0
New Jersey	1972		0	0
New Mexico	1973		0	0
New York	1972		0	0
North Carolina	Non-ratifying state		1	1
North Dakota	1975		0	0
Ohio	1974		0	0
Oklahoma	Non-ratifying state		1	1
Oregon	1973		0	0

(continued)

Table 3.1 (continued)

State	States not ratifying ERA; year ERA was ratified by ratifying states	Year that ratification was rescinded by rescinding states	NONRAT	NONRATRES
Pennsylvania	1972		0	0
Rhode Island	1972		0	0
South Carolina	Non-ratifying state		1	1
South Dakota	1973	1979	0	1
Tennessee	1972	1974	0	1
Texas	1972		0	0
Utah	Non-ratifying state		1	1
Vermont	1973		0	0
Virginia	2020		1	1
Washington	1973		0	0
West Virginia	1972		0	0
Wisconsin	1972		0	0
Wyoming	1973		0	0

Available evidence thus suggests that major and lasting tangible benefits for American women should not be expected from the ERA if it is incorporated into the U.S. Constitution. Instead, the ERA, should it be added to the Constitution, will act sociologically as a symbol.[44] That the ERA will not work as anticipated ought not, however, to be surprising: The inability of the ERA to erase differences between the social place of women and the social place of men is consistent with the apparently general inability of regulatory law to alter the incidence of key forms of social behavior in a modern society.[45] This inability is understandable given that a society is a system: Being a system, a society resists sharp breaks with the past and acts to avoid them by reducing internal pressures for change. As a consequence, American society has moved to maintain social cohesiveness by, inter alia, compensating women indirectly for perceived sex-based disadvantages. An example is that the average White woman in the United States during 1970–1980 received substantially more in family income (as distinct from personal income) than the average White man for each year of formal schooling.[46] The same pattern is likely in earlier decades.

[44] See the text accompanying notes 143 to 145 in *supra* Chap. 1. The ERA would not be "merely" or "simply" a symbol. Symbols exert considerable social influence in a society, and the magnitude of this influence should not be understated. As one court has observed, "symbols speak important messages." Libin v. Town of Greenwich, 625 F. Supp. 393, 394 (D. Conn. 1985).

[45] See the citations in note 135 in *supra* Chap. 1.

[46] Norval D. Glenn & Patricia Ann Taylor, *Education and Family Income: A Comparison of White Married Men and Women in the U.S.*, 63 Soc. Forces 169 (1984).

To sum up, the ERA was regarded by both its advocates and detractors as a mechanism that would transform social life in the United States, but even without the ERA in the Constitution, the social definition and treatment of the sex attribute changed considerably among Americans in and after the last quarter of the twentieth century. Published quantitative social science research, furthermore, supplies no persuasive reason to believe that the sex attribute would have been perceived and dealt with much differently by Americans if the ERA had been added to the Constitution. The foregoing hypothesis is easily accommodated within a framework for law that is rooted in structural-functionalism theory, because under this macrosociological theory, a society is deemed to be an entity that tends to avoid large, quick alterations. Structural-functionalism also suggests that the character of American society determines whether U.S. law content on key social activities changes or remains the same.[47] Understanding political resistance to the ERA requires, therefore, that we examine contemporaneous attributes of American society.

3.1.2 A Macrosociological Account of the ERA

In seeking the reasons that some states balked at ratifying the ERA, I look beneath the surface of social life. I thus avoid consideration of specific individuals and their political actions even though these individuals and actions offer consumers of the mass media an interesting account of state resistance to the ERA. In my view, personalities and events in the political arena are just superficially responsible for the content of law on society-important social topics, including law on the sex attribute. In the history of law on these topics, I argue, individuals are fungible, and whether they engage in sustained political action concerned with law content is explainable by the societal context of this action.

Setting aside individual personalities and political events permits a very different understanding of law content. That understanding, which stems from structural-functionalism theory, is built on the conceptualization of a society as an organized entity whose components form a system. As a system, a society (1) has an existence separate and distinct from the individuals who comprise its population at a given point in time and (2) is pushed to change or remain the same by system-level forces and conditions. Under this conceptualization, a society possesses a tendency to resist disintegration, and the content of its law on important social activities acts to

[47] For a statement of this point by U.S. courts, see Arfons v. E. I. Du Pont De Nemours & Co., Inc., 261 F.2d 434, 436 (2d Cir. 1958) (the content of law "adjust[s] to keep pace with society's growth and present needs"); Arwine v. Bannan, 346 F.2d 458, 469 (1965) (law evolves "to meet the changing needs of society") (quoting Cameron v. State, 112 So.2d 864, 873 (Dist. Ct. App.–1st 1959); internal quotation marks omitted). Also see Sect. 1.2 in *supra* Chap. 1.

promote social cohesion.[48] Accordingly, the appreciable degree of inertia that normally characterizes a society and its law should not be surprising.

I employ the above conceptualization here. I thus focus on macro-level social forces and conditions, because I assume that the content of law on significant social activities is shaped by the attributes of the society in which the law content is embedded. In terms of the ERA, I regard the political resistance that it encountered during the ratification period as evidence that the Amendment touched on central aspects of American social life and was thought by those who mounted the resistance to put these aspects in peril.[49] The continuing effort to place the ERA in the Constitution adds to the evidence that the character of society is the foundation for politics and the law to which it leads. A sizeable political campaign cannot be sustained for a proposal unless the campaign is consistent with and encouraged by aspects of culture and/or social structure.

To bring in the construct on which this book focuses—viz., the concept of societal stress—this chapter is grounded on the premise that the proposed addition of the ERA to the U.S. Constitution stressed American society during the ratification period (1972–1982); that this stress was embodied in opposition to the ERA; and that the opposition can be traced to then-existing social forces and conditions. In ascertaining these forces and conditions—and hence the sources of ERA-induced societal stress—the chapter deems U.S. states and their populations to be involved in a system that has social properties and is characterized by social processes.[50] The chapter thus considers the clash between ERA opponents and ERA supporters, and the outcome of the clash, to have emanated from the sociological properties of American society when the clash occurred and from the drive of every society to maintain if not increase its internal cohesiveness. Notably, the predisposition of American society toward inertia and stability is evidenced in the Constitution of the nation: Amendments to the Constitution are allowed only with the approval of three-fourths of the states.[51] Given this predisposition, Sect. 3.1.3 takes a step beyond what Fig. 3.1 told us about gender-relevant social conditions in the United States when states were deciding whether to ratify the ERA.

---

[48] Larry D. Barnett, Explaining Law: Macrosociological Theory and Empirical Evidence 7–15 (2015) [hereinafter Explaining Law] (listing seven propositions for the macrosociological study of law that addresses society-significant social activities in a nation that is structurally complex and democratically governed). For evidence that macrosociological agents are responsible for the content of law covered by the seven-proposition framework in *id.*, see SAIL vol. 1, *supra* note 26, at 86–116 pt. 2.3.

[49] Bolce et al., *supra* note 27, at 303–05.

[50] Explaining Law, *supra* note 48, at 11–13. My thesis is based on the sociological theory of structural functionalism. *Id.* at 13–14 & nn.23–24, 50–51 n.143, 94–98.

[51] U.S. Const. art. V. See *supra* note 5 for the pertinent text of article V.

3.1.3 *Change in the Social Status of American Women After 1950*

A description of the social environment in which ratification of the ERA was debated will be more informative if it includes a quantitative measure of the social status of women in American society and the data for the measure cover a lengthy period—not only the ERA-ratification years (1972–1982) but also years before and after. The indicator that I have chosen is based on a popular hypothesis in the discipline of economics, namely, that women more than men are attracted to occupations in which job skills are infrequently updated, because women who have minor children, more than men who have minor children, tend to be at home rather than to be employed outside the home.[52] Under this hypothesis, women who have minor children, more than men who have minor children, want types of paid work to which they can easily return after withdrawing from remunerated positions in the economy to raise their children.[53] The result, according to the hypothesis, is that women to a greater extent

---

[52]For evidence supporting the hypothesis, see Amanda McFarland & Sarah Pearlman, *Knowledge Obsolescence and Women's Occupational Sorting: New Evidence from Citation Data*, 20(1) B. E. J. ECON. ANALYSIS & POL'Y, Jan. 2020, at 1, 4, 7, 12 (using data for the United States).

In two national samples of U.S. adults, the first surveyed in 2014 and the second surveyed in 2015, a preference to be at home rather than work outside the home was expressed more than twice as often by women who had a child below age 18 than by men who had a child below age 18 (56 percent versus 26 percent). Lydia Saad, Gallup, *Children a Key Factor in Women's Desire to Work Outside the Home* (2015), https://news.gallup.com/poll/186050/children-key-factor-%20women-desire-work-outside-home.aspx?g_source=mn2-customer.

In a sample of adult residents of California in 1999, seven out of ten respondents took the position that "It is much better for the family if the father works outside the home and the mother takes care of the children." Kathleen Sylvester, *Caring for Our Youngest: Public Attitudes in the United States*, 11 FUTURE OF CHILD. 52, 54 fig. 1 (2001). Working at least 50 h per week became more common from the late 1970s onward in the United States and affected the female-male difference in earnings, but a job engagement of this degree is less frequent among women than among men, possibly because mothers rather than fathers have, under established social norms, primary responsibility for childcare. Youngjoo Cha & Kim A. Weeden, *Overwork and the Slow Convergence in the Gender Gap in Wages*, 79 AM. SOCIOL. REV. 457, 458–59, 476–78 (2014).

[53]Men as well as women experience an earnings penalty for leaving the labor force due to the birth of a first child, but the penalty is larger for women than for men because women spend more time out of the labor force. Marie Evertsson, *Parental Leave and Careers: Women's and Men's Wages After Parental Leave in Sweden*, 29 ADVANCES IN LIFE COURSE RES. 26, 29, 36–37 (2016).

In a nation that is structurally complex and democratically governed, the difference between women and men in the extent of staying home to raise children accounts today for nearly all of the lower earnings of women. Henrik Kleven et al., *Children and Gender Inequality: Evidence from Denmark* 1–3, 7–8, 32–33 (Nat'l Bureau of Econ. Research, Working Paper No. 24219, 2018). Existing female-male economic differences in such a nation thus evidently result almost entirely from female-male social differences. June O'Neill & Dave O'Neill, *Explaining Race and Gender Wage Gaps*, *in* UNITED STATES INCOME, WEALTH, CONSUMPTION, AND INEQUALITY 177, 212 (Diana Furchtgott-Roth ed., 2021) (concluding from social science evidence that invidious discrimination against women in employment is presently "a minimal source of wage differentials" between women and men). Across-the-board increases among women and men in working from home is unlikely to impose an earnings penalty on women, including mothers, relative to men. Jennifer

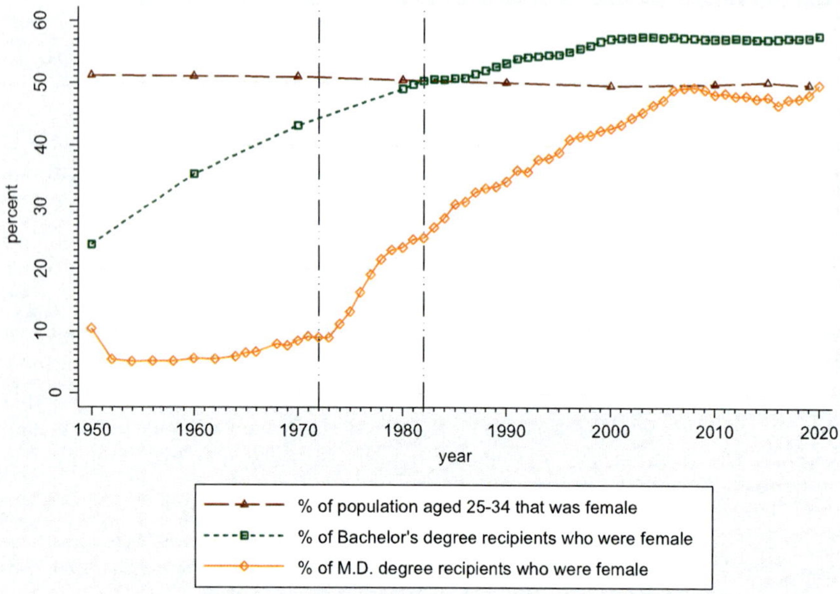

Fig. 3.2 Social position of women: United States since 1950 (Source: see notes 55, 60, and 61)

than men gravitate toward occupations that have "less skill obsolescence for workers who leave and reenter the labor force."[54] The hypothesis supplies the foundation for the empirical indicator that I employ to portray the societal role and status of American women over time. The indicator—the share of all M.D. degrees awarded each year that were conferred on women—is graphed in Fig. 3.2. Vertical lines in the inner region of the figure demarcate the 1972–1982 ratification period.

Figure 3.2 includes three line-connected markers that allow an assessment of social-position dissimilarity between women and men in American society since the middle of the twentieth century. The unbroken line connects markers (hollow

L. Glass & Mary C. Noonan, *Telecommuting and Earnings Trajectories Among American Women and Men 1989-2008*, 95 Soc. Forces 217, 238 (2016).

Sex differences in evolution-created predispositions have been hypothesized as a contributor to the female-male social differences that underlie female-male economic differences; multivariate analyses of data from the U.S. General Social Survey yielded findings consistent with this hypothesis. Satoshi Kanazawa, *Is "Discrimination" Necessary to Explain the Sex Gap in Earnings?*, 26 J. Econ. Psychol. 269, 270, 275–76, 284 (2005).

[54] Women's Bureau, Earnings Differences Between Women and Men 7 (1998), files.eric.ed.gov/fulltext/ED419098.pdf. *See* Michael J. Handel, Org. Econ. Co-operation & Dev., *Trends in Job Skill Demands in OECD Countries* 82 (OECD Social, Employment and Migration Working Paper No. 143, 2012) (finding that, ceteris paribus, the occupations in which women are employed require lower cognitive skills than the occupations in which men are employed), *available at* https://www.oecd-ilibrary.org/employment.

diamonds) that show the percentage of all M.D. degrees in an academic year that were conferred on women in the United States.[55] (For the hollow-diamond markers, the horizontal axis of the figure designates academic year using the calendar year that ended the academic year; for example, 1950 on the horizontal axis designates the 1949–1950 academic year for the markers connected by the unbroken line.) Women who are recipients of the M.D. degree come within the hypothesis advanced by economists, because medicine entails the application of a body of knowledge that is both deep and broadly based—indeed, medicine is among the most knowledge-utilizing occupations in the United States.[56] Inasmuch as knowledge has been rapidly expanding,[57] practitioners in the field of medicine have been subject to relatively rapid skill obsolescence. Medicine, accordingly, is an unconventional occupation for women.

As a barometer of the social status and societal role of women, the percentages of females among all recipients of the M.D. degree gain further credibility from a study of admissions of applicants to U.S. medical schools. Specifically, the study uncovered no evidence of a national pattern of discrimination against women by U.-S. medical schools during the period from the mid-1940s to the mid-1980s (when the data for the study ended). In the United States during this time, the proportion of female applicants who were admitted was roughly the same as the proportion of females in the applicant pool, and acceptance rates were approximately the same for the applicant pool of females as for the applicant pool of males.[58] Consequently, although in the admissions process some individual medical schools may have had a strong preference for applicants of one sex over applicants of the other sex, the schools as a whole did not.

The hollow-diamond markers connected by the unbroken line, in short, reveal how often women went into an occupation that was nontraditional for them when their entry into the occupation was not hampered by favoritism for men. Because the hollow-diamond markers cover the time interval since the middle of the twentieth century, they can be used to gauge the social status of women in the United States before and after, as well as during, the period in which ratification of the ERA was a major political issue. The hollow-diamond markers, however, should not be considered in isolation. Instead, they should be compared to the markers in the two other

[55] Yearly numbers of M.D. degrees, categorized by sex, were used to compute the percentages identified by the markers in the line. The numbers were obtained from NAT'L CTR. FOR EDUC. STAT., DIGEST OF EDUCATION STATISTICS: LIST OF 2021 DIGEST TABLES ch. 3 tbl. 324.40, https://nces.ed.gov/programs/digest/2021menu_tables.asp (last visited Sept. 26, 2022).

[56] Edward J. Feser, *What Regions Do Rather than Make: A Proposed Set of Knowledge-based Occupation Clusters*, 40 URB. STUD. 1937, 1945 tbl. 2, 1947 (2003).

[57] SAIL VOL. 1, *supra* note 26, at 103–05. *See also* Eugenio J. Llanos et al., *Exploration of the Chemical Space and Its Three Historical Regimes*, 116(26) PROC. NAT'L ACAD. SCI. 12660, 12664 (2019) (estimating that new chemical compounds have increased by an average of 4.4 percent per year since 1800).

[58] Stephen Cole, *Sex Discrimination and Admission to Medical School, 1929-1984*, 92 AM. J. SOCIOL. 549, 556–57 tbl. 1., 558, 564 (1986).

lines in Fig. 3.2. The other markers in the figure—one for the female share of the population 25–34 years old and one for the female share of Bachelor's degree recipients—shape the interpretation of the markers for the share of M.D. degrees conferred on women and inform the female share of earners of the M.D. degree as a measure of the female-male social gap.

Because medical-school students in the United States typically receive their M.D. degrees when they are in 25–34 years old,[59] Fig. 3.2 shows the percentages of U.S. residents aged 25–34 who were women. These percentages are marked by hollow triangles that are connected by long broken dashes, and are given in the figure for each decennial-census calendar year from 1950 to 2010 and for calendar years 2015 and 2019.[60] (The years designated on the horizontal axis are, for these percentages, calendar years rather than academic years.) Readers should keep in mind that the percentages referenced by the hollow-triangle markers will not be exactly 50.0% because, inter alia, male-female differentials exist in the sex ratio at birth, in mortality, and in immigration. As a result of these differentials, the female share of the age group 25–34 ranged from 49.6% to 51.2% during the period covered by Fig. 3.2.

The markers in the remaining line—the hollow-square markers connected by the line of short dashes—are also helpful in gauging the social status of women. These markers are based on the sex distribution of Bachelor's degrees awarded in the United States during an academic year, and specify the yearly percentage of all Bachelor's degrees that were conferred on women.[61] (For the hollow-square markers, as for the hollow-diamond markers, the horizontal axis designates the year that ends the designated academic year.) Because the receipt of a Bachelor's degree is a prerequisite to the conferral of the M.D. degree, the pool of female

---

[59] Half of the students who enrolled in U.S. medical schools in 1976 and 1988 were age 22 or 23 when they matriculated, but some of the students (5.5 percent of the 1976 entrants and 12.2 percent of the 1988 entrants) were age 28 or older. The M.D. degree was earned in a maximum of five years by 96 out of each 100 students who matriculated in 1976 and by 91 out of each 100 students who matriculated in 1988. Donald G. Kassebaum & Philip L. Szenas, *The Longer Road to Medical School Graduation*, 69 Acad. Med. 856, 857 tbl. 1 & fig. 1, 860 (1994).

[60] The percentages were calculated from data in the following sources: (1) Data for 1950 to 1980: U.S. Bureau of the Census, 1980 Census of Population. Vol. 1: Characteristics of the Population. Ch. B: General Population Characteristics. Part 1: United States Summary 1-42 tbl. 45 (PC80-1-B1) (1983), *available at* https://www.census.gov/prod/www/decennial.html. (2) Data for 1990: U.S. Bureau of the Census, 1990 Census of Population. General Population Characteristics. United States 19–20 tbl. 14 ([1992]), *available at* https://www.census.gov/prod/www/decennial.html. (3) Data for 2000 and 2010: Lindsay M. Howden & Julie A. Meyer, U.S. Census Bureau, *Age and Sex Composition: 2010*, at 4 tbl. 2 (2011), *available at* https://www.census.gov/prod/cen2010/briefs/c2010br-03.pdf. (4) Data for 2015 and 2019: U.S. Census Bureau, Age and Sex Tables, https://www.census.gov/topics/population/age-and-sex/data/tables.html (sequentially select: year; for the selected year, "Table: Age and Sex Composition in the United States"; under "Detailed Tables by Age and Sex," "Table 1. Population by Age and Sex"). Table 1 was available only through 2019 when I last visited this website (Sept. 26, 2022).

[61] The percentages were obtained from Nat'l Ctr. for Educ. Stat., *supra* note 55, at ch. 3 tbl. 318.10.

recipients of the Bachelor's degree is the source of the pool of female recipients of the M.D. degree. The representation of women among all persons awarded a Bachelor's degree, like the representation of women among all persons in the age range 25–34, thus furnishes a yardstick against which to evaluate the representation of women among M.D.-degree recipients. A caution to keep in mind, however, is that the data on Bachelor's degree recipients cover recipients of all ages and are not confined to recipients in a particular age range.

What does Fig. 3.2 tell us about the social position of women relative to the social position of men in the United States since the midpoint of the twentieth century? As measured by the sex composition of yearly classes of medical-school graduates relative to the sex composition of the age group in which the M.D. is conferred, social equality between young women and young men in the nation as a whole[62] became slightly more common during the 1960s, increased markedly during and after the 1970s, and was attained in the twenty-first century, at which time women achieved representation among all M.D.-degree recipients that matched their representation among all persons 25–34 years old. However, an assessment of gender equality must also include the percentage of Bachelor's degree recipients who were women. Figure 3.2 shows that women were a noticeably smaller share of M.D.-degree recipients than of Bachelor's-degree recipients throughout the post-1950 period (even taking into account that the female share of M.D. degrees typically lags at least 4 years behind the female share of Bachelor's degrees). The gap diminishes in magnitude during and after the ERA-ratification period, but it does not disappear. Why the gap persists is, regrettably, uncertain. That U.S. medical schools do not generally discriminate against female applicants in admitting students[63] suggests that proportionally fewer women than men pursue an M.D. degree because of sex-linked differences in socially acceptable life paths. In particular, American society may give a larger number of social options to women than to men, with the result that women less often than men pursue a career as a physician.[64]

A point that should not be overlooked is that female-male social differences would have been created by societal ideals that prevailed when the women who apply to and complete medical school were younger because the sex-typing of

---

[62] Because the data in Fig. 3.2 are drawn from all of the states in the United States, Fig. 3.2 captures the extent of inequality between women and men nationally, not the extent of inequality in a particular geographic area.

[63] *Supra* note 58 and accompanying text.

[64] Robert Fiorentine & Stephen Cole, *Why Fewer Women Become Physicians: Explaining the Premed Persistence Gap*, 7 Sociol. Forum 469, 473, 493 (1992).

Gender egalitarianism during an historical period as well as in a birth cohort evidently embodies ideals that focus on gender specifically as well as ideals that focus on personal rights generally. Clem Brooks & Catherine Bolzendahl, *The Transformation of US Gender Role Attitudes: Cohort Replacement, Social-Structural Change, and Ideological Learning*, 33 Soc. Sci. Res. 106, 127–28 (2004).

occupations occurs among children.[65] An increase or decrease in the extent of observable gender egalitarianism at a particular time thus involves change in societal ideals that occurred years earlier, that affected mainly young people, and that are manifested in the population as a whole only as aging and mortality alter the make-up of the overall population. As a rule, therefore, social change probably begins in certain parts of (e.g., certain age groups in) a society and usually takes a long time before it is evident across the entire society.

Returning to the question of why the ERA did not become part of the Constitution before the end of the congressionally established ratification period (1972–1982), Fig. 3.2 suggests that, while movement toward female-male social equality had started prior to 1972, the social position of American women was still largely aligned with tradition in 1982. The 1972–1982 ratification period thus took place at a time when convention prevailed in terms of sex and gender. Notably, the retreat of tradition did not stop when the ratification period ended. On the contrary, gender egalitarianism grew after the period passed, and the growth of egalitarianism that took place during the post-ratification period continued into the twenty-first century.

To elaborate, we should not forget that Fig. 3.2 portrays the extent of sex-role equality for women who are relatively young, viz., 25–34 years of age. Older women experienced less-egalitarian gender-relevant teachings when they were in their formative years, and thus the general population of women (and men) was subject to sizeable legacy effects that worked against state acceptance of the ERA during the 1972–1982 ratification period. The preceding point supplies insight into why the ERA was not added to the Constitution during 1972–1982 even though most Americans verbally expressed support for the ERA[66] and even though law (as well as government policy) more often conforms to public opinion than deviates from

[65] Lisa Serbin et al., *The Development of Sex Typing in Middle Childhood*, 58(2) Monographs of the Soc'y for Res. in Child Dev. 4–5, 7, 10–11 (Serial No. 232, 1993).

[66] Benjamin I. Page & Robert Y. Shapiro, The Rational Public: Fifty Years of Trends in Americans' Policy Preferences 102-03 (1992). Gallup surveys found that, among U.S. adults during the years 1975-1982, roughly three out of five approved, and only between one out of four and one out of three disapproved, of the ERA. Rita J. Simon & Jean M. Landis, *Women's and Men's Attitudes About a Woman's Place and Role*, 53 Pub. Opinion Q. 265, 275 (1989). During 1975-1982, women as well as men were split in their attitudes toward the ERA; the split among women differed somewhat from the split among men, and the sex difference in attitudes was not uniform across the years for which data are available. *Id.*

Public opinion surveys, however, may materially overestimate the extent to which gender equality is backed by Americans generally and particular segments of the American population. *See* Matthew J. Streb et al., *Social Desirability Effects and Support for a Female American President*, 72 Pub. Opinion Q. 76, 80–83, 86 (2008) (using a national, probability-selected sample drawn from the U.S. population during 2006; presenting half of the sample with a set of four statements none of which posited a gender-related issue; presenting half of the sample with the same four statements and a statement that posited "a woman serving as president" of the United States; finding that, among female respondents as well as among male respondents, the average number of statements that interviewees said made them "angry or upset" was larger in the latter half-sample than in the former half-sample; and concluding that the foregoing results indicate that the extent to which support exists for the election of a female U.S. president, and by implication for gender it.[67] Simply put, when ratification of the Equal Rights Amendment was being weighed, i.e., during 1972–1982, the adult population in many states was inhospitable to across-the-board social equality between women and men. In historical terms, the ratification period came too early; sex-role ideals had not sufficiently changed to permit ratification of the ERA at this time.[68] The result of the proposal to add the ERA to the federal Constitution was thus societal stress and its manifestation in resistance to the proposal.

3.2 Macrosociological Agents Driving State Opposition to the ERA

If state reluctance to ratify the ERA during the 1972–1982 ratification period was due to society-level stress, the causes of the reluctance do not lie in superficial features of American society. They exist, instead, beneath the surface of social life. In Sect. 3.2, I examine society-embedded factors that differed between states and that theory in macrosociology suggests had the potential to account for whether states opposed or supported the ERA. The study covers all 50 states rather than just the coterminous states, because every state has a voice on a proposed amendment to the Constitution.[69] Several state-level independent variables are tested; all of them are measured as of 1960.[70]

3.2.1 *Dependent Variable*

The information that I employed to code each state on the dependent variable—i.e., whether the state ratified the ERA—is provided in the initial three columns of Table 3.1.[71] Readers should note that the coding resulted from my decisions on a

---

egalitarianism generally, is artificially inflated in responses to public opinion polls in the United States).

[67] Alan D. Monroe, *Public Opinion and Public Policy, 1980-1993*, 62 Pub. Opinion Q. 6, 14 tbl. 2 (1998); Christopher J. Casillas et al., *How Public Opinion Constrains the U.S. Supreme Court*, 55 Am. J. Pol. Sci. 74, 80 & tbl. 1 (2011).

[68] A similar argument has been made by Jo Freeman, *Social Revolution and the Equal Rights Amendment*, 3 Sociol. Forum 145, 151 (1988).

[69] U.S. Const. art. V. See *supra* note 5 for the pertinent text of article V.

[70] Alaska and Hawaii became U.S. states in 1959. Proclamation No. 3269, 24 Fed. Reg. 81–82 (Jan. 6, 1959) (Alaska); Proclamation No. 3309, 24 Fed. Reg. 6868–69 (Aug. 25, 1959) (Hawaii).

[71] The information in the second and third columns of the table was compiled from: Neale, *supra* note 4, at 5–6, 14 n.76; Alice Paul Inst., The Equal Rights Amendment: State Ratifications of the ERA, http://www.equalrightsamendment.org (follow "Ratification" hyperlink to "Ratification Info State by State" page) (last visited Dec. 23, 2019). *See also* Orrin G. Hatch, *The Equal Rights*

pair of issues that involve the ratification history of the ERA. First, five states initially ratified the ERA within the ratification period that had been specified by Congress, viz., 1972–1982, but subsequently (and within this period) they acted to cancel their ratification. Second, three states assented to the ERA after the end of the 1972–1982 period for ratification. Each set of states took a step that may not be permissible, and the questions that these steps raise—whether ratification-repealing actions[72] and post-1982 ratifications[73] are valid and effective—allow the dependent variable to be measured in more than one way. However, I note that post-1982 ratifications occurred in few states, and I therefore confined my coding of states on the dependent variable to actions that were taken by states during 1972–1982. Doing so led to two measurements of the dependent variable, viz., NONRAT and NONRATRES. The coding of every state on each measure is shown in the fourth and fifth columns of Table 3.1.

A description of NONRAT and NONRATRES must begin with the point that every state was coded on the dependent variable as either 0 or 1. Furthermore, states were coded on NONRAT and NONRATRES so as to allow the odds ratios and coefficients estimated by logistic regression[74] to emphasize the states that were *opposed* to the ERA. The ERA-opposing states were thus recorded as 1 on the dependent variable, and they are my focus because opposition by a state to the ERA is presumed to be a manifestation of ERA-induced social stress. The states that blocked the ERA, in other words, can shed light on the conditions and forces producing the social stress that was, under my thesis, embodied in negative state reactions to the ERA.

What differentiates NONRAT from NONRATRES? For NONRAT, the number 1 was assigned to every state that is designated in the second column of Table 3.1 as a "non-ratifying state," and since my focus was on the 1972–1982 ratification period, the number 1 was also assigned to Illinois, Nevada, and Virginia, whose actions to ratify the ERA came after the period set by Congress.[75] On the other hand, the number 0 was applied for NONRAT to every state for which a ratification year is given in the second column as long as the year was within the 1972–1982 period. NONRATRES diverges from NONRAT in one key respect: For NONRATRES, the number 1 was assigned to states that failed to ratify the ERA during 1972–1982, as it was for NONRAT, but the number 1 was *also* applied to states that, after ratifying the ERA during 1972–1982, moved to rescind their ratification. These ratification-rescinding

---

Amendment Extension: A Critical Analysis, 2 HARV. J.L. & PUB. POL'Y 19, 20 nn.3 to 5 (1979). The article authored by Senator Hatch does not list South Dakota as a state that rescinded its ratification of the ERA. Hatch, *supra*, at 20 n.5. However, the article appeared in the Summer 1979 issue of the publishing journal and thus was likely written before the South Dakota legislature passed the session law that rescinded ratification of the ERA by the state. Under the session law, the rescission was effective on March 23, 1979; the session law does not show the date on which it was adopted by the legislature. 1979 S.D. Sess. Laws 28.

[72] Ishikawa, *supra* note 42.

[73] NEALE, *supra* note 4, at 18–26.

[74] See Sect. 1.8 in *supra* Chap. 1.

[75] *Supra* note 6 and accompanying text.

states are Idaho, Kentucky, Nebraska, South Dakota, and Tennessee. Each ratification-rescinding state is identified in the third column of Table 3.1 by the year of its rescinding action.

In sum, NONRAT applied the number 1 to a state that did not assent to the ERA within the 1972–1982 ratification period, while NONRATRES applied the number 1 to a state that, within this period, *either* did not assent to the ERA *or*, after having assented to the ERA, acted formally to cancel its assent. As a result of this difference in coding, 15 states were designated 1 on NONRAT, and 20 states were designated 1 on NONRATRES. The sole reason for the numerical dissimilarity arises from the treatment of the five ratification-canceling states: Although these five states were designated 0 on NONRAT (and hence were considered to have favored the ERA), they were designated 1 on NONRATRES (and hence were considered to have opposed the ERA).

3.2.2 Independent Variables

The indicators of the independent variables in my study use data on each of the 50 states from the 1960 decennial census of the U.S. population. In drawing data from that census, the study looks for social conditions in 1960 that predicted state reactions to the ERA during 1972–1982, i.e., during a time interval that began 12 years later and ended 22 years later. For explaining state reactions to the ERA during the congressionally specified ratification period, the independent variables as measured in 1960 have several advantages. First, the data for the independent variables are uncontaminated by any social conditions in American society that were altered by or arose from the Vietnam war. Social conditions that were caused or intensified by the Vietnam war and that may have affected state reactions to the ERA would not have existed in 1960: The substantial presence of U.S. military ground personnel in Vietnam, especially personnel for combat purposes, started during the middle of the 1960s and concluded during the first half of the 1970s.[76] Sociologically, the U.S. military action in Vietnam at this time must be presumed to have had significant social consequences within the United States since it produced divisions within American social life that were unmatched in degree by any other U.S. military engagement during the twentieth century.[77] A reasonable supposition is that the social disturbances due to the Vietnam war that were visible and are thus

---

[76] JENNIFER KAVANAGH ET AL., RAND CORP., THE PAST, PRESENT, AND FUTURE OF U.S. GROUND INTERVENTIONS: IDENTIFYING TRENDS, CHARACTERISTICS, AND SIGNPOSTS 19 fig. 2.2a, 21 fig. 2.3a (2017). U.S. military ground personnel had been in Vietnam prior to the mid-1960s, but their number was relatively small until after Congress passed the Gulf of Tonkin Resolution in August 1964. Bruce Palmer, Jr., *US Intelligence and Vietnam*, 28 STUDIES IN INTELLIGENCE 1, 24, 35 (special ed., 1984); Pub. L. No. 88-408, 78 Stat. 384 (1964) (Resolution).

[77] BRIAN VANDEMARK, INTO THE QUAGMIRE: LYNDON JOHNSON AND THE ESCALATION OF THE VIETNAM WAR xiii (1995) (writing that the U.S. war in "Vietnam divided America more deeply and painfully than any event since the Civil War" a hundred years earlier).

known were accompanied by other important, albeit subtle, disturbances in social life. In measuring the indicators of the independent variables as of 1960, then, the instant study keeps out war-triggered social factors that potentially affected state responses to the ERA.

The second advantage of measuring the independent variables as of 1960 is that the data are free of the effects of the social movements that were involved in the political battle over ratification of the ERA. In my approach, social movements are assumed to manifest specific societal conditions, and these conditions, rather than the movements per se, are assumed to bring about enduring change in law.[78] The social movement that backed ratification of the ERA would have been helped, and the social movement that resisted ratification of the ERA would have been hurt, by the increased prevalence of gender egalitarianism in the United States during the 1970s,[79] because historical period has a sizeable effect on the level of gender egalitarianism in a society.[80] However, all of the independent variables in my study were measured as of 1960, a year that occurred well before the decade of the 1970s. In looking for the sociological agents that influenced state reactions to the ERA, then, I investigate agents that were untouched by the elevated gender egalitarianism that characterized Americans ten and more years later.

Finally, let me mention a pair of sociological circumstances that further boost the potential of 1960 data on state-level variables to explain the manner in which states reacted to the ERA during the congressionally established ratification period. These circumstances were (1) American society in 1960 was conventional in its cultural norms regarding gender and the institution of marriage[81] and (2) cultural conventionalism was the source of much of the opposition to the ERA.[82] Sociological research on the ERA, accordingly, must include an indicator of cultural conventionalism. In my study, I have such an indicator, but data on attitudes are not used to measure the extent of cultural conventionalism in states (even assuming that state-

[78] A thesis that has become popular in the field of law is that law content is affected by social movements on their own, i.e., by social movements apart from other aspects of the social setting. Scott L. Cummings, *The Puzzle of Social Movements in American Legal Theory*, 64 UCLA L. Rev. 1554, 1556 (2017). In my approach, social movements that are unsupported by their societal environment are considered incapable of bringing about law content that persists for a long time. I assume that social movements, in producing law content that persists, operate just mechanically as a middle link in a chain from societal conditions to law. For evidence supporting the view that social movements concerned with ratification of the ERA constituted the middle link in such a chain, see Karen Oppenheim Mason et al., *Change in U.S. Women's Sex-Role Attitudes, 1964-1974*, 41 Am. Sociol. Rev. 573, 588–89, 594 (1976).

[79] *See* Mason et al., *supra* note 78, at 586–88; Glenna Spitze & Joan Huber, *Changing Attitudes Toward Women's Nonfamily Roles, 1938 to 1978*, 7 Sociol. of Work & Occupations 317, 318–19 & tbl. 1, 323, 329 tbl. 5 (1980).

[80] Spitze & Huber, *supra* note 79, at 333–34; Karin L. Brewster & Irene Padavic, *Change in Gender-Ideology, 1977-1996: The Contributions of Intracohort Change and Population Turnover*, 62 J. Marriage & Fam. 477, 479, 486 (2000).

[81] See the paragraph accompanying *supra* notes 9 to 12; *supra* note 26.

[82] See *supra* note 27.

level data on attitudes could be located for 1960). Evidence exists that the prevalence of unfavorable attitudes toward gender equality is not only underestimated but that the extent of the underestimate differs between the geographic regions of the United States,[83] a situation that creates the possibility that state-level attitudinal data will yield incorrect conclusions regarding the relationship between attitudes (as a measure of culture) and differences between states in their stance on the ERA. I avoid this problem by limiting my independent variables to non-attitudinal features of state populations.

Because resistance to adding the ERA to the Constitution was fueled by concern over the ramifications of the Amendment for marriage and sex roles,[84] I included in my study four of the five independent variables that were tested in *supra* Chap. 2 for their impact on whether a state by law prohibited its residents from marrying a person of a different race. The independent variables that I kept for the study of the ERA were culture, cultural heterogeneity, social disorder, and societal rationality.[85] The empirical indicators of these independent variables were also retained.[86] The independent variable that was in the study of state law on interracial marriage but dropped for the present study was societal fragmentation, which I replaced with *population structure*.[87]

Population structure, however, is not a single phenomenon but a category of phenomena that covers multiple aspects of a bounded group of human beings. In my study, I focused on just one of these aspects, viz., the sex composition of the population, and measured it using the number of males per 100 females in the population of each U.S. state. The measure, which is commonly named the sex ratio, employed data for the year 1960 and aggregated all ages and races.[88]

Why might the sex ratio have affected the posture of states on the ERA? To answer the question, let me begin with the point that the sex ratio at birth in the United States has been roughly in the range of 105–106 since at least the middle of

[83] *See* Streb et al., *supra* note 66, at 80–81, 83 tbl. 2 (finding that the extent of the underestimate is substantially greater in the South than outside the South). The regional difference in the underestimate is consistent with evidence that sex-role conventionalism is more socially influential in the South than elsewhere. J. Scott Carter et al., *The Significance of Place: The Impact of Urban and Regional Residence on Gender-Role Attitudes*, 49 Sociol. Focus 271, 282 (2016).

[84] Sonja K. Foss, *Equal Rights Amendment Controversy: Two Worlds in Conflict*, 65 Q. J. Speech 275, 282–83 (1979).

[85] The rationales for including these independent variables are set forth in Sect. 2.3.1.2 of *supra* Chap. 2.

[86] For the Census Bureau publications that supplied the data for the indicators, see notes 78, 82, 86, 87, and 93 in *supra* Chap. 2.

[87] Independent variables were chosen for the instant study, as they were for the study in Chap. 2, from SAIL vol. 1, *supra* note 26, at ch. 2 pt. 2.3.

[88] State data on the sex ratio in 1960 are from the 1960 census and are provided in U.S. Bureau of the Census, Statistical Abstract of the United States: 1966, at 23 tbl. 20 (87th ed. 1966), *available at* https://www.census.gov/library/publications/1966/compendia/statab/87ed.html.

the twentieth century.[89] The sex ratio at birth, however, is not the sex ratio of the population as a whole. Among all U.S. residents, the sex ratio at a particular time has been affected not only by the higher age-specific mortality rates of males relative to females[90] but also by the sex composition of pools of migrants from other countries.[91] Unsurprisingly, the ratio of males to females in the U.S. population has not remained constant over time; the sex ratio of the population as a whole has changed in response to temporal variation in sex differentials in mortality and in international migration.[92] Similarly, states can differ in the sex ratio of their populations because of state-to-state dissimilarities in sex-specific death rates and sex-specific rates of settlement by immigrants to the United States from other countries. The sex ratio of a state population can also be affected by sex asymmetry among persons who have migrated from other states and settled in the state.

Turning to the relevance of the sex ratio to the content of law, studies have investigated the effects of the sex ratio on what happens to females and to males in the social life of a society. Although the exact effects may depend on and vary with societal culture and structure,[93] this sociological contingency does not foreclose the possibility that the sex ratio has an important influence on social life. For example, the ratio of males to females has been found to affect the extent of labor force participation and marriage among women[94] and the extent of marriage among men.[95] Such evidence suggests that, in some societal circumstances, the sex ratio has the potential to influence aspects of social life that involve gender. If and when the sex ratio does so, the content of gender-pertinent law can be affected.

Through what process might the sex ratio in a state mold the response of the state to the ERA? Returning to the concept of societal stress, a state population that

---

[89] T. J. Mathews & Brady E. Hamilton, Nat'l Ctr. for Health Stat., *Trend Analysis of the Sex Ratio at Birth in the United States*, 53 NAT'L VITAL STAT. REP. 1, 1 fig. 1, 10 tbl. 1 (2005).

[90] Deborah L. Wingard, *The Sex Differential in Morbidity, Mortality, and Lifestyle*, 5 ANN. REV. PUBLIC HEALTH 433, 435–37 (1984) (data on the United States); Elizabeth Arias & Jiaquan Xu, Nat'l Ctr. for Health Stat., *United States Life Tables, 2017*, 68 NAT'L VITAL STAT. REP. 1, 49–50 tbl. 20 (2019) (presenting data for 2017 and for various two-year periods from 1900-1902 to 1999-2001; reporting, for each year, the number of males and the number of females in the United States who survived to specific ages from 1 to 100 out of every 100,000 males/females born alive). For data on the male-female mortality differential in other Western countries, see Hiram Beltrán-Sánchez et al., *Twentieth Century Surge of Excess Adult Male Mortality*, 112 PROC. NAT'L ACAD. SCI. OF U.S. 8993, 8994 fig. 2 (2015), https://www.pnas.org/content/112/29/8993.

[91] SAIL VOL. 2, *supra* note 14, at 51–52.

[92] *Id.* at 49 fig. 2.2; SAIL VOL. 1, *supra* note 26, at 172 fig. 4.4.

[93] Ryan Schacht & Ken R. Smith, *Causes and Consequences of Adult Sex Role Imbalance in a Historical U.S. Population*, 372 PHIL. TRANSACTIONS OF THE ROYAL SOC'Y B, at 1, 8 (art. **20160314**) (2017).

[94] SAIL VOL. 2, *supra* note 14, at 47, 85 nn.63–64; Josh Angrist, *How Do Sex Ratios Affect Marriage and Labor Markets? Evidence from America's Second Generation*, 117 Q. J. ECON. 997, 1033 (2002).

[95] Angrist, *supra* note 94, at 1033; Ryan Schacht & Karen Kramer, *Patterns of Family Formation in Response to Sex Ratio Variation*, 11(8) PLOS ONE, Aug. 24, 2016, at 1, 3–4, 11.

consists of substantially more males than females, or substantially more females than males, would logically experience increased societal stress because of the incompatibility of a severely asymmetrical sex ratio with the traditional way in which social life had been organized around the sex attribute, prompting the government of the state to adopt new law that is aimed at compensating for the current imbalance in the sex ratio and lessening the stress. To illustrate, before women received the right to vote in all elections (federal as well as state) through the addition of the Nineteenth Amendment to the U.S. Constitution in 1920,[96] many U.S. states and territories enacted legislation that allowed women to vote in state/territorial elections, and the states/territories that did so had populations characterized by a relatively high sex ratio.[97] An insufficient number of women, the investigators concluded, was "the single most important" reason that states and territories in the western region of the country were in the vanguard of law that enfranchised women.[98]

Table 3.2 may aid the reader in following the data analysis that I undertake in the next section of this chapter. The table lists all of the variables (dependent and independent) that are in the analysis, gives their mnemonic labels, and summarizes their empirical indicators.

3.2.3 *Data Analysis*

Table 3.3 reports summary descriptive statistics—the mean, the standard deviation, and the highest and lowest numerical value—for the indicator of each independent variable listed in Table 3.2. Readers will notice several differences between the summary statistics for the indicators that were used in both the study in Chap. 2 and the study in the present chapter.[99] The differences exist because the study in Chap. 2 included only the 48 coterminous states while the study in the present chapter includes all (i.e., 50) states.

Since the dependent variable was measured with two dummies (NONRAT and NONRATRES), I divided the data analysis and treated each dummy separately. I did so in order to ascertain whether the results obtained from regressing one of the dependent-variable dummies on the independent variables were similar to the results

---

96 U.S. CONST. amend. XIX ("The right of citizens of the United States to vote shall not be denied or abridged by the United States or by any State on account of sex"); CONSTITUTION OF THE UNITED STATES OF AMERICA: ANALYSIS AND INTERPRETATION – 1992, at 36 & n.11 (S. Doc. 103-6) (1992), https://www.govinfo.gov/app/details/GPO-CONAN-1992/GPO-CONAN-1992-7.

97 Sebastian Braun & Michael Kvasnicka, *Men, Women, and the Ballot: Gender Imbalances and Suffrage Extensions in the United States*, 50 EXPLORATIONS IN ECON. HIST. 405, 415, 423–24, 424–25 tbl. A2 (2013) (measuring the sex ratio in each state and territory as the number of males 15-49 years old for every 100 females in the same age range).

98 *Id.* at 424.

99 Table 2.2 in Chap. 2 reports the summary statistics for the indicators employed by the study in that chapter.

Table 3.2 Variables and their empirical indicators

Variable	Mnemonic label	Empirical indicator (state-level measure)
Dependent variable		
Nonratification/ratification of Equal Rights Amendment during the Congress-specified ratification period (March 1972 through June 1982)	NONRAT	A state was coded 1 on NONRAT if it did *not* ratify the ERA during the 1972–1982 ratification period. A state was coded 0 on NONRAT if it *did* ratify the ERA during this period even if it subsequently acted to cancel its ratification.
	NONRATRES	A state was coded 1 on NONRATRES if, during the 1972–1982 ratification period, it *either* did not ratify the ERA *or* ratified the ERA and later acted to repeal its ratification. A state was coded 0 on NONRATRES if, during the 1972–1982 ratification period, it ratified the ERA and did not subsequently act to repeal its ratification.
Independent variables		
Culture	LABORFORCE	The rate of labor force participation in 1960 among women who were married, were living with their husband, and had a child of their own under the age of six. The rate is expressed as a percentage and is based on females who were at least 14 years old in 1960.
Cultural heterogeneity	FOREIGNBN	The percentage of persons in 1960 who had been born outside the United States and whose parents were not U.S. citizens.
Population structure	SEXRATIO	The number of males per 100 females in 1960.
Social disorder	DIVORCED	The percentage in 1960 of females aged 30–34 who had been married at least once and were currently unmarried because their (only or last) marriage ended in divorce.
Societal rationality	EDUCATION	The median number of years of education that had been completed as of 1960 by persons who were in the age range 25 and older.

obtained from regressing the other dependent-variable dummy on the same independent variables. As an initial matter, let me mention that the regression of NONRAT as well as the regression of NONRATRES revealed that, when the regression model

Table 3.3 Summary statistics for the indicators of the independent variables

Indicator	Mean	Standard deviation	Minimum, Maximum
LABORFORCE	20.2%	4.13 pct. pts.	12.5%, 32.1%
FOREIGNBN	4.2%	3.33 pct. pts.	0.4%, 13.6%
SEXRATIO	99.3	6.04	93.4, 132.3
DIVORCED	3.0%	0.94 pct. pts.	1.3%, 6.5%
EDUCATION	10.5 years	1.09 years	8.7 years, 12.2 years

pct. pts. percentage points

Table 3.4 Regression models for NONRAT

	Model 1A	Model 1B	Model 2A	Model 2B	Model 3A	Model 3B	Model 4A	Model 4B
Odds ratio for								
LABORFORCE	1.028	1.323[b]	1.044	1.354[b]	0.999	1.296[c]	–	–
FOREIGNBN	0.603[c]	0.647[b]	0.616[c]	0.668[b]	–	–	0.607[c]	0.629[c]
DIVORCED	1.132	2.132	–	–	0.808	1.669	1.334	1.939[a]
INTERCEPT	–	0.001[c]	–	0.003[b]	–	0.000[c]	–	0.254
Number of states	50	50	50	50	50	50	50	50
Number of states wrongly predicted	9	7	9	8	15	12	10	11
Accuracy rate (%) for predictions of								
States coded 1	71.4	90.0	75.0	88.9	Δ	66.7	66.7	66.7
States coded 0	86.1	85.0	84.2	82.9	70.0	78.1	85.7	81.6
All states	82.0	86.0	82.0	84.0	70.0	76.0	80.0	78.0

– denotes that the variable/intercept was omitted
Δ denotes that the model predicted that no states would be coded 1 on NONRAT
The superscripts of a, b, and c denote levels of statistical significance: [a] ≤0.10; [b] ≤0.05; [c] ≤0.01

included the indicators of all five independent variables,[100] SEXRATIO and EDUCATION had very high Variance Inflation Factor ("VIF") scores.[101] Further regression models thus omitted both SEXRATIO and EDUCATION, i.e., were confined to LABORFORCE, FOREIGNBN, and DIVORCED. The VIF scores for the indicators of these three independent variables in the subsequent models were less than 10.0 and hence within acceptable limits.

3.2.3.1 NONRAT

The results for NONRAT are shown in Table 3.4. NONRAT was regressed on the independent-variable indicators without the intercept and, separately, with the

[100] Cook's Statistic yielded no evidence that any state in these regressions was an influential outlier, i.e., was skewing the results.

[101] The procedures for computing the VIF scores are described in note 99 in *supra* Chap. 2.

intercept, thereby creating a pair of models within each set of independent variables. The models in a pair are distinguished by the letters A and B: The model that excludes the intercept is identified with the letter A, while the model that includes the intercept is identified with the letter B.

Turning first to Models 1A and 1B, we see that the fit of Model 1B exceeded the fit of Model 1A: Two more states were correctly assigned to the categories of NONRAT by Model 1B than by Model 1A, and predictions overall for the categories of NONRAT were better under Model 1B than under Model 1A. Notably, the superiority of Model 1B in overall predictive accuracy was due to the ability of Model 1B to predict whether states would be coded 1.[102] Between Models 1A and 1B, then, Model 1B is preferable. Model 1A and Model 1B, however, consist of three independent variables. Does a model that uses two independent variables fit the data as well as Model 1B? To answer the question, models containing every combination of two of the independent variables comprising Model 1A and Model 1B were estimated. Among the two-variable models, Model 2A and Model 2B stand out: Their predictions were generally more accurate than the predictions of the other models having two independent variables, and they achieved roughly the same accuracy rates as Model 1A and Model 1B even though they had one less independent variable. Also, the direction of the relationship to the dependent variable for a given independent variable was the same across Models 1A, 1B, 2A, and 2B: In Model 2A and Model 2B as in Model 1A and Model 1B, the relationship to NONRAT was positive for LABORFORCE (the indicator of culture) and negative for FOREIGNBN (the indicator of cultural heterogeneity).

Since the criterion of parsimony gives Model 2A an edge over Model 1A and Model 2B an edge over Model 1B, we turn to the next question: Should conclusions regarding NONRAT be based on Model 2A or on Model 2B? Having posed the question, I concede that a definitive answer is not possible; either model is a reasonable choice. My preference is for Model 2B because it had a much higher accuracy rate than Model 2A in predicting whether states would be coded 1 on NONRAT. Following up on this preference, let us look at the impact of each independent variable. Under Model 2B, we see that the odds of a state being coded 1 on NONRAT rose by 35.4% when LABORFORCE grew by one percentage point (while

---

[102] Model 1A and Model 1B were checked for influential outliers even though Cook's Statistic was below 0.80 for every state under these models. Model 1A was checked by removing, one at a time, the two states that had the largest Cook's Statistic, and then regressing, without the intercept, NONRAT on LABORFORCE, FOREIGNBN, and DIVORCED. Model 1B was checked by removing the state that had the highest Cook's Statistic, and then regressing, with the intercept, NONRAT on LABORFORCE, FOREIGNBN, and DIVORCED. For LABORFORCE and for FOREIGNBN, the re-estimations produced odds ratios that were similar in magnitude to the odds ratios obtained for these indicators when Model 1A and Model 1B were estimated using all fifty states. Under Model 1A, the odds ratio for DIVORCED was below 1.000 when one of the two states was omitted and was above 1.000 when the other state was omitted. In these estimations, however, each odds ratio for DIVORCED was close to 1.000. Consequently, no omitted state was deemed to be an influential outlier. *See* SAIL VOL. 2, *supra* note 14, at 16 (positing the presumption that a U.S. state is not to be designated an influential outlier unless a persuasive reason is found to treat the state as an influential outlier).

FOREIGNBN remained constant), and that the odds of a state being coded 1 on NONRAT fell by 33.2% when FOREIGNBN grew by one percentage point (while LABORFORCE remained constant). A comparison of the impacts on NONRAT of each independent variable, however, ought to be based on standardized regression coefficients,[103] because the standardized coefficients show the factor-change in the odds that a state will be coded 1 on NONRAT when each of the independent-variable indicators increases by one standard deviation while the other independent-variable indicator remains fixed. Under Model 2B, the odds changed by a factor of 3.50 in response to a standard-deviation increase in LABORFORCE and changed by a factor of 0.26 in response to a standard-deviation increase in FOREIGNBN. Since a factor-change above 1.00 is compared to a factor-change below 1.00 by taking the *inverse* of either the former or the latter,[104] I chose FOREIGNBN and computed the inverse of 0.26, i.e., $1.00 \div 0.26 = 3.85$, a numerical value that is close to the factor change (3.50) for LABORFORCE. The magnitude of the effect of LABORFORCE was, accordingly, similar to the magnitude of the effect of FOREIGNBN.[105]

3.2.3.2 NONRATRES

Does treating the five ratification-rescinding states as nonratifying states materially alter the results? To answer the question, I employ NONRATRES as the measure of the dependent variable. Table 3.5 reports the findings of the data analysis for NONRATRES. A comparison of the findings for NONRATRES with the findings for NONRAT, i.e., a comparison of Table 3.5 with Table 3.4, suggests that the question has a negative answer.

Let us begin by looking at the pair of models in Table 3.5 that contain three independent variables, viz., Model 5A and Model 5B. Between the models in this pair, the model that includes the intercept (Model 5B) fits the data better than the model that excludes the intercept (Model 5A), especially in predictions of states coded 1 on NONRATRES. Among the three pairs of models that contain two independent variables each, the models that consist of LABORFORCE and FOREIGNBN (Model 6A and Model 6B) exhibit the best fit. Notably, the direction of the relationship of LABORFORCE to NONRATRES, and the direction of the relationship of FOREIGNBN to NONRATRES, is consistent across Model 5A, Model 5B, Model 6A, and Model 6B: LABORFORCE is positively related to NONRATRES, and FOREIGNBN is negatively related to NONRATRES.

---

[103] See note 187 in *supra* Chap. 1.

[104] J. SCOTT LONG & JEREMY FREESE, REGRESSION MODELS FOR CATEGORICAL DEPENDENT VARIABLES USING STATA 179 (2d ed. 2006).

[105] In the case of Model 2A, the odds that a state will be coded 1 on NONRAT changed by a factor of 1.20 when LABORFORCE rose by one standard deviation and changed by a factor of 0.20 when FOREIGNBN rose by one standard deviation.

Table 3.5 Regression models for NONRATRES

	Model 5A	Model 5B	Model 6A	Model 6B	Model 7A	Model 7B	Model 8A	Model 8B
Odds ratio for								
LABORFORCE	1.066	1.332[b]	1.096[c]	1.385[b]	1.012	1.242[b]	–	–
FOREIGNBN	0.523[c]	0.537[c]	0.536[c]	0.536[c]	–	–	0.539[c]	0.541[c]
DIVORCED	1.230	1.675	–	–	0.849	1.418	1.752[c]	1.805
INTERCEPT	–	0.004[b]	–	0.009[a]	–	0.003[c]	–	0.894
Number of states	50	50	50	50	50	50	50	50
Number of states wrongly predicted	12	9	11	9	19	16	13	13
Accuracy rate (%) for predictions of								
States coded 1	70.0	79.0	73.7	82.4	66.7	66.7	66.7	66.7
States coded 0	80.0	83.9	80.7	81.8	61.7	68.4	79.3	79.3
All states	76.0	82.0	78.0	82.0	62.0	68.0	74.0	74.0

– denotes that the variable/intercept was omitted
The superscripts of a, b, and c denote levels of statistical significance: [a] ≤0.10; [b] ≤0.05; [c] ≤0.01

Under the criterion of parsimony, the three-variable models (Model 5A and Model 5B) must be set aside in favor of the two-variable models (Model 6A and Model 6B)—unless, of course, the criterion of model fit gives the three-variable models a decisive advantage over the two-variable models. As the rows at the bottom of Table 3.5 reveal, however, the former pair of models offers no clear benefit relative to the latter pair of models in fitting the data. Otherwise expressed, three independent variables do not have an obvious edge over two independent variables in predicting the coding of states on NONRATRES. Therefore, the difference in number of independent variables makes Model 6A preferable to Model 5A and Model 6B preferable to Model 5B.

Having selected Model 6A and Model 6B over their alternatives for NONRATRES, I turn to deciding between Model 6A and Model 6B. Is one of these models more appealing than the other? Model 6B correctly predicted two more states than Model 6A, and in predicting states that it expected to be coded 1, Model 6B had an accuracy rate that was appreciably higher than the accuracy rate of Model 6A. Model 6B, accordingly, is preferable to Model 6A. Given the greater appeal of Model 6B, let us look at the odds ratios for the indicators of its independent variables. Table 3.5 shows that, under Model 6B, an increase of one percentage-point in LABORFORCE raised the odds of a state being coded 1 on NONRATRES by 38.5% and that an increase of one percentage-point in FOREIGNBN lowered the odds of a state being coded 1 on NONRATRES by 46.4%. Standardized regression coefficients,[106] which reveal the effect on the dependent variable of an increase of one standard deviation in the indicator of each independent variable while the indicator of the other independent variable is

[106] See note 187 in *supra* Chap. 1.

held constant, show the relative magnitude of the effects of the independent variables in Model 6B. Comparatively, the impact of FOREIGNBN exceeded the impact of LABORFORCE: The odds that a state would be coded 1 on NONRATRES went up by a factor of 3.84 when LABORFORCE rose by one standard-deviation and went down by a factor of 0.13 when FOREIGNBN rose by one standard-deviation.[107] The inverse of the factor for FOREIGNBN is $1.00 \div 0.13 = 7.69$. While the latter is twice the 3.84 obtained for LABORFORCE, the absolute amount of the difference between them may not be large enough to be meaningful.

3.2.4 Summary

Two sociological agents—culture and cultural heterogeneity—were evidently critical to the outcome of the political battle over ratification of the ERA by U.S. states during 1972–1982. Importantly, the concept of societal stress makes sense of the effects of culture and cultural heterogeneity. In terms of culture, social stress can logically be expected to occur insofar as there is deviation from, or a perceived danger of deviation from, tradition in the female role and family life. Therefore, the ERA—a potential change in law that was believed by a sizeable segment of a state population to present a threat to what is highly valued in tradition—presumptively led to social stress in the state, and when the stress passed a threshold, the state did not ratify the ERA. Less tradition in sex roles and family structure, in other words, made the ERA bothersome to a large-enough part of the population of a state to create the social stress that kept the state from ratifying the ERA.

In terms of cultural heterogeneity, the greater presence in a state of a foreign-born population lowered the odds that the state was formally against the ERA. How can this effect be explained? The range of viewpoints on topics such as the female role and family life is expanded by greater diversity in culture, and since law content in a society tends to embody the value-based viewpoints that are shared by the members of the society, social stress (and thus political opposition) is less likely when law pertinent to sex roles and family life is proposed in the context of more-frequent tradition-inconsistent viewpoints, i.e., is less likely in the context of a narrower range of widely accepted viewpoints. Tradition-divergent viewpoints, in other words, push a society to tolerate unconventional beliefs in the interest of maintaining internal cohesiveness and curbing social stress. Consequently, the odds of resistance to the ERA, which deals with a human attribute that is central to the organization of social life in the United States, declined as cultural diversity became greater.

The preceding summary is based on two regression models—Model 2B and Model 6B—that differ in their measure of the dependent variable. Favoring one of

[107] In the case of Model 6A, the odds that a state was coded 1 on NONRATRES changed by a factor of 1.46 for a standard-deviation increase in LABORFORCE and changed by a factor of 0.13 for a standard-deviation increase in FOREIGNBN.

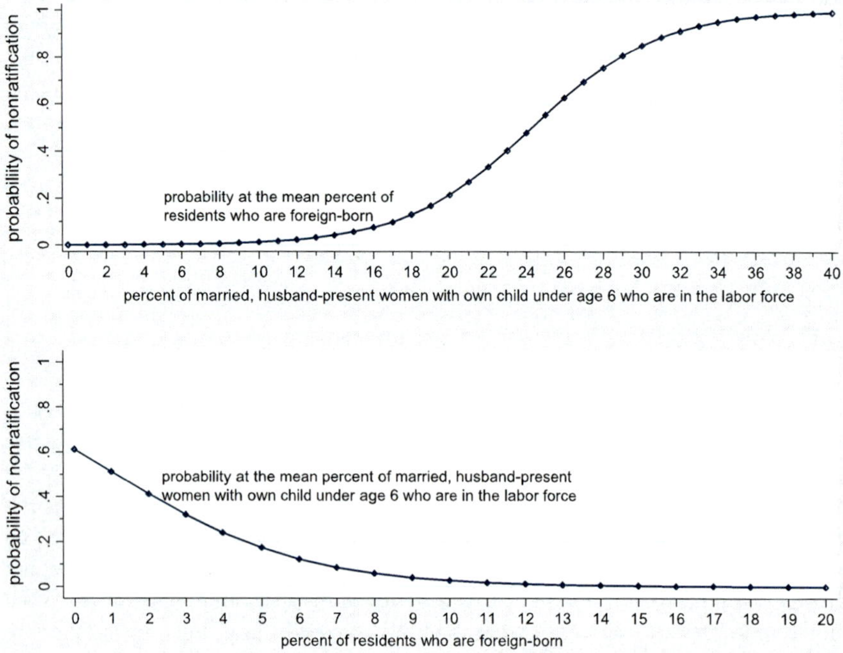

Fig. 3.3 Probability of state nonratification of the Equal Rights Amendment: predictions by Model 2B

the models over the other will simplify the discussion, but doing so requires a choice between NONRAT (Model 2B) and NONRATRES (Model 6B). Everything considered, I think that the advantage is held by Model 2B. This decision has (1) an empirical basis and (2) a basis in constitutional law. As to (1), Model 2B is superior to Model 6B in predicting states that did not ratify the ERA (88.9% for Model 2B and 82.4% for Model 6B). As to (2), Model 2B measures the dependent variable in a way (i.e., with NONRAT) that avoids unanswered questions of law about which states are to be counted as having effectively ratified the ERA. Model 6B, on the other hand, implicates these questions because it measures the dependent variable with NONRATRES.[108]

Additional insight into state reactions to the ERA can be gained from the pair of graphs in Fig. 3.3. Both graphs show the probabilities predicted by Model 2B that a state will be coded 1 on NONRAT and thus yield information on where to expect thresholds at which LABORFORCE and FOREIGNBN altered state responses to the ERA. The vertical axis for each graph in the figure designates the probabilities from 0 to 1.0, and the horizontal axis for each graph shows the numerical values of the named

[108] See the paragraph that accompanies *supra* notes 71–73.

indicator that are generating the probabilities. The top graph thus gives the probabilities for percentages of LABORFORCE when FOREIGNBN was held at its mean; the bottom graph gives the probabilities for percentages of FOREIGNBN when LABORFORCE was held at its mean. In both graphs, the probabilities changed gradually in response to increases in the magnitude of the explanatory variable. However, while the change covered most of the probability range from 0.0 to 1.0 as LABORFORCE increased, it covered just a portion of that range as FOREIGNBN increased.

What do we learn about thresholds from the graphs in Fig. 3.3? Since an increase in LABORFORCE raised the odds that a state did not ratify the ERA, we focus on the numerical values of LABORFORCE above which (with FOREIGNBN at its mean) the probability of a state being coded 1 on NONRAT exceeded 50.0%. This probability—i.e., the probability at which a state had a greater-than-even chance of objecting to the ERA—was reached when LABORFORCE was 25%. (The probability was then 0.55.) When LABORFORCE was seven percentage-points higher, i.e., when LABORFORCE was 32%, the probability of a state being coded 1 on NONRAT was fully 0.91.

Let us turn to FOREIGNBN (with LABORFORCE at its mean). Since an increase in FOREIGNBN lowered the odds that a state did not ratify the ERA, we focus on the numerical values of FOREIGNBN above which a state had a less-than-even chance of objecting to the ERA. When FOREIGNBN was 2%, the probability that a state would be coded 1 on NONRAT was 0.41; when FOREIGNBN was just three percentage-points higher, i.e., when FOREIGNBN was 5%, the probability that a state would be coded 1 on NONRAT was just 0.17.

3.3 American Society and the ERA

A substantial amount of time has passed since 1982, the end of the ERA-ratification period established by Congress. Section 3.2 focused on this period (i.e., 1972–1982) and used data on state-level independent variables measured as of 1960 to explain differences in state reactions to the ERA. Here, i.e., in Sect. 3.3, I build on the conclusions reached in Sect. 3.2 with respect to the indicator of culture and the indicator of cultural heterogeneity. Specifically, Sect. 3.3 aims to understand, in terms of LABORFORCE and FOREIGNBN, the present societal context of the movement to put the ERA (or an equivalent provision) into the Constitution. This movement is ongoing,[109] and its societal setting needs to be understood.

[109] *Supra* notes 6 & 7 and their accompanying text; Press Release, Rep. Carolyn B. Maloney, Rep. Maloney and Women's Rights Advocates Hold Press Conference after DC Circuit Court of Appeals Hears Oral Arguments in Illinois v. Ferriero (Sept. 28, 2022), https://maloney.house.gov/media-center/press-releases/rep-maloney-and-womens-rights-advocates-hold-press-conference-after-dc.

Figure 3.4 graphs time-series data for the United States from the midpoint of the twentieth century to the present. The two trend lines in the figure are for (1) the rate of labor force participation by married, husband-present women who had an own child younger than age 6 and (2) the share of the total U.S. population that consisted of foreign-born persons.[110] Both (1) and (2) are expressed in percentages. Readers should note that Fig. 3.4 shows the percentages for (1) and the percentages for (2) on different vertical axes: For the labor force participation rate of married, spouse-present women who have an own child younger than age 6, the numerical values of the percentages are on the left vertical axis; for the share of the total population that is foreign-born, the numerical values of the percentages are on the right vertical axis. The first year and the last year of the congressionally designated ratification period (i.e., 1972 and 1982) are designated by vertical lines in the inner region of the figure.

Figure 3.4 reveals that, prior to the 1972–1982 ratification period, a rapid increase occurred in labor-force participation by married, spouse-present mothers of children under age 6. Specifically, the labor force participation of these women climbed from 11.9% in 1950 to 30.3% in 1970. Participation continued to grow during the ERA-ratification period, reaching 45.1% in 1980, and while it also went up during the decade of the 1980s, it plateaued at about 60% beginning around 1990. The ERA, therefore, was proposed for ratification at a time when the involvement in the labor force by married mothers of young children was rising quickly and hence would have increasingly perceived as a threat to tradition in sex roles and family life. Because the labor-force participation of married mothers of young children has not changed since about 1990, however, the current level of labor-force engagement by such women has existed for approximately three decades and may have caused

---

[110] Labor force participation rates cover the period 1950 to 2020 and were obtained from: (1) Thomas Snyder & Linda Shafer, Nat'l Ctr. for Educ. Statistics, Youth Indicators, 1996, at 50 (1996). (2) U.S. Census Bureau, Statistical Abstract of the United States: 2012, at 385 tbl. 600 (131st ed., n.d.), https://www.census.gov/library/publications/2011/compendia/statab/131ed.html (follow "Section 12" hyperlink; under "Labor Force Status," select Excel file "600 – Labor Force Participation Rates for Wives, Husband Present by Age of Own Youngest Child"). Percentages for years covered by this report were used when they differed from percentages for years in the Snyder-Shafer report *supra*. (3) Table 6 in the annual issues (2004 to 2021) of U.S. Bureau of Labor Statistics, Women in the Labor Force: A Databook. The annual issues are available at https://www.bls.gov/opub/reports/archive.htm.

For the definition of "labor force," see note 82 in *supra* Chap. 2.

Decennial census data for 1950 to 2010 on foreign-born persons in the U.S. population are used in the figure. The data were obtained from: (1) Campbell Gibson & Kay Jung, U.S. Census Bureau, *Historical Census Statistics on the Foreign-Born Population of the United States: 1850 to 2000*, at [60–62] tbl. 14 (Working Paper No. 81, 2006). (2) Elizabeth M. Grieco et al., U.S. Census Bureau, *The Foreign-Born Population in the United States: 2010*, at 2 tbl. 1 (ACS-19) (2012).

The percentage of the U.S. population represented by foreign-born persons in 2019 (the latest year for which data have been released) was computed from: U.S. Census Bureau, Foreign Born: 2019 Current Population Survey Detailed Tables tbl. 1.1, https://www.census.gov/data/tables/2019/demo/foreign-born/cps-2019.html.

The foreign-born population of the United States includes males as well as females and covers all ages, ethnic groups, and races.

Fig. 3.4 Labor force participation rate of married spouse-present women who have an own child under age 6, and share of the population that is foreign-born: United States since 1950 (Source: see note 110)

American society to adapt to it.[111] If this adaptation took place, participation in the labor force by married mothers of young children would likely be producing less social stress now than when states were presented with the ERA for possible ratification, and all else being equal, the ERA would be encountering less political resistance today than it did during 1972–1982.

Figure 3.4 also reveals that the foreign-born share of the U.S. population, while contracting from 1950 to 1970, expanded afterward and that the expansion has yet to end. In 1970, foreign-born residents were 4.7% of the population, but they represented 11.1% of the population in 2000 and 14.1% in 2019. This change is likely to have brought into American society a greater variety of worldviews.[112] If

[111] Although such an adaptation is certainly possible, the fraction of mothers of a young child who are outside the labor force has also been sizeable and stable over the last three decades. The magnitude and persistence of this fraction implies that societal uneasiness with labor-force participation by mothers of a young child has not diminished since around 1990 and that it is still considerable.

[112] A language channels the perceptions of its users. Explaining Law, *supra* note 48, at 170–71. Therefore, groups that differ in language will have dissimilar worldviews. Notably, in the United States, the fraction of the foreign-born population aged 5 and older that did not speak English at home underwent a secular increase between 1980 and 2010-2012 while the fraction of the foreign-

the range of tolerated viewpoints was enlarged by a societal drive to reduce social stress emanating from the post-1980 increase in foreign-born residents, as the reasoning in Sect. 3.2.4 suggests, the greater tolerance makes American society more amenable to the ERA today than in 1972–1982.

What, then, should we conclude about the impact of the current societal context on the outcome of the ongoing political fight over the ERA? Explaining what has already happened and been observed is rarely hard, but forecasting what has not yet been observed is invariably perilous. To quote a well-known adage, "[i]t's difficult to make predictions, especially about the future."[113] In macrosociological forecasts, the risk of error is magnified because a human society of even modest size contains feedback loops, the number of which may increase geometrically as lines of communication in the society grow arithmetically. Feedback loops raise the degree of complexity in social life, and as complexity mounts, inaccurate predictions are likely to be more frequent.

Nonetheless, an assessment of the evidence pertaining to the Equal Rights Amendment permits two general (and related) predictions. First, the addition of the ERA to the U.S. Constitution will not materially alter how American society structures sex roles and family life. The ERA will thus not produce what its opponents fear or what its proponents promise. Incorporation of the ERA into the Constitution would follow the very substantial change in patterns of gender-related behavior that has taken place in the United States under a Constitution without the ERA,[114] and such change after the ERA, like such change before the ERA, would be due to the alteration of society-level properties by broad sociological forces. The ERA would symbolize the character of social life that these forces have produced, but although symbols normally promote societal cohesiveness, they do not reshape a society.[115] Second, the addition of the ERA to the Constitution, if it happens, should not be a surprise. Ceteris paribus, new law content on a significant social aspect of a democratically governed population develops only after—and not necessarily soon after—the social nature and treatment of that aspect has appreciably changed. The social evolution that has occurred in terms of gender in the United States since the end of World War II could, therefore, bring the ERA into the text of the

---

born population aged 25 and older that had "high" fluency in English underwent a secular decrease among immigrants who arrived after 1987. Christine P. Gambino et al., U.S. Census Bureau, *English-Speaking Ability of the Foreign-Born Population in the United States: 2012*, at 2, 11 fig. 8 (top graph) (ACS-26) (2014).

[113] The adage is of uncertain origin. Quote Investigator, https://quoteinvestigator.com/2013/10/20/no-predict; *The Perils of Prediction, June 2nd*, Economist, https://www.economist.com/letters-to-the-editor-the-inbox/2007/07/15/the-perils-of-prediction-june-2nd.

[114] See *supra* Sect. 3.1.3.

[115] *Cf.* Martha F. Davis, *The Equal Rights Amendment: Then and Now*, 17 Colum. J. Gender & L. 419, 458–59 (2008) (concluding from a review of equal rights provisions in state constitutions that such a provision in the federal Constitution is unlikely to bring about a major change in U.S. law but that it would nonetheless benefit women by, inter alia, ending "the continued denial of full and explicit constitutional *recognition* of women") (italics added).

U.S. Constitution. Given what Model 2B and Fig. 3.4 tell us, a principal force pushing adoption of the ERA today is evidently the long-term increase in the share of foreign-born persons in the U.S. population, an increase that has enlarged the range of viewpoints in American social life and promoted, in the interest of social cohesion, the acceptance of nontraditional social ideas.

Chapter 4
Same-Sex Marriage

4.1 Same-Sex Marriage in the United States

> [M]arriage and family [are] the foundation of civilization, the source of virtue and the wellspring of society. ... [L]egalization of same-sex marriage ... inevitably would be detrimental to the institution of marriage, children and society as a whole.[1]

> It is the traditional values served by civil marriage — responsibility, fidelity, commitment, and stability, among others — that . . . justify its equal availability under law. Those values would be served by ending governmental exclusion of same-sex couples from the institution of civil marriage, not by perpetuating it.[2]

The above-quoted passages are illustrative of the division that presently exists among Americans in their views toward whether law should allow same-sex couples to marry. The passages appear in friend-of-the-court briefs that were submitted to the U.S. Supreme Court in Obergefell v. Hodges,[3] a case in which the validity of state statutory bans against same-sex marriage were challenged under the Due Process Clause and the Equal Protection Clause of the Fourteenth Amendment to the national Constitution.[4] The Court, which announced its decision on June 26, 2015,[5] ruled that law prohibiting same-sex marriage violated both Clauses because it was inconsistent with the basic social ideals that these clauses recognize. To quote the Court:

---

[1]Brief of Family Research Council as Amicus Curiae Supporting Respondents, Obergefell v. Hodges, 135 S. Ct. 2584 (2015) (No. 14-556), at 1.

[2]Brief of Kenneth B. Mehlman et al. as Amicus Curiae Supporting Petitioners, Obergefell v. Hodges, 135 S. Ct. 2584 (2015) (No. 14-556), at 26 (italics omitted from quoted passage).

[3]Obergefell v. Hodges, 135 S. Ct. 2584 (2015).

[4]U.S. CONST. amend. XIV, § 1 ("nor shall any state deprive any person of life, liberty, or property, without due process of law; nor deny to any person within its jurisdiction the equal protection of the laws"). The guarantees of due process and equal protection are explained in the portion of Sect. 2.2 that precedes Sect. 2.2.1 in *supra* Chap. 2.

[5]J. SUP. CT. U.S., Oct. Term 2014, at 919.

L. D. Barnett, *Societal Stress and Law*,
https://doi.org/10.1007/978-3-031-30875-8_4

> No union is more profound than marriage, for it embodies the highest ideals of love, fidelity, devotion, sacrifice, and family. In forming a marital union, two people become something greater than once they were. . . . [Those who are here challenging same-sex marriage bans] hope . . . not to be condemned to live in loneliness, excluded from one of civilization's oldest institutions. They ask for equal dignity in the eyes of the law. The Constitution grants them that right.[6]

I will delve into state proscriptions against same-sex marriage in *infra* Sect. 4.2.1. Here, however, I want to underscore the historical-demographic context of the societal treatment of same-sex marriage.

Hominids have been on planet Earth for at least 4,000,000 years and *Homo sapiens* has been present for at least 100,000 years,[7] but during almost all of this time, the number of individuals was small[8] and growing slowly.[9] Survival of the species was, therefore, not assured. The possibility of extinction would logically have been a potent reason for human groups to exert social pressure on their members to have many offspring and to avoid practices such as same-sex intimacy that were not conducive to pregnancy. Understandably, then, social beliefs favorable to reproduction and to interpersonal arrangements that facilitate reproduction have deep sociological roots in human societies. This depth is evidenced in Western nations by the support that the beliefs receive in Judeo-Christian religious teachings. The Old Testament of the Bible, for example, expressly condemns homosexuality.[10]

---

[6] Obergefell v. Hodges, 135 S. Ct. at 2608. The opinion of the Court in *Obergefell* is not alone in linking a Court decision to American social ideals. Interpretations by the Court of the provisions of the Constitution that are concerned with personal liberties commonly express these ideals. LARRY D. BARNETT, SOCIETAL AGENTS IN LAW: A MACROSOCIOLOGICAL APPROACH 14–15 (2019) [hereinafter SAIL VOL. 1].

[7] Fiorenzo Facchini, *Man, Origin and Nature*, *in* INTERDISCIPLINARY ENCYCLOPEDIA OF RELIGION AND SCIENCE (G. Tanzella-Nitti et al. eds., 2002), http://inters.org/origin-nature-of-man (last visited Oct. 2, 2022).

[8] During the geologic period that ended 1,200,000 years ago, hominids evidently had a remarkably small population, which is thought to have been no more than 26,000 individuals. Chad D. Huff et al., *Mobile Elements Reveal Small Population Size in the Ancient Ancestors of Homo sapiens*, 107 PROC. NAT'L ACAD. SCI. 2147, 2149 (2010). *Cf.* Nelson J. R. Fagundes et al., *Statistical Evaluation of Alternative Models of Human Evolution*, 104 PROC. NAT'L ACAD. SCI. 17614, 17615 tbl. 1 (2007) (estimating that human beings who have the anatomy of human beings today evolved around 141,000 years ago and that, if they originated in Africa, they numbered only about 12,800 individuals when they began to colonize other continents).

[9] Estimates of the size and growth of the human population of the world from 1,000,000 B.C. to the mid-1970s are in Ansley J. Coale, *The History of the Human Population*, SCI. AM., Sept. 1974, at 40, 42–43. For example, Professor Coale estimates that ten thousand years ago, i.e., in 8000 B.C., the total number of human beings was around 8,000,000 and that this number was growing each year by just roughly 15 per 1,000,000 population, i.e., by 0.0015 percent. *Id.* at 43. For estimates covering the period since 1920, see Part 1.2 and Figure 1.1 in LARRY D. BARNETT, DEMOGRAPHY AND THE ANTHROPOCENE (2021).

[10] *Leviticus* 18:22 (King James) ("Thou shalt not lie with mankind, as with womankind: it is abomination"); *Leviticus* 20:13 (King James) ("If a man also lie with mankind, as he lieth with a woman, both of them have committed an abomination: they shall surely be put to death; their blood

Because religious ideas derive from important societal concerns and experiences,[11] the Judeo-Christian condemnation of homosexuality provided social support in Western societies to the societal imperative of procreation.

Given the interest of *Homo sapiens* in avoiding extinction—and the tendency of every human society to be socially stable[12]—same-sex marriage has, unsurprisingly, had limited acceptance in Judeo-Christian nations.[13] This point is illustrated by the United States: In 2021 (i.e., six years after the U.S. Supreme Court decided *Obergefell*), same-sex married-couple households in the United States comprised just 0.6 percent of all married-couple households in the country.[14] Furthermore, the organized movement for homosexual rights in the United States did not originate until around or shortly after the middle of the twentieth century.[15] By that point, of course, human beings were numerous and adding to their number rapidly. The United Nations estimates, for example, that the world had 2.5 billion people in 1950 and 7.8 billion people in 2020[16]—a more than threefold increase in just seven decades. Indeed, the large size and continuing numerical growth of the human population was probably a factor that promoted the emergence of same-sex marriage as a topic for public debate and law. In the United States, higher population density is

---

shall be upon them"). Passages in the Old Testament linked to reproduction are analyzed in JOHN MCKEOWN, GOD'S BABIES: NATALISM AND BIBLE INTERPRETATION IN MODERN AMERICA (2014).

[11]Adam J. Powell, *The Ideal — One Possibility for the Future of Religious Identity*, 6 INTERMOUNTAIN W. J. RELIGIOUS STUD. 112, 116 (2015) (observing that "[r]eligion reflects society, both through abstract idealizations and integrations of reality"), https://digitalcommons.usu.edu/imwjournal/vol6/iss1/7.

[12]See Sect. 1.2 in *supra* Chap. 1.

[13]William N. Eskridge, Jr., *A History of Same-Sex Marriage*, 79 VA. L. REV. 1419, 1447–48, 1469 (1993) (contending that, in Christian societies, social teachings against same-sex marriage date to at least the thirteenth century A.D. and possibly to the fourth century A.D., if not earlier).

[14]U.S. Census Bureau, *Coupled Households by Type* tbl. B11009 (2021), https://censusreporter.org/tables/B11009 (in window "Show data by choosing a place or summary level," type "United States" and enter)) (last visited Oct. 2, 2022). Same-sex cohabiting couple households were 0.4 percent of all cohabiting couple households in 2021. *Id.*

Among cohabiting young-adult couples, same-sex couples exhibit a substantially higher break-up rate than different-sex couples. Kara Joyner et al., *Gender and the Stability of Same-Sex and Different-Sex Relationships Among Young Adults*, 54 DEMOGRAPHY 2351, 2359–60, 2366 fig. 2, 2367 tbl. 3 (2017) (using data on a national probability-selected sample of U.S. young adults from 1995 to 2007–2008). When marrying is an available option, therefore, considerably fewer same-sex couples than opposite-sex couples will evidently proceed to marriage. *Cf.* JULIANA HOROWITZ ET AL., PEW RES. CTR., MARRIAGE AND COHABITATION IN THE U.S. 4, 5–6 (2019) (finding that, in the first and second decades of the twenty-first century, somewhat more than half of U.S. adults aged 18–44 cohabited).

[15]Eskridge, *supra* note 13, at 1483; Andrew M. Jacobs, *Romer Wasn't Built in a Day: The Subtle Transformation in Judicial Argument Over Gay Rights*, 1996 WIS. L. REV. 893, 897 & n.14.

[16]United Nations Dep't of Econ. & Soc. Aff., World Population Prospects 2022 (data on estimated mid-year population, extracted Oct. 2, 2022)), https://population.un.org/wpp/Download/Standard/CSV/.

associated with more social acceptance of homosexuality[17] and less tolerance in U.S. law of discrimination against homosexuals.[18]

4.1.1 Law on Same-Sex Marriage

Section 4.2 of the current chapter is concerned with the macrosociological agents that determined whether, when the U.S. Supreme Court issued its ruling in *Obergefell*, states had law that forbid same-sex marriage. A study of these agents requires, of course, an accurate, state-by-state enumeration of the presence or absence of such law. Because the states that possessed a law-based ban on same-sex marriage could not enforce their ban after the U.S. Supreme Court announced *Obergefell*—which occurred on June 26, 2015[19]—my study will deal with state law as it existed on that day.

In studying state law on same-sex marriage, I focus on state statutes and state constitutions. In democracies, statutes and constitutions offer the advantage that they come from the broadest set of elected representatives (viz., legislators) or from the electorate itself. Legislation and constitutions in democratic nations, therefore, are directly and firmly rooted in the citizenry. Judicial rulings, on the other hand, have a weaker footing in the body politic since judges are not invariably elected. Indeed, no federal court judges in the United States are elected, and in a substantial number of states, judges on the highest appellate court are not elected either.[20] Consequently, in assembling the state same-sex marriage law that was "on the books" when the *Obergefell* ruling appeared, I gave just minimal consideration to what the judiciary had already said about the validity and enforceability of such law.

4.1.2 Attitudes in the United States Toward Same-Sex Marriage

By definition, a democracy conforms its law to fundamental aspects of public opinion. Indeed, an established democracy in which law generally stops manifesting

[17] Robert Andersen & Tina Fetner, *Cohort Differences in Tolerance of Homosexuality: Attitudinal Change in Canada and the United States, 1981-2000*, 72 Pub. Opinion Q. 311, 316, 322, 323 tbl. 3 (2008).

[18] Kenneth D. Wald et al., *The Politics of Gay Rights in American Communities: Explaining Antidiscrimination Ordinances and Policies*, 40 Am. J. Pol. Sci. 1152, 1155, 1164, 1165 tbl. 2, 1168 (1996).

[19] J. Sup. Ct. U.S., Oct. Term 2014, at 919.

[20] Brennan Ctr. for Just., *Judicial Selection: Significant Figures* (2015, updated 2021), https://www.brennancenter.org/our-work/research-reports/judicial-selection-significant-figures (last visited Oct. 2, 2022).

public opinion seems unlikely to remain a democracy.[21] Accordingly, let us look at the extent to which Americans believed, when the U.S. Supreme Court decided *Obergefell*, that same-sex marriage should be permitted by law. These beliefs are important in the sociology of law, because when the Court evaluates the acceptability of a society-significant social arrangement under a personal-rights provision of the Constitution, its decision is usually shaped by what the public in general then thinks about the acceptability of the arrangement.[22] Despite the popular notion that courts are independent of external influences and their rulings are determined by the individuality of judges, the judiciary operates within a societal context. Moreover, this context does not remain the same over time. Large-scale social forces change the societal context in which the judiciary works and, in turn, the substance of court rulings.[23]

Figure 4.1 supplies data for two longitudinal measures of the attitudes of the American public regarding the issue of same-sex marriage. The data for the measures were obtained from questions in probability-sample surveys of U.S. adults that asked interviewees about their views on "allowing gays and lesbians to marry legally" and that presented interviewees with four explicit choices for their answers, viz., "strongly favor," "favor," "strongly oppose," or "oppose."[24] Data from these surveys have been published for eighteen years in the period from 1996 through 2019 and include a pair of percentages—(1) the percentage of respondents who said that they "strongly favor" law that permits gays and lesbians to marry and (2) the percentage of respondents who said that they "strongly oppose" such law.[25] I relied on just the percentages of respondents whose attitudes were intense, i.e., who responded "strongly favor" or "strongly oppose," because on logical grounds these percentages are probably indicators of the potency of pertinent social movements.[26] Using

[21] *Cf.* Damarys Canache, *Citizens' Conceptualizations of Democracy: Structural Complexity, Substantive Content, and Political Significance*, 45 Comp. Pol. Stud. 1132, 1137, 1139, 1150 (2012) (analyzing answers to an open-ended question on the meaning of democracy to respondents in probability-sample surveys, conducted during 2006 and 2007, of residents of thirteen Latin American nations; concluding that meanings centered on personal liberty and freedom were most favorable to the maintenance of a stable democracy).

[22] Alan D. Monroe, *Public Opinion and Public Policy, 1980-1993*, 62 Pub. Opinion Q. 6, 14 tbl. 2 (1998); Christopher J. Casillas et al., *How Public Opinion Constrains the U.S. Supreme Court*, 55 Am. J. Pol. Sci. 74, 80 & tbl. 1 (2011).

[23] *See* SAIL vol. 1, *supra* note 6, at ch. 4.

[24] The data for Fig. 4.1 are from Pew Res. Ctr., Majority of Public Favors Same-Sex Marriage, But Divisions Persist 14–15 (2019). © Pew Research Center 2019. No more than 13 percent of interviewees in any survey declined to answer or volunteered a "don't know" response. *Id.*

For a description of the procedure used to gather the data, see Pew Res. Ctr., U.S. Survey Methodology at https://www.pewresearch.org/our-methods/u-s-surveys/u-s-survey-methodology (last visited Oct. 2, 2022).

[25] In years when more than one survey was done, mean percentages were computed from the surveys in each year, and the mean percentages are used in Fig. 4.1.

[26] Strong personal beliefs regarding a topic appear to trigger individuals' endorsement of and engagement in social movements that attempt to shape law and policy on the topic. Thus, lifetime

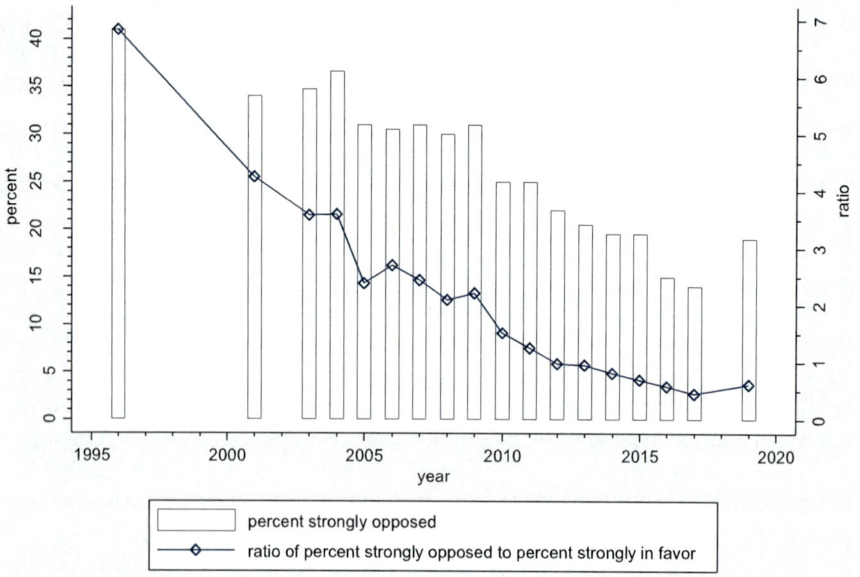

Fig. 4.1 Opposition to legalization of same-sex marriage: United States. Source: footnote 24 and calculations by author

(1) and (2), I calculated the *ratio* of the latter to the former in each year. The ratio for a given year, therefore, results from mathematically dividing the numerical value of (2) by the numerical value of (1) for that year.

Figure 4.1 presents both the yearly percentages for (2) and the yearly ratios of (2) divided by (1). The measures in the figure thus indicate, respectively, the absolute and relative prevalence of strong resistance to law that allows same-sex couples to marry. The prevalence of such resistance is pertinent to the instant book because it gauges whether American society would have been stressed at a given point in time by the legalization of same-sex marriage—and was stressed in 2015 by the Supreme Court ruling in *Obergefell.*

---

participation of individuals in organizations working for, and lifetime participation of individuals in organizations working against, access to abortion has been found to be most prevalent among individuals to whom abortion is an important topic and among individuals who have highly polarized attitudes toward abortion. Debra Kaysen & Jayne E. Stake, *From Thought to Deed: Understanding Abortion Activism*, 31 J. Applied Soc. Psychol. 2378, 2383-84, 2390 tbl. 3, 2394 (2001) (using data from nonprobability samples of pro-abortion organization members and anti-abortion organization members). *See* Soon Seok Park & Rachel L. Einwohner, *Becoming a Movement Society? Patterns in the Public Acceptance of Protest, 1985-2006*, 52 Sociol. Focus 186 (2019) (analyzing data from national probability samples of U.S. adults; finding that support for political protest rises with the degree of interest in politics).

Let me point out that, in perusing Fig. 4.1, readers will need to refer to the two vertical axes.[27] The left vertical axis, which is labelled "percent," shows the numerical values for (2), i.e., the percentages of U.S. adults who strongly felt that law should not permit same-sex marriage; these percentages are represented by the bars in the plot region of the graph. The right vertical axis, which is labelled "ratio," supplies the numerical values of the ratio of (2) to (1); the ratios are denoted by the line-connected diamonds in the plot region.

A close examination of Fig. 4.1 and its data leads to four observations. First, the share of the U.S. public that strongly disapproved of legalization of same-sex marriage moved in a generally downward direction over time. To illustrate, at the beginning of the time interval covered by the figure (i.e., in 1996), 41 percent of adults strongly opposed legalization; at the end of the interval (i.e., in 2019), only 19 percent did. The prevalence of strong objections to legalization was thus cut roughly in half during this period. Second, the ratio, which also fell secularly, reached approximate unity in 2012 (when the ratio was 0.98). In 2012, that is, the share of the U.S. public that was most negative toward legalization of same-sex marriage was approximately the same size as the share that was most positive. Third, strong opposition to law that permits same-sex couples to marry was less common in 2014 and 2015 than strong approval of such law, which pushed the ratio below unity in these years (0.81 in 2014 and 0.70 in 2015). Because *Obergefell* was announced in mid-2015,[28] the years 2014 and 2015 supply the immediate context in which the U.S. Supreme Court decided the case. In holding that government prohibitions of same-sex marriage violate the Constitution of the nation, *Obergefell* accordingly conformed to the general tendency of rulings by the Court on society-central social activities to embody the dominant view of the American public regarding these activities.[29]

I turn now to the fourth and final observation. Figure 4.1 shows that a strong aversion to legalization of same-sex marriage was less prevalent in 2016 and 2017 than in 2015, but that in 2019 it was essentially as prevalent as in 2015.[30] The post-2015 shifts—an initial, short-term decrease followed by a sizeable increase—in highly unfavorable attitudes warrant mention because they may signal reactions by the public to the ruling in *Obergefell*. The 2019 jump in strongly negative attitudes

[27]Changes over time in the two measures in Fig. 4.1 are not perfectly parallel because of temporal differences in the percentage of interviewees who did not respond or who answered "don't know." See *supra* note 24.

[28]Text accompanying *supra* note 5.

[29]Casillas et al., *supra* note 22, and accompanying text.

[30]The decline in 2016 and 2017 may have been a reaction to *Obergefell*. *Cf.* Andrew R. Flores & Scott Barclay, *Backlash, Consensus, Legitimacy, or Polarization: The Effect of Same-Sex Marriage Policy on Mass Attitudes*, 69 Pol. Res. Q. 43, 47, 51–52 (2016) (analyzing data on U.S. adults from a pair of national sample surveys, one done several months before, and one done about a month after, two U.S. Supreme Court decisions in 2013 that were precursors of *Obergefell*; finding that the net effect of the decisions was to increase the incidence of favorable attitudes toward same-sex marriage).

should be juxtaposed with the observation that, when the eighteen years of data in Fig. 4.1 are combined, the average share of all respondents who strongly opposed law that allows same-sex couples to marry was noticeably larger than the average share of all respondents who strongly supported such law: To be exact, strong opposition was expressed by a mean of 26.6 percent while strong support was expressed by a mean of 17.8 percent. During the 1996–2019 period as a whole, therefore, strong disapproval was more frequent than strong approval. Notably, the standard deviations of the two attitudes across all of the years in the period were very similar, viz., 7.8 percentage points for strong disapproval and 8.0 percentage points for strong approval. Because the standard deviation of an attitude represents the degree of spread in the occurrence of the attitude over multiple occurrences, year-to-year variation in strong opposition did not differ overall from year-to-year variation in strong support. Substantial hostility toward same-sex marriage, consequently, may remain in American society for many years and have significant sociological effects, which effects may include social stress from the adoption of law allowing this form of marriage. The latter point warrants elaboration.

As pointed out earlier, the United States had very few same-sex married couples in 2021,[31] six years after the U.S. Supreme Court ruling in *Obergefell*. However, while same-sex marriage is statistically rare among Americans, the frequency of same-sex marriage may not affect, or may not be the chief factor that affects, whether same-sex marriage and its legalization produce societal stress. A much more influential factor may be the symbolism of law[32] (here, constitutional law requiring U.S. jurisdictions to permit same-sex couples to marry), especially the impact of this symbolism on the segment of the U.S. population that is averse to the legalization of same-sex marriage. By its ruling in *Obergefell*, the Court evidently increased the prevalence of views that Americans are moving toward acceptance of same-sex marriage.[33] *Obergefell*, accordingly, would have alienated the population segment that did not want same-sex marriage to be legalized. This segment, notably, does not draw proportionally from all subpopulations in the United States; instead, it tends to be a product of religious conservativism and, hence, disproportionately present

[31] See the text accompanying *supra* note 14. Similarly, U.S. same-sex couples having a sexually intimate relationship were a small proportion of all married and unmarried U.S. couples at the turn of the twenty-first century. David M. Smith & Gary J. Gates, *Gay and Lesbian Families in the United States: Same-Sex Unmarried Partner Households: A Preliminary Analysis of 2000 United States Data* 1, 5 tbl. 2 (2001) (estimating gay and lesbian couples in the year 2000 to have been 0.99 percent of all U.S. couples), *available at* https://eric.ed.gov/?id=ED457285.

[32] Larry D. Barnett, The Place of Law: The Role and Limits of Law in Society 203–04, 394–404 (2011); Larry D. Barnett, Explaining Law: Macrosociological Theory and Empirical Evidence 15–16 (2015) [hereinafter Explaining Law].

[33] Margaret E. Tankard & Elizabeth Levy Paluck, *The Effect of a Supreme Court Decision Regarding Gay Marriage on Social Norms and Personal Attitudes*, 28 Psychol. Sci. 1334, 1336–37, 1339, 1341–42 (2017).

among persons who base their worldview on the traditional teachings of religion.[34] Importantly, religious conservatives are a sizeable portion of the current U.S. population.[35]

In sum, American society would have been stressed by the *Obergefell* ruling. As one scholar put the matter, the ruling of the Court was thought by many Americans to be "the work of a partisan elite imposing its policy preferences."[36] Sociologically, the ruling would have (1) placed a wedge between the institution of religion and the institution of law, i.e., weakened system integration, and/or (2) widened the social distance between religious conservatives and other groups, i.e., weakened social integration.[37]

4.2 Macrosociological Causes of the Content of State Law on Same-Sex Marriage

This chapter rests on the proposition that the content of law on society-important activities is generated by large-scale forces and conditions and that, as a result, the content of law is patterned, not random.[38] Under the proposition, a society is considered to be a system of interconnected institutions that exists apart from the individuals who populate the system at any given time, and the content of its law is assumed to be molded by macro-level agents that individuals do not control. Section 4.2 is devoted to a study aimed at unearthing the macrosociological agents that pushed some states to have law that barred same-sex marriage. In this study, all states, not just continental states, comprise the universe, because the social consequences of the change in law content on which I focus occurred fully half a century after the nation admitted its last states, viz., Alaska and Hawaii.[39] The substantial length of the interval minimizes the risk that Alaska and Hawaii were outliers that materially influenced the relationship between the macrosociological agents and the content of law.

---

[34] Samuel L. Perry, *Bible Beliefs, Conservative Religious Identity, and Same-Sex Marriage Support: Examining Main and Moderating Effects*, 54 J. SCI. STUDY OF RELIGION 792, 792–93, 798–801, 810 (2015).

[35] SAIL VOL. 1, *supra* note 6, at 38–40 & fig. 1.4; MARK CHAVES, AMERICAN RELIGION: CONTEMPORARY TRENDS 85–91 (2011).

[36] Emily Buss, *The Divisive Supreme Court*, 2017 SUP. CT. REV. 25, 25.

[37] For the distinction between the two forms of sociological integration, see David Lockwood, *Social Integration and System Integration*, *in* EXPLORATIONS IN SOCIAL CHANGE 244 (George K. Zollschan & Walter Hirsch eds., 1964).

[38] SAIL VOL. 1, *supra* note 6, at pt. 1.1.1.

[39] Alaska and Hawaii were made states in 1959. Proclamation No. 3269, 24 Fed. Reg. 81 (Jan. 6, 1959) (Alaska); Proclamation No. 3309, 24 Fed. Reg. 6868 (Aug. 25, 1959) (Hawaii).

4.2.1 Dependent Variable

Section 4.2 seeks to identify society-level forces and conditions that determined whether same-sex couples were prohibited or permitted by state law to marry as of June 26, 2015, the date on which the U.S. Supreme Court published its ruling in *Obergefell*.[40] In states that on this date had law banning same-sex marriage, *Obergefell* would logically have produced social stress, and the macro-level forces and conditions that gave rise to the law would have been responsible for the stress. As a result, the dependent variable was coded using the number 1 for states whose law at this time prohibited same-sex marriage and the number 0 for states whose law at this time did not prohibit same-sex marriage. Coding the dependent variable in the foregoing manner facilitates identification of sociological agents that increased, and sociological agents that decreased, the social stress caused by the ruling: When the Court in *Obergefell* held that law banning same-sex marriage violated the national Constitution and could not be enforced, the states that were coded 1—i.e., the states that forbade same-sex marriage—were pushed into accepting change in a society-significant arrangement, viz., marriage. This was, of course, change that the states having a prohibition on same-sex marriage did not want. In the states having such law, therefore, *Obergefell* would have generated social stress, and the macrosociological agents behind their law on same-sex marriage would be underlying causes of the stress.

The information employed to code the states on the dependent variable is mainly in the Appendix to the present chapter,[41] but for certain states, the information in the Appendix is supplemented in the discussion below. Sixteen states were coded 0: California, Connecticut, Delaware, Hawaii, Illinois, Maine, Maryland, Massachusetts, Minnesota, New Hampshire, New Jersey, New Mexico, New York, Rhode Island, Vermont, and Washington. The other thirty-four states were coded 1. Notably, during the year before *Obergefell* (i.e., during 2014), three-fifths or more of the residents in each of the sixteen states that were coded 0, i.e., that did not prohibit same-sex marriage, favored law that allowed same-sex couples to marry.[42]

---

[40] J. Sup. Ct. U.S., Oct. Term 2014, at 919.

[41] The information in the Appendix for each state was obtained using at least three of the following sources:

- The HeinOnline session laws library.
- The Statutes & Court Rules database in Westlaw Edge.
- The Statutes & Legislation database in Lexis Advance®.
- State statute codes and session laws on the websites of state legislatures.
- Obergefell v. Hodges, 135 S. Ct. 2584, 2611 (2015).
- Office of the Attorney General of Maryland, The State of Marriage Equality in America (April 2015).

[42] Andrew R. Flores & Scott Barclay, Williams Inst., *Trends in Public Support for Marriage for Same-Sex Couples by State* [3] fig. 1 (2015), *available at* https://williamsinstitute.law.ucla.edu/publications/pub-support-ss-marriage-by-state.

Let me turn to seven states for which the coding process was either not straightforward or may be open to question. The states were California, Hawaii, Massachusetts, New Jersey, New Mexico, Oregon, and Wisconsin. I explain below the reasons for coding each of them as I did. However, readers should keep in mind that my explanation for a state may be aided by the Appendix entry for the state.

- *California*. Since November 2008, the state constitution has contained a provision that denies same-sex marriages lawful status in California. In August 2010, the provision became unenforceable when a federal court held that the provision offended the Fourteenth Amendment to the national Constitution.[43] Of importance to the present study, however, is that the state legislature in 2014 passed a measure, which came into force on January 1, 2015, that permitted same-sex couples to marry in the state and that accepted same-sex marriages lawfully contracted outside the state.[44] Since the legislation was adopted after the provision in the state constitution, I regarded it as expressing the current electorate-anchored law of California on same-sex marriage. California, as a result, was coded 0 on the dependent variable, i.e., was designated a state that did not forbid same-sex marriage when the U.S. Supreme Court decided *Obergefell*.
- *Hawaii*. A provision in the state constitution allows the legislature to bar same-sex couples from marrying, but the provision was adopted in 1998. In 2013, state legislation was approved that permits same-sex marriage. Hawaii, consequently, was coded 0 on the dependent variable.
- *Massachusetts*. Although the state constitution was held in 2003 by the Supreme Judicial Court of the state (the highest Massachusetts state appellate court) to confer a right to marry on otherwise-qualified same-sex couples, the statutes of the state on the subject are somewhat opaque.[45] A pair of acts—Chapter 216 and Chapter 217—passed by the state legislature on July 31, 2008 evidence electorate-based acceptance of same-sex marriage. Chapter 216 dropped residence in another state as a bar to marrying in Massachusetts.[46] Since pursuant to the 2003 ruling of the Supreme Judicial Court, a Massachusetts resident was able before *Obergefell* to marry a person of the same sex in the state, Chapter 216 allowed nonresidents to marry a person of the same sex in Massachusetts. Chapter 217 made a spouse in a same-sex marriage eligible for health and dental services that a Massachusetts government program provided to low-income and disabled individuals.[47] Notably, Chapter 217 explicitly rejected a federal statute

[43] Perry v. Schwarzenegger, 704 F. Supp. 2d 921 (N.D. Cal. 2010), *aff'd sub. nom.* Perry v. Brown, 671 F.3d 1052 (9th Cir. 2012), *vacated on other grounds sub. nom.* Hollingsworth v. Perry, 570 U.S. 693 (2013).

[44] Ch. 82, 2013-2014 CAL. STAT. 1965.

[45] For a chronicle of political events pertaining to law on same-sex marriage in Massachusetts, see Anthony Michael Kreis, *Stages of Constitutional Grief: Democratic Constitutionalism and the Marriage Revolution*, 20 U. PA. J. CONST. L. 871, 915–22 (2018).

[46] Ch. 216, 2008 MASS. ACTS 1014.

[47] Ch. 217, 2008 MASS. ACTS 1014 (codified at MASS. ANN. LAWS ch. 118E, § 61 (LexisNexis 2020)).

under which the U.S. government defined marriage to include just opposite-sex couples.[48] Taken together, Chapter 216 and Chapter 217 signal electorate consent to same-sex marriage. Massachusetts, accordingly, was coded 0 on the dependent variable.

- *New Jersey*. A bill that was passed in 2012 by the New Jersey legislature ("the 2012 bill") would have defined marriage as "the legally recognized union of two consenting persons in a committed relationship"[49] and allowed same-sex couples to marry in the state. The 2012 bill did not become law, however, because the governor of the state did not approve it; instead, the governor returned the bill to the legislature,[50] which took no further action. The 2012 bill, which declared that it was intended "to end the pernicious practice of discrimination in civil marriage in New Jersey,"[51] constitutes the last formal position on same-sex marriage taken by the state legislature.

  A statute that had been adopted in New Jersey in December 2006 (and effective in February 2007) allowed same-sex couples to contract "civil unions," but not marriages, in the state.[52] Approximately a year-and-a-half after the state governor kept the 2012 bill from becoming law, a New Jersey Superior Court ruled that civil unions are not equivalent to marriage and that the state statute creating civil unions thus violated the equal protection guarantee of the state constitution.[53] Shortly thereafter, the Supreme Court of New Jersey agreed that the availability of civil unions but not marriage to same-sex couples was inconsistent with the state constitutional guarantee of equal protection and declined to stay the order that the Superior Court had issued to the state of New Jersey directing the state to grant marriage licenses to same-sex couples.[54]

  Because the 2012 bill is the last official statement of the New Jersey legislature on same-sex marriage, it was the principal (but not sole) basis for coding the state on the dependent variable. An additional factor was that the New Jersey legislature failed to act on multiple proposals for an amendment to the state constitution that would have confined marriage to opposite-sex couples[55] and on proposals

[48] 1 U.S.C. § 7 (2020).

[49] S. B. 1, 215th Leg., at 4 (N.J. 2012). The bill was introduced in January 2012 and passed both chambers of the state legislature in February 2012. The bill and its legislative history were retrieved from N.J. Office of Legislative Services, Bills 2012-2013, https://www.njleg.state.nj.us. The Bill Search utility on this website covers legislative sessions starting in 1996–1997.

[50] Gov. Chris Christie, Senate Bill 1 (conditional veto, received in the Senate on Feb. 21, 2012), retrieved from https://www.njleg.state.nj.us.

[51] S. B. 1, § 2*l*, 215th Leg., at 3 (N.J. 2012).

[52] Ch. 103, §§ 1 to 5, 96, 2006 N.J. Laws 975, 975–79, 1038.

[53] Garden State Equality v. Dow, 82 A.3d 336, 342, 367–68 (N.J. Super. Ct. Law Div. Sept. 27, 2013).

[54] Garden State Equality v. Dow, 79 A.3d 1036, 1042–44 (N.J. Oct. 18, 2013).

[55] *E.g.*, Assemb. Con. Res. No. 212, 211th Leg. (N.J. 2005); Assemb. Con. Res. No. 39, 215th Leg. (N.J. 2012).

calling for a comparable amendment to the national Constitution.[56] Its inaction on these proposals is evidence that the citizenry of the state was not hostile to legalizing same-sex marriage. Indeed, New Jersey was among the eight states in 2014 whose residents exhibited attitudinally the highest estimated level of support for law that permitted same-sex marriage and whose residents after 2004 experienced the greatest estimated increase in such support.[57] Given the foregoing, New Jersey was coded 0 on the dependent variable, i.e., was treated as a state whose electorate-approved law did not forbid same-sex marriage.

- *New Mexico*. While the law of New Mexico does not explicitly confine marriage to opposite-sex couples, state statutes imply that same-sex marriage is not allowed.[58] In December 2013, however, the Supreme Court of New Mexico ruled that the government of the state, by denying same-sex couples the right to marry, violated the equal protection guarantee of the state constitution.[59] Notably, during the decade-and-a-half prior to the New Mexico Supreme Court ruling, multiple bills and resolutions were introduced in the state legislature seeking to limit marriage to opposite-sex couples,[60] but none of these bills and resolutions was approved. That all of the bills failed to pass is an indicator that, well before *Obergefell*, same-sex marriage was accepted by the New Mexico electorate and, in turn, by their state legislators.[61] Consequently, New Mexico was treated as a state whose electorate-approved law did not prohibit same-sex marriage when the U.S. Supreme Court decided *Obergefell*, i.e., New Mexico was coded 0 on the dependent variable.
- *Oregon*. In November 2004, Oregon voters approved a proposal to add to the state constitution a provision that restricted marriage to opposite-sex couples.[62] Although the restriction was in the Oregon constitution when the U.S. Supreme Court decided *Obergefell* on June 26, 2015, it had been held by a federal court on

---

[56] Assemb. Res. No. 179, 211th Leg. (N.J. 2004); Assemb. Res. No. 102, 212th Leg. (N.J. 2006).

[57] Flores & Barclay, *supra* note 42, at [3] fig. 1, [5] fig. 2.

[58] Griego v. Oliver, 316 P.3d 865, 871, 876 (N.M. 2013).

[59] *Id.* at 865, 872, 877, 889. The Supreme Court of New Mexico in *Griego* was reviewing a decision by a trial court, which in September 2013 had concluded that state law, in disallowing same-sex marriage, was unenforceable under the provision of the state constitution that forbade discrimination on the basis of sex. Griego v. Oliver, 2013 WL 5768197 (Dist. Ct. N.M. 2013).

[60] *E.g.*, H.R. B. 640, 43rd Leg. (N.M. 1997) (proposing amendments to state statutes); H.R.J. Res. 4, 51st Leg. (N.M. 2013) (proposing an amendment to the state constitution). From the 43rd Legislature through the 51st Legislature, only the 46th Legislature had no such bill and/or resolution introduced.

Bills and resolutions from 1996 to the present are retrievable from: New Mexico Legislature, https://www.nmlegis.gov (under "Legislation" tab, select "Bill Finder") (last visited Oct. 3, 2022).

[61] Jeffrey R. Lax & Justin H. Phillips, *Gay Rights in the States: Public Opinion and Policy Responsiveness*, 103 Am. Pol. Sci. Rev. 367, 371–72, 374–75, 383 (2009) (finding, inter alia, that the content of state law on same-sex marriage is sensitive to and corresponds with public opinion within states regarding same-sex marriage).

[62] Or. Const. art. XV, § 5a (adopted by the electorate on Nov. 2, 2004) ("only a marriage between one man and one woman shall be valid or legally recognized as a marriage").

May 19, 2014 to be a violation of the equal protection guarantee of the Fourteenth Amendment to the national Constitution.[63] As a consequence of the May 2014 federal court ruling, a same-sex couple in Oregon could obtain a license to marry.

Because the restriction in the state constitution was unenforceable once it was deemed to be inconsistent with the Fourteenth Amendment, the state legislature was able, for approximately a year before *Obergefell*, to alter Oregon statutes on marriage and explicitly allow same-sex couples to marry. No such legislation, however, was passed. An act that replaced sex-specific words with sex-neutral words in existing Oregon state statutes pertinent to marriage was approved in 2015 and became effective in 2016,[64] but evidently because the invalidation in 2014 of the provision in the state constitution ended organized advocacy for further change in law containing sex-based criteria applicable to whether a couple is eligible to marry,[65] no legislation that explicitly permitted same-sex marriage in Oregon was adopted prior to the ruling in *Obergefell* on June 26, 2015.[66] Given the content of its constitution and statutes at the time of *Obergefell*, Oregon was deemed to be a state whose electorate-based law did not allow same-sex marriage and was thus coded 1 on the dependent variable.

- *Wisconsin*. Two events during the first decade of the twenty-first century indicate that electorate-anchored law in Wisconsin did not accept same-sex marriage when *Obergefell* was decided. The first event occurred in 2003: The Wisconsin legislature approved a bill that excluded same-sex couples from marrying.[67] Although the bill did not become law because the state governor vetoed it and the legislature was unable to override the veto,[68] the bill is evidence that public

[63] Geiger v. Kitzhaber, 994 F. Supp.2d 1128, 1133, 1147 (D. Or. 2014). The Attorney General of Oregon, in response to the plaintiffs' complaint, declined to defend the provision in the state constitution that barred same-sex marriage. Oregon Dep't of Justice, *Statement of Oregon Attorney General on Pending Litigation Challenging Same-Sex Marriage Ban*, Feb. 20, 2014, https://www.doj.state.or.us/media-home/news-media-releases/statement-of-oregon-attorney-general-ellen-rosenblum-on-the-subject-of-pending-litigation-challenging-same-sex-marriage-ban.

[64] Ch. 629, 2015 Or. Laws 1552 (eff. Jan. 1, 2016). The act, which had been House Bill 2478, was passed by the state Senate on June 16, 2015; the act was passed by the state House of Representatives on June 22, 2015, and was approved by the governor of Oregon on July 1, 2015. Oregon Legislature, Legislative Information, 2015 Regular Session, https://olis.oregonlegislature.gov/liz/2015R1/Measures/Overview/HB2478 (last visited Oct. 3, 2022). The act took effect on January 1, 2016. 2015 Or. Laws at 1580.

[65] Edith Honan, *After Gay Marriage Legalized in Oregon, Advocates Abandon Ballot Push*, Reuters, May 23, 2014, https://www.reuters.com/article/us-usa-gaymarriage-oregon/after-gay-marriage-legalized-in-oregon-advocates-abandon-ballot-push-idUSBREA4M0OH20140524 (last visited Oct. 3, 2022).

[66] In 2016, the Oregon legislature adopted an act that, inter alia, extended to spouses in a same-sex marriage the same law-created benefits and burdens as spouses in an opposite-sex marriage. Ch. 46, § 3, 2016 Or. Laws 2641, 2642 (eff. March 14, 2016) (codified at Or. Rev. Stat. Ann. § 106.345 (LexisNexis 2020)).

[67] Assembly Bill 475, 2003–2004 Leg. (Wis. 2003).

[68] The legislative history and text of Assembly Bill 475 are at: http://docs.legis.wisconsin.gov/2003/proposals/ab475 (last visited Oct. 3, 2022). In Wisconsin, a veto of a bill by the governor is

sentiment in Wisconsin was generally unfavorable to same-sex marriage. The second event occurred in 2006: Wisconsin voters amended the state constitution to prohibit not only same-sex marriage in the state but also any equivalent of same-sex marriage.[69] Although a federal court ruled eight years later that the prohibition was invalid under the Equal Protection Clause of the Fourteenth Amendment to the national Constitution,[70] thereby ending enforcement of the prohibition, electorate-grounded law in Wisconsin evidently disfavored same-sex marriage. The state, accordingly, was coded 1 on the dependent variable, i.e., was deemed a state that prohibited same-sex marriage.

My discussion of the dependent variable should not end without mentioning two prior studies that, like mine, sought to unearth the antecedents of U.S. state law on same-sex marriage.[71] In coding states on the dependent variable, the prior studies and I disagreed as to certain states in terms of the content of their law on same-sex marriage.[72] These disagreements—which may have yielded substantially dissimilar estimates of the relationship to the dependent variable of any independent variable that was included in all three studies—are partly due to the years included in each study. One study covered state law through calendar year 2000;[73] the other study covered state law through 2014.[74] My study covered state law until June 26, 2015, the day on which the U.S. Supreme Court announced its ruling in *Obergefell*.[75] The foregoing differences in time period and their impact on the coding of the dependent variable is illustrated by California. In the prior studies, California was deemed to prohibit same-sex marriage, but in my study, it was classified as permitting same-sex marriage. The reason for the divergence in coding is that California adopted legislation that permitted same-sex marriage beginning on January 1, 2015, which is after the time intervals used in the earlier studies but prior to *Obergefell*.[76]

Differences between the studies in the years that each covered, however, do not account for all of the between-study inconsistencies in coding the states on the

overridden if, subsequent to the veto, each chamber of the legislature again passes the bill and, in doing so, at least two-thirds of the members of each chamber vote in favor of the bill. Wis. Const. art V, § 10(2)(a).

[69]The text of the prohibition is reproduced in the Appendix entry for Wisconsin.

[70]Baskin v. Bogan, 766 F.3d 648 (7th Cir.), *cert. denied*, 574 U.S. 876 (2014).

[71]Sarah A. Soule, *Going to the Chapel? Same-Sex Marriage Bans in the United States, 1973-2000*, 51 Soc. Prob. 453 (2004); Giulia Mariani, *Religious Diversity and Party Control in the States: Explaining Adoptions of Same-Sex Marriage Laws*, 17 Sexuality Res. & Soc. Pol'y 119 (2020).

[72]*Compare* the Appendix to the present chapter and the discussion in the text regarding the eight states *with* Soule, *supra* note 71, at 457 tbl. 1, *and* Mariani, *supra* note 71, at 120 & tbl. 1, 122.

[73]Soule, *supra* note 71, at 457 tbl. 1, 463.

[74]Mariani, *supra* note 71, at 120 & tbl. 1, 122.

[75]J. Sup. Ct. U.S., Oct. Term 2014, at 919.

[76]The U.S. Supreme Court ruling in *Obergefell* is referenced by Mariani, *supra* note 71, at 120, 122, 126. However, the last year of the period covered by her study is 2014. *Id.* at 122. No explanation seems to have been furnished by her for omitting any change(s) in state law that occurred during the first half of 2015, i.e., during the months of 2015 that preceded the *Obergefell* ruling.

dependent variable. I focus here on just one of the two previous studies because the *Obergefell* ruling is mentioned in it. This research (the Mariani study) deemed ten states to have legislation that permitted same-sex marriage.[77] The study that I report in the present chapter concurs as to these ten states but includes six others, namely, California, Connecticut, Maine, Massachusetts, New Jersey, and New Mexico.[78] California was included for the reason given in the above discussion of that state; see also the entry for California in the Appendix. Connecticut and Maine were included because they had law that allowed same-sex marriage during the period that the Mariani study covered, viz., calendar years through 2014; the Mariani study was thus mistaken in treating Connecticut and Maine as not having such law.[79] The remaining states—Massachusetts, New Jersey and New Mexico—were considered by me but not by Dr. Mariani to be states that allowed same-sex marriage because we relied on different criteria in determining law content on same-sex marriage. The difference in criteria led to conflicting classifications of the three states on the dependent variable, i.e., Dr. Mariani designated the three states as not having law that permitted same-sex marriage while I designated the three states as having such law.[80]

4.2.2 Independent Variables

Pedagogically, the two studies that preceded mine offer a contrast to, and thereby illuminate, the theory that underlies my study and the independent variables that I chose. In particular, one of the prior studies emphasized political antecedents of law content while the other emphasized political and religious antecedents.[81] My study, on the other hand, does not look at either political or religious factors because it considers the content of law on society-significant social behavior to be a function of out-of-sight drivers of everyday social life. Political events, personalities, and processes are, in my approach, sociologically superficial; they are deemed to be manifestations of macro-level societal conditions and forces. Religious activities and teachings are treated by me as an aspect or product of culture, a phenomenon that

[77] Mariani, *supra* note 71, at 120 & tbl. 1, 122.

[78] For a list of all sixteen states, see the paragraph accompanying *supra* notes 41 & 42.

[79] See the entry for Connecticut in the Appendix to the instant chapter. Connecticut is omitted by Dr. Mariani from the list of states that she treated as having law that permitted same-sex marriage. Mariani, *supra* note 71, at 120 tbl. 1. I could not find in her article any explanation for why Connecticut was left off the list.

As to Maine, *compare* Mariani, *supra* note 71, at 122 n.2, *with* the entry for Maine in the Appendix to the present chapter.

[80] See the discussion of Massachusetts, New Jersey, and New Mexico in Sect. 4.2.1.

[81] Soule, *supra* note 71, at 458–62; Mariani, *supra* note 71, at 122–23. The political independent variables that were selected by Dr. Mariani led her to exclude one state (Nebraska) from her data. Mariani, *supra* note 71, at 122.

possesses multiple dimensions.[82] In short, I trace the political and the religious to other societal properties.[83] Given the sharp differences between my premises and those of prior investigators, I do not attempt to explain law content on key social matters in the ways that they do, and my study thus does not rely on their works for assistance in selecting independent variables.

Since law on marriage is the dependent variable here as it was in Chap. 2, the present study retains all but one of the independent variables that were used in Chap. 2.[84] Each independent variable that was used in both chapters is expected to have the relationship (positive or negative) to the dependent variable in this chapter that was posited for the dependent variable in Chap. 2. The independent variable that was employed in Chap. 2 but omitted here is societal fragmentation, which I replaced with an aspect of population structure (discussed below).[85] The data for all of the independent variables are for the year 1960, because the ideals that American society at that time had for marriage were traditional.[86] Ideals for marriage that are conventional do not accept same-sex marriage, of course, and if and where these ideals persist, they logically are a driver of law that forbids a male to marry a male and a female to marry a female. As can be seen in the Appendix, a half-dozen states adopted law barring same-sex marriage during the 1970s, but most of the thirty-four states that adopted such law did so during or after the 1990s. If the adopting states acted as they did because of any independent variable, the effect of the independent variable would be detectible using 1960 data on the independent variable.

To measure the *population structure* of each state, I employed the percentage of state residents in 1960 who lived in a "metropolitan area" in the state.[87] Conceptually, a metropolitan area is "an integrated economic and social unit with a recognized large population nucleus" of at least 50,000 people.[88] Sociologically, the percentage

---

[82] An attempt to identify some key dimensions of culture is made in SAIL VOL. 1, *supra* note 6, at 91–98.

[83] *Id.* at 5, 88–91, 121 nn.30, 31.

[84] See Sect. 2.3.1.2 in Chap. 2 for the rationales underlying the choice of these independent variables.

[85] SAIL VOL. 1, *supra* note 6, at 114–16.

[86] See Sect. 3.1.1 in *supra* Chap. 3.

[87] The data on metropolitan residence in 1960 were gathered in the 1960 decennial census and were included in U.S. BUREAU OF THE CENSUS, STATISTICAL ABSTRACT OF THE UNITED STATES: 1970, at 17 tbl. 16 (91st ed. 1970) [hereinafter STATISTICAL ABSTRACT 1970], *available at* https://www.census.gov/library/publications/time-series/statistical_abstracts.html.

[88] U.S. BUREAU OF THE BUDGET, STANDARD METROPOLITAN STATISTICAL AREAS: 1967, at vii ([1967]), *available at* https://catalog.hathitrust.org/Record/007123419.

Empirically, an area was "metropolitan" in the 1960 census when it included a city that had a minimum of 50,000 residents ("central city") *or* included two cities that shared a common boundary ("twin cities"). For an area to be metropolitan when it did not have a central city but had twin cities, one of the twin cities must have had a minimum of 15,000 residents and the other city must have had a sufficient number of residents to bring the combined population of the twin cities to a minimum of 50,000. The twin cities, furthermore, must have been "a single community" economically as well as socially. *Id.* at 1. The preceding empirical criteria for a U.S. metropolitan area were applicable of a state population that resides in a metropolitan area is an indicator of the extent of urbanism in the state. The instant study employs this percentage to test whether urbanism theory is correct in predicting that lower population density, i.e., less urbanism, raises the odds that jurisdictions will have law that prohibits same-sex marriage.[89] Urbanism theory, in other words, anticipates a negative relationship between the percentage of residents in a state who are in a metropolitan area and the odds that the state will have put in place law that keeps same-sex couples from marrying.

What does urbanism theory say that yields an expectation of this negative relationship? In broad terms, urbanism theory proposes that a populous setting differs sociologically, and not just demographically, from a sparsely settled setting. The sociological difference, according to urbanism theory, exists for several reasons.[90] First, a geographic location that has many people, relative to a geographic location that has few people, will have a larger number of distinct subgroups each of which is defined by one or more unconventional activities. In high-density locations, accordingly, unconventional behaviors are more frequent than in low-density locations. Second, a location in which many people are present, relative to a location in which few people are present, enables contacts between individuals who engage, or who are predisposed to engage, in the activity or activities characterizing a subgroup. These person-to-person contacts between similar individuals produce, in turn, an expansion of the subgroup. Third, high-density locations are more likely to involve interactions between the dominant group in a society and the subgroups in the society, allowing the latter to influence the former. Fourth, mounting population density in a location expands the number and variety of stimuli in the location. It does so partly because the individuals in a highly populated location are exposed to the more numerous and greater range of subgroups that exist there. Fifth, exposure to

---

except in New England. The criteria applied to New England were not identical to those used for other parts of the United States. *Id.* at 2.

[89]The earlier studies on causes of same-sex marriage included urbanization in several years as an independent variable and obtained the data for this variable from publications of the U.S. Census Bureau. Soule, *supra* note 71, at 465–66; Mariani, *supra* note 71, at 123. (Professor Soule cites the publication *Statistical Abstract of the United States* as the source of her data; Dr. Mariani does not cite a source.) Notably, the data that both appear to have used were for the percentage of the population in each state that resided in an *urban* area, not a metropolitan area. Under the criteria applied by the Census Bureau, an area that has 2500 inhabitants could be designated as "urban." Statistical Abstract 1970, *supra* note 87, at 2; U.S. Census Bureau, Statistical Abstract of the United States: 2000, at 4 (120th ed. 2000). As explained in *supra* note 88, a metropolitan area has a population much larger than 2500. Since the population necessary for urbanism to emerge undoubtedly exceeds 2500, the impact of urbanism on whether states by law forbid same-sex marriage may not be accurately ascertained using the share of state populations that is in an urban area. Ceteris paribus, research on this impact is preferably conducted using the share of state populations that is in a metropolitan area.

[90]Claude S. Fischer, *The Subcultural Theory of Urbanism: A Twentieth-Year Assessment*, 101 Am. J. Sociol. 543, 544–46 (1995); Georg Simmel, *The Metropolis and Mental Life*, *in* The Sociology of Georg Simmel 409 (ed. & trans. Kurt H. Wolff, 1950), *available at* https://archive.org/details/sociologyofgeorg030082mbp/page/n1/mode/2up (last visited Oct. 4, 2022).

a larger number and variety of stimuli in high-density locations undermines societal directives that seek to suppress socially distinct subgroups.[91] Growth in the number and density of human beings, in other words, increases skepticism of and resistance to teachings that hold back social innovation. To quote Georg Simmel, people in a metropolitan setting are subjected to "rapidly changing and closely compressed contrasting stimulations," which lead to "a heightened awareness and a predominance of intelligence"—put colloquially, a person in a metropolitan environment "reacts with his head instead of his heart."[92] As the concentration of human beings grows, people are thus more likely to question societal rules, more predisposed to subject these rules to critical analysis, and less inclined to rely on established assumptions, including stereotypes.[93]

Not surprisingly, urbanism theory has significant implications for the content of law on society-significant activities, including law on same-sex marriage. I discuss two of these implications here. First, the higher incidence of nontraditional social behaviors in densely populated environments supplies, by itself, an impetus for rejecting law that disapproves of such behaviors and for substituting law that approves of them.[94] Although the assumption is popular that the behavior of individuals is shaped by law, the assumption in metaphorical terms reverses the horse and the cart: In a structurally complex, democratically governed nation, law that addresses society-important social activities is, ceteris paribus, a response to rather than a cause of the frequency of the activities. The result is that, as the incidence of an unconventional social behavior rises, the institution of law becomes more disposed to accept the behavior.

Second, dense populations create a setting that produces resistance to law that endorses dominant social forms, thereby weakening law that attempts to prevent activities that deviate from these forms. Densely populated places, in other words, generate social philosophies that push people to decide for themselves whether to engage in particular activities, even nontraditional activities. Accordingly, social experimentation is more prevalent in geographic areas where people live closely together than in areas where they do not, and this experimentation is a headwind to law content that is seen as getting in the way of the experimentation. Since law arises from societal conditions and forces,[95] population growth raises the odds that

---

[91] In the United States, the cited proposition may be manifested in the greater prevalence of life dissatisfaction that occurs when population size and density increase. Adam Okulicz-Kozaryn & Joan Maya Mazelis, *Urbanism and Happiness: A Test of Wirth's Theory of Urban Life*, 55 Urb. Stud. 349, 352–53, 358–59 (2016) (finding that population size and density directly affect the extent of life dissatisfaction and operate separately from the impact on dissatisfaction of urban-related socio-economic problems).

[92] Simmel, *supra* note 90, at 410, 414.

[93] Larry D. Barnett, Societal Agents in Law: Quantitative Research 165 (2015) [hereinafter SAIL vol. 2].

[94] Explaining Law, *supra* note 32, at 16–17, 47–52.

[95] SAIL vol. 1, *supra* note 6, at ch. 2 pts. 2.3, 2.4.

law-based provisions aimed at deterring nontraditional activities will be slowly subverted and eventually abandoned.

Urbanism theory, in sum, is relevant to law content that tries to regulate society-significant social behaviors. Indeed, it is potentially of major import to this content. Notably, the theory and its application to law receive some backing from empirical research. Large population size has been found to be the principal determinant of law that prohibits discrimination against persons whose sexuality involves relationships with persons of the same sex, i.e., whose sexuality is out of line with prevailing social ideology.[96] Similarly, population density has been found to affect attitudes toward whether same-sex marriage should be lawful. As urbanism theory predicts, the inhabitants of metropolitan areas favor the legalization of same-sex marriage more often than the inhabitants of nonmetropolitan areas.[97]

Table 4.1 lists the variables that are included in my study and briefly describes the statistical indicator that I employed for each variable. Readers may find the table a helpful reference as they proceed through the data analysis in Sect. 4.2.3.

4.2.3 Data Analysis

I start with the summary statistics—the mean, standard deviation, and range—for the empirical indicator of each of the independent variables. The summary statistics are presented in Table 4.2 and aggregate all fifty U.S. states, which constitute the universe for the study.[98]

In reporting the results of the regression models that were used, I leave out the results for the full, five-variable model, i.e., the results obtained from regressing GAYMARR on the indicators of the five independent variables as a group. Although no state appeared to be an influential outlier under the five-variable model,[99] the indicators for three of the independent variables in this model had Variance Inflation

---

[96] Wald et al., *supra* note 18, at 1165 tbl. 2, 1168.

[97] Thomas C. Wilson, *Urbanism and Unconventionality: The Case of Sexual Behavior*, 76 Soc. Sci. Q. 346, 349, 356–57 & tbl. 3 (bottom panel) (1995).

[98] See the text accompanying *supra* note 39.

[99] SAIL vol. 2, *supra* note 93, at 16, 31 nn.55, 56. The largest Cook's Statistic for a state under the five-variable model was 0.99, but almost half the states had a Cook's Statistic in the range of 0.90 to 0.99. The state having the largest Cook's Statistic, accordingly, did not stand out.

In addition to computing Cook's Statistic, I used the LEASTLIKELY command in Stata as a further check on whether any state was an influential outlier under the five-variable model. *Id.* at 16, 31n.58. As discussed in *supra* Sect. 4.2.1, New Mexico was coded on the dependent variable as not banning same-sex marriage. The LEASTLIKELY command estimated that the probability that New Mexico would not ban same-sex marriage was very low, an outcome that led me to regress GAYMARR on the indicators of the five independent variables without New Mexico in the data. Excluding New Mexico yielded odds ratios for the indicators that were similar to those estimated when New Mexico was included. New Mexico, consequently, was deemed not to be an influential outlier.

Table 4.1 Variables and their empirical indicators

Variable	Mnemonic label	Empirical indicator (state-level measure)
Dependent variable		
Whether, as of June 26, 2015, state law proscribed same-sex marriage	GAYMARR	States whose law as of this date banned same-sex marriage were coded 1; states whose law as of this date did not ban same-sex marriage were coded 0.
Independent variables		
Culture	LABORFORCE	The rate of labor force participation in 1960 among women who were married, were living with their husband, and had a child of their own under the age of six. The rate covers females who were at least 14 years old in 1960 and is expressed as a percentage.
Cultural heterogeneity	FOREIGNBN	The percentage of persons in 1960 who had been born outside the United States and whose parents were not U.S. citizens.
Population structure	POPDENSITY	The percentage of residents in 1960 who lived in a metropolitan area.
Social disorder	DIVORCED	The percentage in 1960 of females aged 30–34 who had been married at least once and were currently unmarried because their (only or last) marriage ended in divorce.
Societal rationality	EDUCATION	The median number of years of education that had been completed as of 1960 by persons who were in the age range 25 and older in 1960.

Table 4.2 Summary statistics for the indicators of the independent variables[a]

Indicator	Mean	Standard deviation	Minimum, Maximum
LABORFORCE	20.2%	4.13 pct. pts.	12.5%, 32.1%
FOREIGNBN	4.2%	3.33 pct. pts.	0.4%, 13.6%
POPDENSITY	51.5%	26.64 pct. pts.	0.0%, 97.4%
DIVORCED	3.0%	0.94 pct. pts.	1.3%, 6.5%
EDUCATION	10.5 yrs.	1.09 yrs.	8.7 yrs., 12.2 yrs.

[a] "pct. pts." represents "percentage points"; "yrs." represents "years"

Factor ("VIF") scores evidencing excessive collinearity.[100] In addition, both the slope and standard error of the intercept in the five-variable model were very high, which suggested that the intercept suffered from an unacceptable degree of

[100] In the regression model that left out the intercept, the VIF scores of the three variables ranged from 15.7 to 34.3. A VIF score of 10.0 or above is a signal of inordinate collinearity. DAMODAR N. GUJARATI & DAWN C. PORTER, BASIC ECONOMETRICS 140 (5th ed. 2009). The procedures for computing the VIF scores are described in note 99 in *supra* Chap. 2.

collinearity.[101] Therefore, the models that I subsequently estimated had fewer independent variables and omitted the intercept.

Which among the five independent variables that I am considering should be retained in models for the sociological determinants of whether a state outlawed same-sex marriage? Culture is an especially promising determinant in light of the statistical results obtained in the prior two chapters, where culture (measured by LABORFORCE) was in the preferred regression model for predicting whether interracial marriage would be banned by a state and in the preferred regression model for predicting whether the Equal Rights Amendment would be opposed by a state. Notably, these models exhibited an excellent fit to the data even though they contained just two independent variables, giving rise to the possibility that a two-variable model for state law on same-sex marriage will fit the data as well as the preferred models in Chaps. 2 and 3. I explored this possibility by testing two-variable regression models consisting of culture and one of the other four independent variables. Two-variable pairs that excluded culture were studied, too, because every independent variable in Table 4.1 had a basis in theory for being considered a potential source of differences between states in law on same-sex marriage. Consequently, two-variable regression models were formed using all pairs of independent variables and estimated to ascertain how well each fit the data.

The regression of GAYMARR, the dependent variable, on the pairs of independent variables led to the two models—Model 1 and Model 2—whose results are reported in Table 4.3. Other two-variable models had a poorer fit to the data.[102] The two-variable models in Table 4.3 thus offer the most appealing explanations for the differences that existed between states in law on same-sex marriage.

From the odds ratios in the table, we see that, under Model 1, LABORFORCE and FOREIGNBN had opposing effects on whether a state would be coded 1 on GAYMARR. Specifically, a one percentage-point rise in LABORFORCE was associated with a 23.8 percent *increase* in the odds that a state had law prohibiting same-sex marriage while a one percentage-point rise in FOREIGNBN was associated with a 52.7 percent *decrease* in the odds that a state had law forbidding same-sex marriage. Model 1 produced no evidence of either excessive collinearity[103] or influential outliers.[104] Standardized

[101] DAVID W. HOSMER & STANLEY LEMESHOW, APPLIED LOGISTIC REGRESSION 140–41 (2d ed. 2000).

[102] I tested, and rejected, a three-variable model that consisted of the independent variables whose indicator odds ratios appear in Table 4.3, viz., culture (measured by LABORFORCE), cultural heterogeneity (measured by FOREIGNBN), and societal rationality (measured by EDUCATION). When GAYMARR was regressed on the indicators of the variables in this model (viz., LABORFORCE, FOREIGNBN, and EDUCATION), the odds ratio for each indicator was similar to the odds ratio for that indicator in Model 1 and in Model 2. Additionally, the accuracy rates of predictions made by the three-variable model as to where states would be on the dependent variable were identical to the accuracy rates of the predictions made by Model 2. The indicators for two of the three variables in the three-variable model, however, had VIF scores substantially exceeding 10.0.

[103] The VIF score for the indicators in Model 1 was 2.25.

[104] Under Model 1, Cook's Statistic did not exceed 0.38 for any state, and the odds ratios for LABORFORCE and FOREIGNBN did not materially change when I excluded the one state (New Mexico)

Table 4.3 Regression models for GAYMARR

	Model 1	Model 2
Odds ratio for		
LABORFORCE	1.238^{c}	–
FOREIGNBN	0.473^{c}	0.460^{c}
POPDENSITY	–	–
DIVORCED	–	–
EDUCATION	–	1.491^{c}
INTERCEPT	–	–
Number of states	50	50
Number of states wrongly predicted	7	6
Accuracy rate (%) for predictions of		
States coded 1	88.6	88.9
States coded 0	80.0	85.7
All states	86.0	88.0

Notes to table:
The superscript c denotes the .01 level of statistical significance, i.e., $c \leq .01$
– denotes that the variable/intercept was omitted

regression coefficients revealed that the influence exerted by FOREIGNBN on GAYMARR was much larger than the influence exerted by LABORFORCE on GAYMARR. To be precise, an increase of one standard deviation in LABORFORCE altered the odds of a state being coded 1 on the dependent variable by a factor of 2.411, while an increase of one standard deviation in FOREIGNBN altered the odds by a factor of 0.082. Since a factor change above 1.00 is compared to a factor change below 1.00 by taking the *inverse* of either the former or the latter,[105] we find that $1.00 \div 0.082 = 12.195$, which far surpasses the factor for LABORFORCE (i.e., 2.411).

We turn now to Model 2. In terms of their effects on the dependent variable, the Model 2 independent variables, like the Model 1 independent variables, worked in opposite directions: The odds that a state possessed law prohibiting same-sex marriage, i.e., was coded 1 on GAYMARR, fell by 54.0 percent when FOREIGNBN increased one percentage-point but rose by 49.1 percent when EDUCATION increased one year. An increment in EDUCATION promoted law against same-sex marriage presumably because an additional median year of schooling produced more societal rationality; greater societal rationality, in turn, would have diminished social support for, and hence imperiled, tradition; and the enhanced threat to tradition would have triggered a societal reaction manifested in law that backs traditional social forms such as opposite-sex marriage.

that had the lowest probability of being in the dependent-variable category where it was placed. The results for Model 1, consequently, did not appear to have been affected by an influential outlier.

105 J. SCOTT LONG & JEREMY FREESE, REGRESSION MODELS FOR CATEGORICAL DEPENDENT VARIABLES USING STATA 179 (2d ed. 2006).

The results for Model 2, like the results for Model 1, did not seem to have been affected by either excessive collinearity[106] or influential outliers.[107] Standardized regression coefficients disclosed that the odds that a state had law forbidding same-sex marriage changed by a factor of 0.075 when FOREIGNBN increased one standard deviation and changed by a factor of 1.544 when EDUCATION increased one standard deviation. The inverse of the former is $1.00 \div 0.075 = 13.33$, which materially exceeds the factor for EDUCATION (i.e., 1.544). Comparatively, then, FOREIGNBN had a much greater impact on GAYMARR than did EDUCATION.

With regard to how well the models performed when predicting the category of GAYMARR in which each state would fall, we do not find a large difference. (See the bottom four rows of Table 4.3.) As to the number of states wrongly predicted, Model 2 bettered Model 1 by one state. As to rates of correct forecasts, Model 2 has an advantage over Model 1 with regard to states that were expected not to ban same-sex marriage (i.e., states coded 0). However, the edge that Model 2 has over Model 1 is small and can be discounted if the two models diverge on another criterion and the other criterion supplies a credible, persuasive basis for preferring Model 1. Since FOREIGNBN (the indicator of cultural heterogeneity) was in both models, only LABORFORCE (the indicator of culture) and EDUCATION (the indicator of societal rationality) distinguish the models. Should Model 1 be selected because it includes LABORFORCE? Or is Model 2 more attractive due to its advantage in predicting states coded 0?

Unfortunately, the choice between the models is not easily made, but I am inclined toward Model 1 because theory in the macrosociology of law content will be simpler if Model 1 instead of Model 2 is used. At least one of the independent variables in Model 1 (culture and cultural heterogeneity) was in the preferred models in the two preceding chapters.[108] Societal rationality (measured by EDUCATION), on the other hand, was not in these models. Given that societal rationality was absent from Model 1, any theory built on the findings in this and the preceding two chapters will be less complex with the use of Model 1 than with the use of Model 2. However, readers may well have a different reason for choosing between the models and for that reason may favor Model 2.

Let me now present visualizations of the relationships between the independent variables and the dependent variable. The visualizations offer answers to the question: Across the range of numerical values for the indicator of each independent variable, what are the probabilities that, when the U.S. Supreme Court announced its ruling in *Obergefell* (June 26, 2015), a state possessed law that banned same-sex marriage? I present the estimated probabilities under Model 1 as well as the

[106]The VIF score for the indicators in Model 2 was 2.87.

[107]Under Model 2, the Cook's Statistic for each state 0.47 or lower. New Mexico had the largest Cook's Statistic and the lowest probability of being coded as it was on the dependent variable. However, the exclusion of New Mexico from the data produced odds ratios for FOREIGNBN and EDUCATION that were very similar to the odds ratios for all fifty states under Model 2. New Mexico, therefore, did not appear to be, and was not treated as, an influential outlier under Model 2.

[108]In *supra* Chap. 2, see Model 2A in Table 2.3. In *supra* Chap. 3, see Model 2B in Table 3.4.

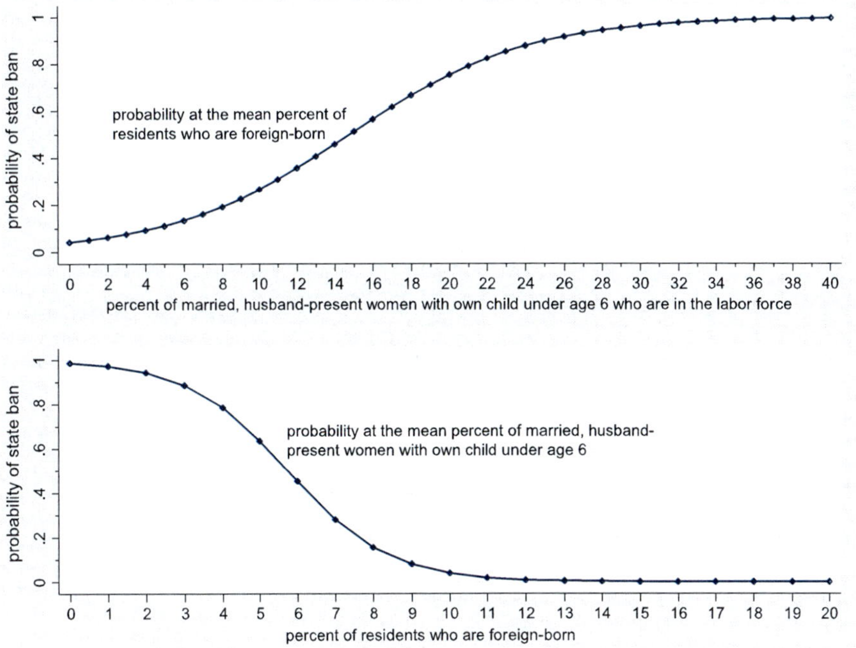

Fig. 4.2 Probability of a state ban on same-sex marriage: predictions by Model 1

estimated probabilities under Model 2 so that readers are able to consider both models. The estimated probabilities for Model 1 are in the pair of graphs in Fig. 4.2; the estimated probabilities for Model 2 are in the pair of graphs in Fig. 4.3. For each model, the pair of graphs lay out the probabilities predicted by one of the empirical indicators used in the model when the other empirical indicator in the model is held at its mean.[109] In the graphs, the vertical axis covers probabilities from 0 to 1.0, and the horizontal axis shows numerical values of the indicator that is the source of the probabilities. As the figures show, the gradient of the probabilities is sharpest for FOREIGNBN (the indicator of cultural heterogeneity) under both Model 1 and Model 2.

What do the graphs in Figs. 4.2 and 4.3 tell us about when states are likely to have law that forbids same-sex marriage and when states are not likely to have such law? The "when" represents, in essence, the expected points of thresholds for the presence/absence of a ban on same-sex marriage. Since we are dealing with four graphs covering two sets of independent variables, the visualizations in the two figures turnish much more information than the visualizations in the prior chapters. To make

[109] See Table 4.2 for the mean of each indicator. Since the indicator of EDUCATION was the median number of years of schooling that had been finished by persons who were 25 years of age or older, the mean of EDUCATION in Table 4.2 is the mean of the minimum and maximum of EDUCATION.

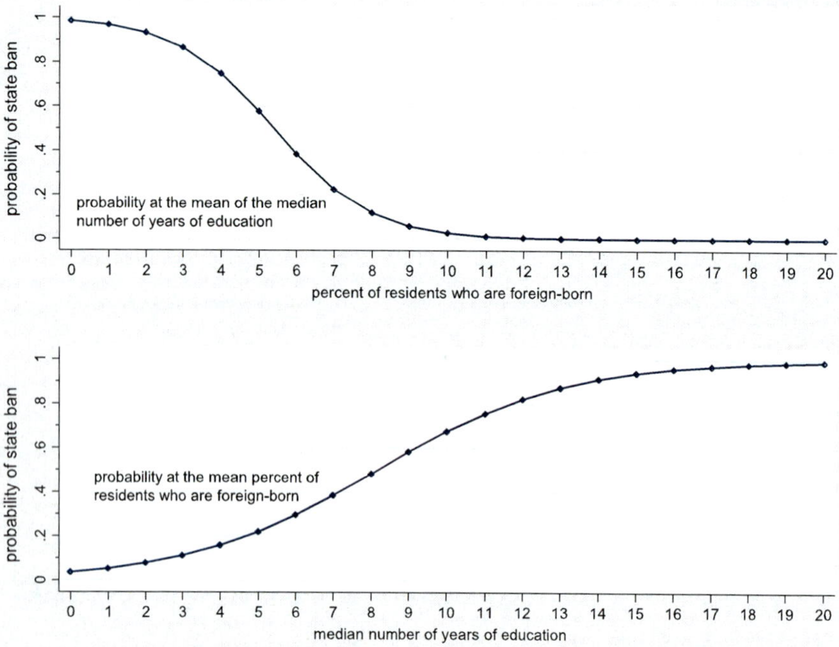

Fig. 4.3 Probability of a state ban on same-sex marriage: predictions by Model 2

Table 4.4 Model 1 and Model 2 probabilities of a state ban on same-sex marriage at selected numerical values of each indicator in the models

Indicator at selected numerical values	Probabilities under Model 1[a]	Indicator at selected numerical values	Probabilities under Model 2[a]
LABORFORCE		EDUCATION	
15 percent	0.51	9 years[b]	0.58
25 percent	0.90	14 years[b]	0.91
FOREIGNBN		FOREIGNBN	
6 percent	0.45	6 percent	0.39
9 percent	0.08	9 percent	0.06

[a] Probabilities for the indicator of each independent variable in a model when the indicator of the other independent variable in the model is kept at its mean
[b] Median years of education completed

the information easier to understand, I have summarized, in Table 4.4, key points in the graphs.

I begin with Model 1. Since an increase in LABORFORCE raised the odds that a state prohibited same-sex marriage, I focus on the numerical values of LABORFORCE above which (with FOREIGNBN at its mean) the probability of a state being coded 1 on GAYMARR exceeded 50.0 percent. This probability—i.e., the probability at which state law against same-sex marriage had a greater-than-even chance of existing was reached when LABORFORCE was 15 percent. The probability was then 0.51. An additional ten percentage-points of LABORFORCE (i.e., LABORFORCE at 25 percent) moved the probability of a state being coded 1 on GAYMARR up to 0.90.

Let us turn to FOREIGNBN (with LABORFORCE at its mean). Since an increase in FOREIGNBN lowered the odds that a state banned same-sex marriage, I focus on the numerical values of FOREIGNBN above which a state had a less-than-even chance of outlawing same-sex marriage. When FOREIGNBN was six percent, the probability that a state would be coded 1 on GAYMARR was 0.45, and when FOREIGNBN was nine percent, the probability fell to just 0.08.

Under Model 2, the odds that a state banned same-sex marriage was raised by EDUCATION and lowered by FOREIGNBN. Consequently, I focus on numerical values of the former at which the probability of a ban was over 0.50 and on numerical values of the latter at which the probability of a ban was under 0.50. As seen in Table 4.4, the chance of a ban on same-sex marriage rose above even when the population of a state had nine median years of completed schooling and fell below even when the foreign-born share of the state population was six percent.

4.3 Conclusion

This chapter stems from the June 2015 ruling by the U.S. Supreme Court that two guarantees of the federal Constitution—the equal protection guarantee and the due process guarantee—are breached by law that prohibits marriage between two people who would be legally qualified to marry if they were not of the same biological sex. The premise of the chapter is that the ruling, by upending the traditional family form, caused social stress in the thirty-four states that had such law when the ruling was announced. If so, the agents that raised and the agents that lowered the likelihood of experiencing this stress are the state-level sociological forces and conditions that affected the odds that a state banned same-sex marriage. For more than eight-five percent of U.S. states, two sets of explanatory variables were able to predict whether, at the time of the ruling, state law forbid same-sex marriage. One set (i.e., model) consisted of culture and cultural heterogeneity; the other set (model) consisted of societal rationality and cultural heterogeneity. While greater cultural heterogeneity in a state (measured by the foreign-born share of the state population) reduced the odds that the state prohibited same-sex marriage and hence experienced the Court-induced social stress, greater deviation from the family form that has been ensconced in American culture (measured by the labor-force participation rate of husband-present married mothers of young children) increased the odds of a state bar to same-sex marriage and thus of the Court-induced social stress. A strengthening of societal rationality (measured by the median number of years of schooling completed) moved a state in the same direction as a departure from tradition in culture. In each model, however, cultural heterogeneity had a measurably larger impact on the presence/absence of such law than the other explanatory variable in the model.

The evidence from Sect. 4.2 underscores the strong relationship that exists generally between the sociological attributes of a society and the content of its law on society-important social activities. But how did the attributes work with respect to law on same-sex marriage? What did the attributes do to influence the formulation of law pertaining to same-sex marriage? Cultural heterogeneity was in both models, and I therefore start with it. A society having more subcultures (i.e., a society in which foreign-born persons are a larger share of the population) contains a wider range of world views, and the more numerous world views warm the society to viewpoints besides those its traditions presently embody. Since a culturally rich society, in order to protect social cohesiveness, necessarily accommodates alternatives to its conventional beliefs, including conventional beliefs regarding marriage and the family, a culturally diverse society is, ceteris paribus, more receptive to law that allows same-sex couples to marry. Unsurprisingly, then, a larger number of subcultures lowers the inclination of a society to have law limiting marriage to opposite-sex couples, and an inverse relationship exists between cultural heterogeneity and the presence of law that forbids same-sex marriage. More cultural heterogeneity, in turn, meant a reduced potential for social stress when the U.S. Supreme Court ruled that law against same-sex marriage was unconstitutional.

In terms of culture as an explanatory variable, the erosion of the culturally backed family form is logically a threat to all aspects of tradition in marriage, including the tradition of opposite-sex marriage. Thus, a weakening of culture as measured in Sect. 4.2 had a positive relationship to (i.e., promoted) the presence of state law banning same-sex marriage. Less adherence to the traditional family form, in turn, would have been responsible for social stress when the U.S. Supreme Court held that the Constitution disallowed law that aimed to safeguard tradition by keeping two persons of the same sex from marrying one another.

The third independent variable—societal rationality—also exhibited a positive relationship to the dependent variable, i.e., fostered state prohibitions of same-sex marriage. A positive relationship between societal rationality and the presence of a ban on same-sex marriage is entirely plausible because more rationality in a society increases social scrutiny of societal traditions, including the tradition of opposite-sex marriage, and raises questions about the desirability of these traditions. Greater societal rationality would therefore be socially destabilizing. To defend itself against this destabilization, a societal system will logically react by, inter alia, adopting and retaining law that prohibits same-sex marriage. When the U.S. Supreme Court ruled that law against same-sex marriage violated the Constitution, the social stress from the ruling would, of course, be due partly to the societal rationality that was responsible for the adoption of the invalidated law.

To conclude this chapter, I return to and clarify the proposition, discussed in Sect. 1.6 of *supra* Chap. 1, that the frequency of a society-significant social activity such as marriage is not in the long run a material function of law directed at these activities. I maintain that the proposition is correct for same-sex marriage in the United States even though government counts of such marriages would typically be affected by whether law allows same-sex couples to marry.[110] The proposition is defensible as it applies to same-sex marriage because same-sex marriages are a statistical rarity in American society.[111] Law that prohibited same-sex marriage did not, therefore, substantially alter the overall pattern of American marriage. Further support for the proposition is the finding that the rate at which opposite-sex marriages occur in the United States has not been affected by state law that allows a same-sex marriage or a same-sex civil union.[112] Same-sex sexuality outside of marriage would also not have been appreciably affected by law, because law that criminalized same-sex sexual acts was unenforced when these acts took place in a private setting,[113] as they undoubtedly almost always did. In brief, then, the content of law on same-sex relationships, like the content of law on any other society-important form of social behavior, is not a mechanism that controls how often individuals engage in a core behavior. A proscription or prescription of law addressed to a key social activity is, rather, a symbol of societal values and an adhesive that bonds individuals to their society.

Appendix. State Law on the Sex Composition of Couples Allowed to Marry: June 26, 2015

State	Law
Alabama	" . . . . (b) Marriage is inherently a unique relationship between a man and a woman. . . . A marriage contracted between individuals of the same sex is invalid in this state. (c) Marriage is a sacred covenant, solemnized between a man and a woman . . . . (d) No marriage license shall be issued in the State of Alabama to parties of the same sex. (e) The State of Alabama shall not recognize as valid any marriage of parties of the same sex that occurred or was alleged to have occurred as a result of the law

(continued)

[110] In Sweden, the government-recorded incidence of same-sex marriage was not affected by legislation that permitted formal same-sex marriage. However, the legislation was preceded by law, adopted about a decade-and-a-half earlier, that allowed same-sex "registered partnerships" and that was subsequently amended so that the rights of these partnerships were equivalent to the rights of same-sex marriage before the same-sex marriage legislation was adopted. Martin Kolk & Gunnar Andersson, *Two Decades of Same-Sex Marriage in Sweden: A Demographic Account of Developments in Marriage, Childbearing, and Divorce*, 57 DEMOGRAPHY 147, 149, 151–52, 155–56, 165–66 (2020).

[111] See the text accompanying *supra* note 14.

[112] Alexis Dinno & Chelsea Whitney, *Same-Sex Marriage and the Perceived Assault on Opposite-Sex Marriage*, PLOS ONE, June 11, 2013, https://journals.plos.org/plosone/article?id=10.1371/journal.pone.0065730.

[113] Susan Ayres, *Coming Out: Decision-Making in State and Federal Sodomy Cases*, 62 ALB. L. REV. 355, 362 (1998); Lawrence v. Texas, 539 U.S. 558, 569 (2003).

State	Law
	of any jurisdiction regardless of whether a marriage license was issued. . . ." ALA. CONST., art. 1, § 36.03 (2020) (approved by the electorate, and declared ratified, in June 2006). Provisions identical to sections (b), (c), (d), and (e) above are in Act No. 98-500, § 2, 1998 Ala. Laws 1077 (codified at ALA. CODE § 30-1-19 (LexisNexis 2020)).
Alaska	"(a) Marriage is a civil contract entered into by one man and one woman that requires both a license and solemnization. . . ." Ch. 21, § 1, 1996 Alaska Sess. Laws 1 (eff. May 7, 1996) (codified at ALASKA STAT. § 25.05.011 (2020)).
	"(a) A marriage entered into by persons of the same sex, either under common law or under statute, that is recognized by another state or foreign jurisdiction is void in this state . . . . (b) A same-sex relationship may not be recognized by the state as being entitled to the benefits of marriage." Ch. 21, § 2, 1996 Alaska Sess. Laws 1 (eff. May 7, 1996) (codified at Alaska Stat. § 25.05.013 (2020)).
Arizona	"Only a union of one man and one woman shall be valid or recognized as a marriage in this state." ARIZ. CONST. art. 30, § 1 (2019) (eff. Dec. 16, 2008).
	"Marriage between persons of the same sex is void and prohibited." Ch. 348, § 1, 1996 Ariz. Sess. Laws 1839 (codified at ARIZ. REV. STAT. § 25-101(C) (LexisNexis 2020)).
	"A. Marriages valid by the laws of the place where contracted are valid in this state, except marriages that are void and prohibited by section 25-101. . . . C. Parties residing in this state may not evade the laws of this state relating to marriage by going to another state or country for solemnization of the marriage." Ch. 348, § 2, 1996 Ariz. Sess. Laws 1839 (codified at ARIZ. REV. STAT. § 25-112 (LexisNexis 2020)).
Arkansas	"Marriage consists only of the union of one man and one woman." ARK. CONST. amend. 83, § 1 (2020) (eff. Dec. 2, 2004).
	"(a) All marriages contracted outside this state that would be valid by the laws of the state or country in which the marriages were consummated and in which the parties then actually resided shall be valid in all the courts in this state. (b) This section shall not apply to a marriage between persons of the same sex." Act 144, 1997 Ark. Acts 825, § 2 (codified at ARK. CODE ANN. § 9-11-107 (2020)).
	"Marriage shall be only between a man and a woman. A marriage between persons of the same sex is void." Act 144, 1997 Ark. Acts 825, § 1 (codified at ARK. CODE ANN. § 9-11-109 (2020)).
California	"Only marriage between a man and a woman is valid or recognized in California." CAL. CONST. art. I, § 7.5 (Deering 2020) (eff. Nov. 5, 2008).
	"The Legislature finds and declares that the purpose of this act is to clarify that all laws relating to marriage and the rights and responsibilities of spouses apply equally to opposite-sex and same-sex spouses." Ch. 82, § 1, 2013-2014 CAL. STAT. 1965, 1966 (reproduced as note to CAL. FAM. CODE § 300 (Deering 2020)). Chapter 82, which took effect on January 1, 2015, repealed the following statute: "Only marriage between a man and a woman is valid or recognized in California." Prop. 22, § 2, 2000 CAL. STAT. A-302 (initiative statute approved by the electorate on March 7, 2000) (codified at CAL. FAM. CODE § 308.5) (repealed eff. Jan. 1, 2015, Ch. 82, § 7, 2013-2014 CAL. STAT. 1965, 1967 (eff. Jan. 1, 2015)).

(continued)

State	Law
	"Marriage is a personal relation arising out of a civil contract between two persons . . . ." Ch. 82, § 2, 2013-2014 CAL. STAT. 1965, 1966 (codified at CAL. FAM. CODE § 300(a) (Deering 2020)) (eff. Jan. 1, 2015)).
	"A marriage contracted outside this state that would be valid by laws of the jurisdiction in which the marriage was contracted is valid in this state." Ch. 82, § 6, 2013-2014 CAL. STAT. 1965, 1967 (codified at CAL. FAM. CODE § 308 (Deering 2020)) (eff. Jan. 1, 2015)).
	See the discussion of California in *supra* Sect. 4.2.1.
Colorado	"Only a union of one man and one woman shall be valid or recognized as a marriage in this state." COLO. CONST. art. II, § 31 (2019) (eff. Dec. 31, 2006).
	"(1) . . . a marriage is valid in this state if . . . (b) It is only between one man and one woman. (2) . . . any marriage contracted within or outside this state that does not satisfy paragraph (b) of subsection (1) of this section shall not be recognized as valid in this state. . . ." Ch. 233, § 1, 2000 COLO. SESS. LAWS 1054 (eff. May 26, 2000) (codified at COLO. REV. STAT. § 14-2-104 (2020)).
Connecticut	"Marriage means a legal union of two persons." Pub. Act No. 09-13, § 3, 2009 CONN. ACTS 78, 79 (Reg. Sess.) (eff. April 23, 2009) (codified at CONN. GEN. STAT. § 46b-20(4) (2020)). Pub. Act No. 09-13 was titled "An Act Implementing the Guarantee of Equal Protection under the Constitution of the State for Same Sex Couples."
	"Wherever in the general statutes or the public acts the term 'husband', 'wife', 'groom', 'bride', 'widower' or 'widow' is used, such term shall be deemed to include one party to a marriage between two persons of the same sex." Pub. Act No. 09-13, § 8, 2009 CONN. ACTS 78, 80 (Reg. Sess.) (eff. April 23, 2009) (codified at CONN. GEN. STAT. § 1-1m (2020)).
	"A marriage, or a relationship that provides substantially the same rights, benefits and responsibilities as a marriage, between two persons entered into in another state or jurisdiction and recognized as valid by such other state or jurisdiction shall be recognized as a valid marriage in this state, provided such marriage or relationship is not expressly prohibited by statute in this state." Pub. Act No. 09-13, § 1, 2009 CONN. ACTS 78, 78 (Reg. Sess.) (eff. April 23, 2009) (codified at CONN. GEN. STAT. § 46b-28a (2020)).
Delaware	"(a) All laws of this State applicable to marriage or married spouses or the children of married spouses, whether derived from statutes, administrative rules or regulations, court rules, governmental policies, common law, court decisions, or any other provisions or sources of law, including in equity, shall apply equally to same-gender and different-gender married couples and their children. . . ." Ch. 19, § 4, 79 DEL. LAWS 1, 3 (2013) (eff. July 1, 2013) (codified at DEL. CODE ANN. tit. 13, § 129(a) (2020). Chapter 19 is intended to "allow[] two persons to marry regardless of their genders, [and] to recognize same-gender marriages and substantially similar legal unions solemnized outside of Delaware as marriages . . . ." Ch. 19, pmbl., 79 DEL. LAWS 1 (2013).
Florida	"Inasmuch as marriage is the legal union of only one man and one woman as husband and wife, no other legal union that is treated as marriage or the substantial equivalent thereof shall be valid or recognized." FLA. CONST. art. I, § 27 (2019) (adopted 2008).

(continued)

State	Law
	"(1) Marriages between persons of the same sex entered into in any jurisdiction, whether within or outside the State of Florida, the United States, or any other jurisdiction, either domestic or foreign, or any other place or location, or relationships between persons of the same sex which are treated as marriages in any jurisdiction, whether within or outside the State of Florida, the United States, or any other jurisdiction, either domestic or foreign, or any other place or location, are not recognized for any purpose in this state. . . ." Ch. 97-268, § 1, 1997 FLA. LAWS 4957 (eff. June 5, 1997) (codified at FLA. STAT. § 741.212 (2020)).
Georgia	"(a) This state shall recognize as marriage only the union of man and woman. Marriages between persons of the same sex are prohibited in this state. (b) No union between persons of the same sex shall be recognized by this state as entitled to the benefits of marriage. This state shall not give effect to any public act, record, or judicial proceeding of any other state or jurisdiction respecting a relationship between persons of the same sex that is treated as a marriage under the laws of such other state or jurisdiction. . . . ." GA. CONST. art. I, § IV, ¶ I (approved by the electorate on Nov. 2, 2004).
	"(a) It is declared to be the public policy of this state to recognize the union only of man and woman. Marriages between persons of the same sex are prohibited in this state. (b) No marriage between persons of the same sex shall be recognized as entitled to the benefits of marriage. Any marriage entered into by persons of the same sex pursuant to a marriage license issued by another state or foreign jurisdiction or otherwise shall be void in this state. . . ." Act No. 755, 1996 GA. LAWS 624, § 1 (eff. July 1, 1996) (codified at GA. CODE ANN. § 19-3-3.1 (2020)).
Hawaii	"The legislature shall have the power to reserve marriage to opposite-sex couples." HAW. CONST. art. I, § 23 (approved Nov. 3, 1998).
	". . . [T]he marriage contract . . . shall be permitted between two individuals without regard to gender . . . ." Act 1, § 3, 2013 HAW. SESS. LAWS 1, 3 (2d Spec. Sess.) (eff. Dec. 2, 2013) (codified at HAW. REV. STAT. § 572-1 (2020)). Act 1 was intended to "recognize marriages between individuals of the same sex in the State of Hawaii." Act 1, §§ 1, 16, 2013 HAW. SESS. LAWS 1, 2, 8 (2d Spec. Sess.).
	See the discussion of Hawaii in *supra* Sect. 4.2.1.
Idaho	"A marriage between a man and a woman is the only domestic legal union that shall be valid or recognized in this state." IDAHO CONST. art. III, § 28 (approved by the electorate on Nov. 7, 2006).
	"(1) Marriage is a personal relation arising out of a civil contract between a man and a woman . . . ." Ch. 104, § 3, 1995 IDAHO SESS. LAWS 334 (eff. Jan. 1, 1996) (codified at IDAHO CODE ANN. § 32-201 (2020)).
	"All marriages contracted without this state, which would be valid by the laws of the state or country in which the same were contracted, are valid in this state, unless they violate the public policy of this state. Marriages that violate the public policy of this state include, but are not limited to, same-sex marriages . . . ." Ch. 331, § 1, 1996 IDAHO SESS. LAWS 1126 (eff. March 18, 1996) (codified at IDAHO CODE ANN. § 32-209 (2020)).
Illinois	"(a) All laws of this State applicable to marriage, whether they derive from statute, administrative or court rule, policy, common law, or any other source of civil or criminal law, shall apply equally to marriages of same-sex and different-sex couples and their children.

(continued)

State	Law
	(b) Parties to a marriage and their children, regardless of whether the marriage consists of a same-sex or different-sex couple, shall have all the same benefits, protections, and responsibilities under law, whether they derive from statute, administrative or court rule, policy, common law, or any other source of civil or criminal law. ..." Pub. Act 98-597, § 10, 2013 ILL. LAWS 7141, 7142 (eff. June 1, 2014) (codified at 750 ILL. COMP. STAT. ANN. § 80/10 (2020)).
	"... A marriage, whether of the same sex or different sexes and providing that it is not a common law marriage, legally entered into in another jurisdiction, shall be recognized in this State as a marriage ...." Pub. Act 98-597, § 60, 2013 ILL. LAWS 7141, 7145 (eff. June 1, 2014) (codified at 750 ILL. COMP. STAT. ANN. § 75/60 (2020)).
Indiana	"(a) Only a female may marry a male. Only a male may marry a female. (b) A marriage between persons of the same gender is void in Indiana even if the marriage is lawful in the place where it is solemnized." Pub. L. 198-1997, § 1, 1997 IND. ACTS 2897 (eff. May 13, 1997) (codified at IND. CODE § 31-11-1-1 (2020)).
Iowa	"1. Only a marriage between a male and a female is valid." Ch. 1099, § 1, 1998 IOWA ACTS 182 (eff. July 1, 1998) (codified at IOWA CODE § 595.2 (2020)).
	"A marriage which is solemnized in any other state, territory, country, or any foreign jurisdiction which is valid in that state, territory, country, or other foreign jurisdiction, is valid in this state if the parties meet the requirements for validity pursuant to section 595.2, subsection 1, and if the marriage would not otherwise be declared void." Ch. 1099, § 3, 1998 IOWA ACTS 182, 183 (eff. July 1, 1998) (codified at IOWA CODE § 595.20 (2020)).
Kansas	"... Marriage shall be constituted by one man and one woman only. All other marriages are declared to be contrary to the public policy of this state and are void." KAN. CONST. art. 15, § 16(a). Ch. 211, 2005 KAN. SESS. LAWS 1560; approved by the electorate on April 5, 2005.
	"The marriage contract is to be considered in law as a civil contract between two parties who are of opposite sex. All other marriages are declared to be contrary to the public policy of this state and are void. ..." Ch. 26, § 1, 2011 KAN. SESS. LAWS 95 (eff. July 1, 2011) (codified at KAN. STAT. ANN. § 23-2501 (2020)).
	"... It is the strong public policy of this state only to recognize as valid marriages from other states that are between a man and a woman." Ch. 142, § 3, 1996 KAN. SESS. LAWS 438, 440 (codified at KAN. STAT. ANN. § 23-2508 (2020)).
Kentucky	"Only a marriage between one man and one woman shall be valid or recognized as a marriage in Kentucky. ..." KY. CONST. § 233a (ratified Nov. 2, 2004).
	"As used and recognized in the law of the Commonwealth, 'marriage' refers only to the civil status, condition, or relation of one (1) man and one (1) woman united in law for life, for the discharge to each other and the community of the duties legally incumbent upon those whose association is founded on the distinction of sex." Ch. 258, § 4, 1998 KY. ACTS 984 (eff. July 15, 1998) (codified at KY. REV. STAT. § 402.005 (LexisNexis 2020)).
	"(1) Marriage is prohibited and void: ... (d) Between members of the same sex; ..." Ch. 258, § 2(1), 1998 KY. ACTS 984 (eff. July 15, 1998) (codified at KY. REV. STAT. § 402.020(1) (LexisNexis 2020)).

(continued)

State	Law
	"(1) If any resident of this state marries in another state, the marriage shall be valid here if valid in the state where solemnized, unless the marriage is against Kentucky public policy. (2) A marriage between members of the same sex is against Kentucky public policy and shall be subject to the prohibitions established in KRS 402.045." Ch. 258, § 3, 1998 KY. ACTS 984 (eff. July 15, 1998) (codified at KY. REV. STAT. § 402.040 (LexisNexis 2020)).
	"A marriage between members of the same sex which occurs in another jurisdiction shall be void in Kentucky." Ch. 258, § 1(1), 1998 KY. ACTS 984 (eff. July 15, 1998) (codified at KY. REV. STAT. § 402.045(1) (LexisNexis 2020)).
Louisiana	"Marriage in the state of Louisiana shall consist only of the union of one man and one woman. . . . No official or court of the state of Louisiana shall recognize any marriage contracted in any other jurisdiction which is not the union of one man and one woman." LA. CONST. art. 12, § 15. Article 12, section 15 was approved by the electorate on Sept. 18, 2004. Act. No. 926, 2004 LA. ACTS 2933.
	"Marriage is a legal relationship between a man and a woman that is created by civil contract. . . ." Act. No. 886, § 1, 1987 LA. ACTS 2409, 2410 (eff. Jan. 1, 1988) (codified at LA. CIV. CODE ANN. art. 86 (2020)).
	"Persons of the same sex may not contract marriage with each other. . . ." Act. No. 886, § 1, 1987 LA. ACTS 2409, 2413 (eff. Jan. 1, 1988) (codified at LA. CIV. CODE ANN. art. 89 (2020)).
	"A purported marriage between persons of the same sex violates a strong public policy of the state of Louisiana and such a marriage contracted in another state shall not be recognized in this state for any purpose . . . ." Act. No. 890, 1999 LA. ACTS 2503, 2504 (eff. Aug. 1, 1999) (codified at LA. CIV. CODE ANN. art. 3520 (B) (2020)).
Maine	"Marriage is the legally recognized union of 2 people. Gender-specific terms relating to the marital relationship or familial relationships must be construed to be gender-neutral for all purposes throughout the law . . . ." Ch. 1, 2011 Initiated Bill 3 – Legis. Doc. 1860, § 1 (approved by the electorate on Nov. 6, 2012; eff. Dec. 29, 2012), 2013 MAINE LAWS 1125 (codified at ME. REV. STAT. ANN. tit. 19-A, § 650-A (2020)). Initiated Bill 3, inter alia, "repeals the provision that limits marriage to one man and one woman and replaces it with the authorization for marriage between any 2 persons that meet the other requirements of Maine law." H.R. Doc., 125th Leg., 2d Reg. Sess., Leg. Doc. 1860, Summary (Me. 2012) (downloaded from the Law and Legislative Digital Library, Maine State Law and Legislative Reference Library, http://legislature.maine.gov/lawLibrary).
	"A marriage of a same-sex couple that is validly licensed and certified in another jurisdiction is recognized for all purposes under the laws of this State." Ch. 1, 2011 Initiated Bill 3 – Legis. Doc. 1860, § 2 (approved by the electorate on Nov. 6, 2012; eff. Dec. 29, 2012), 2013 MAINE LAWS 1125 (codified at ME. REV. STAT. ANN. tit. 19-A, § 650-B (2020)).
Maryland	"Only a marriage between two individuals who are not otherwise prohibited from marrying is valid in this State." Ch. 2, § 1, 2012 MD. LAWS 9 (eff. Jan. 1, 2013) (codified at MD. CODE ANN., FAM. LAW § 2-201(b) (LexisNexis 2020)). Chapter 2 made changes to section 2-201(b) of the Maryland Family Law Code, removing the phrase "a man and a woman" and replacing it with the phrase "two individuals who are not otherwise prohibited from marrying." Ch. 2, §§ 1, 7, 2012 MD. LAWS 9, 14.

(continued)

State	Law
Massachusetts	In November 2003, the highest state appellate court in Massachusetts concluded that, although state statutory provisions covering marriage were intended to limit marriage to couples composed of opposite-sex persons, guarantees in the state constitution required the state to issue marriage licenses to same-sex couples. Goodridge v. Dep't of Pub. Health, 798 N.E.2d 941, 952–53, 968 (Mass. 2003). The court directed that implementation of its ruling in *Goodridge* be delayed 180 days so that the state legislature could act "as it may deem appropriate in light of this opinion." *Id.* at 969–70. The Massachusetts legislature has not adopted a measure that explicitly allows a same-sex couple to marry. However, in 2008 it repealed state statutes that prevented residents of other jurisdictions from marrying in Massachusetts. Ch. 216, 2008 MASS. ACTS 1014. Chapter 216 allowed residents of other jurisdictions to contract a same-sex marriage in Massachusetts because, pursuant to *Goodridge*, same-sex couples who were Massachusetts residents had been marrying in Massachusetts since 2004. Anthony Michael Kreis, *Stages of Constitutional Grief: Democratic Constitutionalism and the Marriage Revolution*, 20 U. PA. J. CONST. L. 871, 919 (2018).
	See the discussion of Massachusetts in *supra* Sect. 4.2.1.
Michigan	"To secure and preserve the benefits of marriage for our society and for future generations of children, the union of one man and one woman in marriage shall be the only agreement recognized as a marriage or similar union for any purpose." MICH. CONST. art. I, § 25 (eff. Dec. 18, 2004).
	"Marriage is inherently a unique relationship between a man and a woman. . . . A marriage contracted between individuals of the same sex is invalid in this state." Act. No. 324, 1996 MICH. PUB. ACTS 1026, 1027 (eff. June 26, 1996) (codified at MICH. COMP. LAWS SERV. § 551.1 (2020)).
	"A man shall not marry . . . another man." Act No. 324, 1996 MICH. PUB. ACTS 1026, 1027 (eff. June 26, 1996) (codified at MICH. COMP. LAWS SERV. § 551.3 (2020)).
	"A woman shall not marry . . . another woman." Act No. 324, 1996 MICH. PUB. ACTS 1026, 1027 (eff. June 26, 1996) (codified at MICH. COMP. LAWS SERV. § 551.4 (2020)).
	"This state recognizes marriage as inherently a unique relationship between a man and a woman, as prescribed by . . . section 551.1 of the Michigan Compiled Laws, and therefore a marriage that is not between a man and a woman is invalid in this state regardless of whether the marriage is contracted according to the laws of another jurisdiction." Act No. 334, 1996 MICH. PUB. ACTS 1047, 1048 (eff. June 26, 1996) (codified at MICH. COMP. LAWS SERV. § 551.272 (2020)).
Minnesota	"A civil marriage, so far as its validity in law is concerned, is a civil contract between two persons . . . ." Ch. 74, § 2, 2013 MINN. LAWS 404, 405 (substituting the words "two persons" for the words "a man and a woman") (eff. Aug. 1, 2013) (codified at MINN. STAT. ANN. § 517.01 (West 2020)).
	"The following civil marriages are prohibited: . . . ." Ch. 74, § 3, 2013 MINN. LAWS 404, 405 (amending MINN. STAT. ANN. § 517.03(1)(a) by deleting two subsections that prohibited marriages between "persons of the same sex") (eff. Aug. 1, 2013).
	"When necessary to implement the rights and responsibilities of spouses or parents in a civil marriage between persons of the same sex under the laws of this state, . . . gender-specific terminology, such as 'husband,' 'wife,' 'mother,'

(continued)

State	Law
	'father,' 'widow,' 'widower,' or similar terms, must be construed in a neutral manner to refer to a person of either gender." Ch. 74, § 6(2), 2013 MINN. LAWS 404, 407 (eff. Aug. 1, 2013) (codified at MINN. STAT. ANN. § 517.201(2) (West 2020)).
Mississippi	"Marriage may take place and may be valid under the laws of this State only between a man and a woman. A marriage in another State or foreign jurisdiction between persons of the same gender, regardless of when the marriage took place, may not be recognized in this State and is void and unenforceable under the laws of this State." MISS. CONST. art. 14, § 263A (eff. Dec. 11, 2004).
	"Any marriage between persons of the same gender is prohibited and null and void from the beginning. Any marriage between persons of the same gender that is valid in another jurisdiction does not constitute a legal or valid marriage in Mississippi." Ch. 301, 1997 MISS. LAWS 1 (eff. Feb. 12, 1997) (codified at MISS. CODE ANN. § 93-1-1(2) (2020)).
Missouri	"That to be valid and recognized in this state, a marriage shall exist only between a man and a woman." MO. CONST. art.1, § 33 (adopted Aug. 3, 2004).
	"1. It is the public policy of this state to recognize marriage only between a man and a woman. 2. Any purported marriage not between a man and a woman is invalid. 3. No recorder shall issue a marriage license, except to a man and a woman. 4. A marriage between persons of the same sex will not be recognized for any purpose in this state even when valid where contracted." HB 157, 2001 MO. LAWS 357, 358 (eff. Aug. 28, 2001) (codified at MO. ANN. STAT. § 451.022 (LexisNexis 2020)).
Montana	"Only a marriage between one man and one woman shall be valid or recognized as a marriage in this state." MONT. CONST. art. XIII, § 7 (approved Nov. 2, 2004).
	"Marriage is a personal relationship between a man and a woman . . . ." Ch. 536, §§ 4, 46, 1975 MONT. LAWS 1514, 1515, 1533 (eff. Jan. 1, 1976) (codified at MONT. CODE ANN. § 40-1-103 (2019)).
	"The following marriages are prohibited: . . . (d) a marriage between persons of the same sex." Ch. 424, § 1, 1997 MONT. LAWS 2088 (eff. Oct. 1, 1997) (codified at MONT. CODE ANN. § 40-1-401(1) (2019)).
Nebraska	"Only marriage between a man and a woman shall be valid or recognized in Nebraska. The uniting of two persons of the same sex in a civil union, domestic partnership, or other similar same-sex relationship shall not be valid or recognized in Nebraska." NEB. CONST. art. I, § 29 (approved by the electorate in November 2000).
	"At the time of the marriage the male must be of the age of seventeen years or upward, and the female of the age of seventeen years or upward. . . ." Legis. Bill 165, § 1, 1978 NEB. LAWS 87 (eff. July 1978) (codified at NEB. REV. STAT. ANN. § 42-102 (LexisNexis 2020)).
Nevada	"Only a marriage between a male and female person shall be recognized and given effect in this state." NEV. CONST. art. 1, § 21 (adopted 2002).
	"1. Except as otherwise provided in this section, a male and a female person, at least 18 years of age, . . . and not having a husband or wife living, may be joined in marriage. 2. A male and a female person who are the husband and wife of each other may be rejoined in marriage if the record of their marriage has been lost or destroyed or is otherwise unobtainable.

(continued)

State	Law
	..." Ch. 336, 2009 NEV. STAT. 1503 (eff. July 1, 2009) (codified at NEV. REV. STAT. ANN. § 122.020), amended as of July 1, 2017 to read: "1. Except as otherwise provided in this section, two persons, regardless of gender, at least 18 years of age, ... and not having a spouse living, may be joined in marriage. 2. Two persons, regardless of gender, who are married to each other may be rejoined in marriage if the record of their marriage has been lost or destroyed or is otherwise unobtainable. ..." Ch. 167, §§ 1, 91, 2017 NEV. STAT. 755, 756, 799 (eff. July 1, 2017) (codified as amended at NEV. REV. STAT. ANN. § 122.020 (LexisNexis 2020)).
New Hampshire	"Marriage is the legally recognized union of 2 people. Any person who otherwise meets the eligibility requirements of this chapter may marry any other eligible person regardless of gender. ..." Ch. 59, 2009 N.H. LAWS 60 (eff. Jan. 1, 2010) (codified at N.H. REV. STAT. ANN. § 457:1-a (LexisNexis 2020)).
New Jersey	In 2012, the New Jersey legislature approved a bill that would have permitted same-sex marriage in the state, but the state governor did not sign the bill into law. Marriage Equality and Religious Exemption Act, Senate Bill 1 (215th New Jersey Legislature). The bill is the last formal position taken by the state legislature on same-sex marriage.
	See the discussion of New Jersey in *supra* Sect. 4.2.1.
New Mexico	See the discussion of New Mexico in *supra* Sect. 4.2.1.
New York	"1. A marriage that is otherwise valid shall be valid regardless of whether the parties to the marriage are of the same or different sex. 2. No government treatment or legal status, effect, right, benefit, privilege, protection or responsibility relating to marriage, whether deriving from statute, administrative or court rule, public policy, common law or any other source of law, shall differ based on the parties to the marriage being or having been of the same sex rather than a different sex. ..." Ch. 95, § 3, 2011 N.Y. LAWS 749 (eff. July 24, 2011) (codified at N.Y. DOM. REL. LAW § 10-a (Consol. 2020)).
North Carolina	"Marriage between one man and one woman is the only domestic legal union that shall be valid or recognized in this State. ..." N.C. CONST. art. XIV, § 6 (eff. May 23, 2012).
	"Marriages, whether created by common law, contracted, or performed outside of North Carolina, between individuals of the same gender are not valid in North Carolina." Ch. 588, 1995 N.C. SESS. LAWS 67 (eff. June 20, 1996) (codified at N.C. GEN. STAT. § 51-1.2 (2020)).
North Dakota	"Marriage consists only of the legal union between a man and a woman. ..." N.D. CONST. art. XI, § 28 (approved by the electorate on Nov. 2, 2004).
	"Marriage is a personal relation arising out of a civil contract between one man and one woman to which the consent of the parties is essential. ... A spouse refers only to a person of the opposite sex who is a husband or a wife." Ch. 145, § 1, 1997 N.D. LAWS 755 (codified at N.D. CENT. CODE § 14-03-01 (2019)).
	"Except when residents of this state contract a marriage in another state which is prohibited under the laws of this state, all marriages contracted outside this state, which are valid according to the laws of the state or country where contracted, are valid in this state. This section applies only to a marriage contracted in another state or country which is between one man and one woman as husband and wife." Ch. 145, § 2, 1997 N.D. LAWS 755 (eff. Aug. 1, 1997) (codified at N.D. CENT. CODE § 14-03-08 (2019)).

(continued)

State	Law
	Chapter 145 was passed in a regular session of the North Dakota legislature, approved by the North Dakota governor, and filed with the North Dakota secretary of state on March 25, 1997. Under the North Dakota constitution, Chapter 145 would have been effective on August 1, 1997. N.D. CONST. art. 4, § 13. However, Chapter 145 provided that, if same-sex marriage became lawful in another state prior to August 1, 1997, the chapter would be effective on the date that the law of the other state allowed same-same sex marriage. Ch. 145, § 3, 1997 N.D. LAWS 755.
Ohio	"Only a union between one man and one woman may be a marriage valid in or recognized by this state and its political subdivisions. This state and its political subdivisions shall not create or recognize a legal status for relationships of unmarried individuals that intends to approximate the design, qualities, significance or effect of marriage." OHIO CONST. art. XV, § 11 (eff. Dec. 2, 2004).
	"... (B) (1) Any marriage between persons of the same sex is against the strong public policy of this state. Any marriage between persons of the same sex shall have no legal force or effect in this state and, if attempted to be entered into in this state, is void ab initio and shall not be recognized by this state. (2) Any marriage entered into by persons of the same sex in any other jurisdiction shall be considered and treated in all respects as having no legal force or effect in this state and shall not be recognized by this state. ..." Act of Feb. 3, 2004, § 1, 2003 OHIO LAWS 3403, 3404 (eff. May 7, 2004) (codified at OHIO REV. CODE ANN. § 3101.01(B) (2020)).
Oklahoma	"A. Marriage in this state shall consist only of the union of one man and one woman. ... B. A marriage between persons of the same gender performed in another state shall not be recognized as valid and binding in this state as of the date of the marriage. ..." OKLA. CONST. art. II, § 35 (approved by the electorate on Nov. 2, 2004).
	"Any unmarried person who is at least eighteen (18) years of age and not otherwise disqualified is capable of contracting and consenting to marriage with a person of the opposite sex." Ch. 39, § 1, 1975 OKLA. SESS. LAWS 57 (eff. Oct. 1, 1975) (codified at OKLA. STAT. ANN. tit. 43, § 3(A) (LexisNexis 2020)).
	"A marriage between persons of the same gender performed in another state shall not be recognized as valid and binding in this state as of the date of the marriage." Ch. 131, § 9, 1996 OKLA. LAWS 473, 475 (eff. Jan. 1, 1997) (codified at OKLA. STAT. ANN. tit. 43, § 3.1 (LexisNexis 2020)).
Oregon	See the discussion of Oregon in *supra* Sect. 4.2.1.
Pennsylvania	"The following words and phrases when used in this part shall have the meanings given to them in this section unless the context clearly indicates otherwise: ... 'Marriage.'—A civil contract by which one man and one woman take each other for husband and wife. ..." Act No. 124, § 1, 1996 PA. LAWS 706 (eff. 60 days after Oct. 16, 1996) (codified at 23 PA. CONSOL. STAT. § 1102 (2020)).
	"It is hereby declared to be the strong and longstanding public policy of this Commonwealth that marriage shall be between one man and one woman. A marriage between persons of the same sex which was entered into in another state or foreign jurisdiction, even if valid where entered into, shall be void in this

(continued)

State	Law
	Commonwealth." Act No. 124, § 2, 1996 PA. LAWS 706 (eff. 60 days after Oct. 16, 1996) (codified at 23 PA. CONSOL. STAT. § 1704 (2020)).
Rhode Island	"Any person who otherwise meets the eligibility requirements of chapters 15-1 and 15-2 may marry any other eligible person regardless of gender." Ch. 4, §§ 1, 8, 2013 R.I. PUB. LAWS 7 (eff. Aug. 1, 2013) and Ch. 5, §§ 1, 8, 2013 R.I. PUB. LAWS 15 (eff. Aug. 1, 2013) (codified at R.I. GEN. LAWS § 15-1-1 (2020)). Chapter 51-1 prohibits bigamy, marriage between designated kin, and marriage of a person who, when marrying, is "mentally incompetent." Chapter 15-2 prohibits marriage without a license; requires that, to obtain a license, a person who has been married provide evidence that the prior marriage has been duly dissolved; and establishes the conditions under which a minor is allowed to marry.
South Carolina	"A marriage between one man and one woman is the only lawful domestic union that shall be valid or recognized in this State. This State and its political subdivisions shall not create a legal status, right, or claim respecting any other domestic union, however denominated. This State and its political subdivisions shall not recognize or give effect to a legal status, right, or claim created by another jurisdiction respecting any other domestic union, however denominated. ..." S.C. CONST. art. XVII, § 15 (eff. March 27, 2007).
	"A marriage between persons of the same sex is void ab initio and against the public policy of this State." Act No. 327, §§ 1, 4, 1996 S.C. ACTS 2048 (eff. May 20, 1996)) (codified at S.C. CODE UNANN. § 20-1-15 (2020)).
South Dakota	"Only marriage between a man and a woman shall be valid or recognized in South Dakota. ..." S.D. CONST. art. 21, § 9 (approved by the electorate on Nov. 7, 2006).
	"Marriage is a personal relation, between a man and a woman, arising out of a civil contract to which the consent of parties capable of making it is necessary. ..." Ch. 161, 1996 S.D. SESS. LAWS 221 (eff. ninety days after March 11, 1996) (codified at S.D. CODIFIED LAWS § 25-1-1 (2020)).
Tennessee	"The historical institution and legal contract solemnizing the relationship of one (1) man and one (1) woman shall be the only legally recognized marital contract in this state. ... If another state or foreign jurisdiction issues a license for persons to marry and if such marriage is prohibited in this state by the provisions of this section, then the marriage shall be void and unenforceable in this state." TENN. CONST. art. 11, § 18 (approved by the electorate on Nov. 7, 2006). The foregoing provision is a rephrasing of Ch. 1031, § 1, 1996 Pub. Acts 822 (eff. May 15, 1996) (codified at TENN. CODE ANN. § 36-3-113 (2020)).
Texas	"Marriage in this state shall consist only of the union of one man and one woman." TEX. CONST. art. I, § 32(a) (approved by the electorate on Nov. 8, 2005).
	"(a) A man and a woman desiring to enter into a ceremonial marriage must obtain a marriage license from the county clerk of any county of this state. (b) A license may not be issued for the marriage of persons of the same sex." Ch. 7, 1997 TEX. SESS. LAWS 8, 9, 43 (eff. April 17, 1997) (codified at TEX. FAM. CODE ANN. § 2.001 (2019)).
	"... (b) A marriage between persons of the same sex or a civil union is contrary to the public policy of this state and is void in this state. (c) The state or an agency or political subdivision of the state may not give effect to a:

(continued)

State	Law
	(1) public act, record, or judicial proceeding that creates, recognizes, or validates a marriage between persons of the same sex or a civil union in this state or in any other jurisdiction; or (2) right or claim to any legal protection, benefit, or responsibility asserted as a result of a marriage between persons of the same sex or a civil union in this state or in any other jurisdiction." Ch. 124, § 1, 2003 TEX. SESS. LAWS 171 (eff. Sept. 1, 2003) (codified at TEX. FAM. CODE ANN. § 6.204 (2019)).
Utah	"(1) Marriage consists only of the legal union between a man and a woman. (2) No other domestic union, however denominated, may be recognized as a marriage or given the same or substantially equivalent legal effect." UTAH CONST. art. 1, § 29 (eff. Jan. 1, 2005).
	"(1) (a) It is the policy of this state to recognize as marriage only the legal union of a man and a woman as provided in this chapter. (b) Except for the relationship of marriage between a man and a woman recognized pursuant to this chapter, this state will not recognize, enforce, or give legal effect to any law creating any legal status, rights, benefits, or duties that are substantially equivalent to those provided under Utah law to a man and a woman because they are married." Ch. 261, § 1, 2004 Utah Laws 1158 (eff. March 23, 2004) (codified at UTAH CODE ANN. § 30-1-4.1 (2020)).
	"The following marriages are prohibited and declared void:
	. . . (5) between persons of the same sex." Ch. 1, § 1, 1977 UTAH LAWS 1, 2 (eff. July 15, 1977) (codified as amended at UTAH CODE ANN. § 30-1-2 (2018)). Subsection 5 was repealed effective May 14, 2019 by Ch. 300, §1, 2019 UTAH LAWS 1989, and Ch. 317, § 2, 2019 UTAH LAWS 2071.
Vermont	"Marriage is the legally recognized union of two people. . . ." Act No. 3, §§ 5, 13, 2009 VT. ACTS & RESOLVES 33, 37 (redefining marriage by substituting the words "two people" for "one man and one woman") (eff. Sept. 1, 2009) (codified at VT. STAT. ANN. tit. 15, § 8 (2019)). Act No. 3 declares that its objective is, inter alia, "to recognize legal equality in the civil marriage laws . . . ." Act No. 3, § 2, 2009 VT. ACTS & RESOLVES 33.
Virginia	"That only a union between one man and one woman may be a marriage valid in or recognized by this Commonwealth and its political subdivisions. . . ." VA. CONST. art. I, § 15-A (approved by the electorate on Nov. 7, 2006).
	"A marriage between persons of the same sex is prohibited. Any marriage entered into by persons of the same sex in another state or jurisdiction shall be void in all respects in Virginia and any contractual rights created by such marriage shall be void and unenforceable." Ch. 644, 1975 VA. ACTS 1336, 1337; Ch. 354, 1997 VA. ACTS 513 (eff. July 1, 1997); Ch. 365, 1997 VA. ACTS 538 (eff. July 1, 1997) (codified at VA. CODE ANN. § 20-45.2 (LexisNexis 2019)); repealed eff. July 1, 2020 by Ch. 75 (HB 1490), Ch. 195 (SB 17), and Ch. 900 (HB 623), 2020 VA. LEGIS. INFO. SYS., https://lis.virginia.gov (retrieved Sept. 8, 2020).
Washington	"(1) Marriage is a civil contract between two persons who have each attained the age of eighteen years, and who are otherwise capable. . . . (3) Where necessary to implement the rights and responsibilities of spouses under the law, gender-specific terms such as husband and wife used in any statute, rule, or other law must be construed to be gender neutral and applicable to spouses of the same sex.

(continued)

State	Law
	. . ." Ch. 3, § 1, 2012 WASH. SESS. LAWS 199 (redefining marriage by, inter alia, substituting the words "two persons" for "a male and a female" in subsection 1 and adding subsection 3) (eff. June 7, 2012) (codified at WASH. REV. CODE ANN. § 26.04.010 (LexisNexis 2020)). Chapter 3, which is titled "Same Sex Marriage," declares that its objectives include "creating equality in civil marriage." Ch. 3, 2012 WASH. SESS. LAWS 199.
West Virginia	"(a) The application for a marriage license must contain a statement of the full names of both the female and the male parties . . . . (c) Every application for a marriage license must contain the following statement: 'Marriage is designed to be a loving and lifelong union between a woman and a man. . . .' " Ch. 91, 2001 W. VA. ACTS 374, 431 (eff. March 22, 2001) (reenacted by Ch. 49, 2012 W. VA. ACTS 567, 568 (eff. 90 days after March 10, 2012)) (codified at W. VA. CODE § 48-2-104 (LexisNexis 2020)).
	". . . Celebration or solemnization of a marriage means the performance of the formal act or ceremony by which a man and woman contract marriage and assume the status of husband and wife. . . ." Ch. 91, 2001 W. VA. ACTS 374, 437 (eff. March 22, 2001) (codified at W. VA. CODE § 48-2-401 (LexisNexis 2020)).
Wisconsin	"Only a marriage between one man and one woman shall be valid or recognized as a marriage in this state. A legal status identical or substantially similar to that of marriage for unmarried individuals shall not be valid or recognized in this state." WIS. CONST. art. XIII, § 13 (adopted by the electorate on November 7, 2006).
	See the discussion of Wisconsin in *supra* Sect. 4.2.1.
Wyoming	"Marriage is a civil contract between a male and a female person to which the consent of the parties capable of contracting is essential." Ch. 152, 1977 WYO. SESS. LAWS 479, 480, 508 (eff. May 27, 1977) (codified at WYO. STAT. ANN. § 20-1-101 (2020)).

Notes to Appendix: (a) Sources are cited in *supra* note 41. (b) Abbreviations used: amend. = amendment; Ann. = Annotated; art. = article; Cent. = Century; Ch. = Chapter; Civ. = Civil; cl. = clause; Comp. = Compiled; Consol. = Consolidated; Const. = Constitution; Doc. = Document; eff. = effective date; Fam. = Family; Gen. = General; HB = House Bill; H.R. = House of Representatives; Leg. = Legislature; Legis. = Legislative; Pub. = Public; Reg. = Regular; Rev. = Revised; SB = Senate Bill; Serv. = Service; Sess. = Session; Spec. = Special; Stat. = Statutes; Unann. = Unannotated

Chapter 5
Wrapping Up

5.1 The Rationale for the Concept of Societal Stress in Scholarship on Law

Although a vast amount of scholarly time has been invested in studying the institution of law, the societal accompaniments of change in law content are poorly understood. Why has more progress not been made in uncovering what happens in and to social life when change takes place in proscriptions and prescriptions of law? One reason is undoubtedly that the institution of law has many aspects, and the complexity of the institution makes study of the institution difficult. Another reason appears to lie in the premises employed, and the premises not employed, in scholarship on law. Premises can have a major bearing on the depth and extent of knowledge that emerges from scholarship. In particular, I direct attention to one premise and argue that it is pertinent to change over time in what law says and does not say about social activities and arrangements. Regrettably, this premise has had just limited success in contributing insights into societal reactions to actual and possible modifications of law despite its potential to add a great deal.

The premise on which I focus asserts that the institution of law is embedded in a society. The premise, which I label the law-in-society premise, has a long and impressive pedigree,[1] but in the United States, the push it might provide for engagement with the social sciences, especially the quantitative social sciences, has been largely neutralized in the first instance by intellectual blinders that are common in U.S. law schools. These law schools, which produce much if not most of the scholarship on the content of American law, have unfortunately preferred to rely on the discipline of philosophy, or more precisely on the specialty of philosophy known as jurisprudence, for their inquiries into the essence of law. The reliance on jurisprudence has been an obstacle to maximizing the quality of scholarship on law

[1] Brian Z. Tamanaha, *The Third Pillar of Jurisprudence: Social Legal Theory*, 56 Wm. & Mary L. Rev. 2235, 2241–50 (2015).

L. D. Barnett, *Societal Stress and Law*,
https://doi.org/10.1007/978-3-031-30875-8_5

content, in part because there is no theory in jurisprudence that explicitly expands on and develops the ramifications of the law-in-society premise.[2] The result is that attention is directed away from, or at least is not directed toward, the quantitative social sciences, and the potential benefits of the law-in-society premise are not fully realized in law-school scholarship. The limited contribution of the premise is perhaps surprising since the U.S. Supreme Court has pointed out that judicial bodies, which are a primary concern of law schools, require "legitimacy, a product of substance and perception that shows itself in the people's acceptance of the Judiciary as fit to determine what the Nation's law means and to declare what it demands."[3] As the Court points out, the degree of legitimacy that judicial bodies possess is due to societal conditions, but scholarship emanating from U.S. law schools almost always avoids the social-science disciplines that can quantitively assess how these conditions interact with the institution of law.[4]

Can the problem be solved if law-school scholarship makes the law-in-society premise its centerpiece? The answer, unfortunately, appears to be negative. Such scholarship would not be better-positioned to understand the societal accompaniments of change in the content of law, because the law-in-society premise by itself furnishes a superficial perspective on law. In particular, scholarship based on the premise suffers from difficulties in theory as well as research and is handicapped by a political bias.[5] In the remainder of Sect. 5.1, accordingly, I address the law-in-society premise. To be exact, I use the premise as a stepping stone to what I argue is a more fruitful way to think about and study change in what law says (and does not say) in a society. Such an approach necessarily involves an appreciation of what law does (and does not do) in a society.

To take a step beyond the law-in-society premise, I draw on structural-functionalism theory.[6] In my view, because the institution of law exists within a society, it exists and operates within a system, i.e., within an entity whose elements mutually influence each other rather than work independently of one another.[7] Law, in other words, is one of a set of societal institutions that are interconnected and interdependent. The importance of the system context of law cannot be overemphasized. In every jurisdiction (e.g., nation or state), the character of the societal system is critical to not just the substance of the law-based proscriptions and

---

[2] *Id.* at 2237, 2275, 2277.

[3] Planned Parenthood v. Casey, 505 U.S. 833, 865 (1992).

[4] Scholarship on comparative law may prove to be an early adopter of social science concepts and research methods. Larry D. Barnett, Societal Agents in Law: A Macrosociological Approach 7–8 (2019) [hereinafter SAIL vol. 1]. *See* Anne Meuwese & Mila Versteeg, *Quantitative Methods for Comparative Constitutional Law*, *in* Practice and Theory in Comparative Law 230, 231, 255 (Maurice Adams & Jacco Bomhoff eds., 2012) (describing quantitative research as permitting "comparativists to address a series of new questions as well as to generate new insights into existing debates," and as being "a new methodological frontier for comparative (constitutional) law").

[5] SAIL vol. 1, *supra* note 4, at 8–10.

[6] See Sect. 1.2 in *supra* Chap. 1.

[7] Alexander Backlund, *The Definition of System*, 29 Kybernetes 444 (2000).

prescriptions that develop, but also to the social consequences that the proscriptions and prescriptions generate. Since a jurisdiction whose population is numerically sizeable, socially subdivided, and technologically advanced has a societal system that unavoidably is intricate and possesses feedback loops, change in the proscriptions and prescriptions of law in a jurisdiction will produce unanticipated, and often-unwanted, social effects, and as the complexity of the societal system increases, the frequency of law-generated side effects can be expected to mount as well. The operation of the institution of law, accordingly, should not be thought to be free of side effects.

In the instant book, I have dealt with two United States Supreme Court decisions interpreting the Constitution of the nation and a proposal to amend the text of the Constitution. Because these three law-based events had a direct bearing on social arrangements at the heart of American society, I have argued that each event was responsible for a significant amount of social stress. In other words, the three events, although beneficial in important ways to American society, were not entirely harmless in sociological terms. Being socially salient, they had social costs. The three events, furthermore, were intended by me to be merely illustrations; other actual and possible adoptions of new law have undoubtedly produced unforeseen, unwanted side effects, too. An example involves the U.S. flag, "a symbol of our Nation and certain national ideals."[8] The power of the flag as a symbol has meant that destroying or even physically disfiguring the flag for political ends is conduct that is unacceptable to a sizeable portion of the American population.[9] Accordingly, considerable social stress would have been caused by the U.S. Supreme Court when it ruled that the free-expression guarantee of the First Amendment[10] protects persons who destroy or deface a U.S. flag that they own for the purpose of expressing an objection to a policy or action of the government of the country.[11]

---

[8]United States v. Eichman, 496 U.S. 310, 316 (1990). The U.S. flag has been described as "the quintessential symbol of the American community." Steven G. Gey, *This is Not a Flag: The Aesthetics of Desecration*, 1990 Wis. L. Rev. 1549, 1592.

[9]Joseph Carroll, Gallup Inc., *Public Support for Constitutional Amendment on Flag Burning* (2006) (finding that, in 2006, two out of five U.S. adults said that they would be "upset" if the Constitution was not amended to permit the federal government and state governments to outlaw burning the American flag), https://news.gallup.com/poll/23524/public-support-constitutional-amendment-flag-burning.aspx.

[10]The text of the First Amendment is reproduced in note 121 in *supra* Chap. 1.

[11]Texas v. Johnson, 491 U.S. 397, 400 n.1, 404, 418, 420 (1989) (acknowledging that "there is a special place reserved for the flag in this Nation, and thus we do not doubt that the government has a legitimate interest in making efforts to 'preserv[e] the national flag as an unalloyed symbol of our country'"; observing that government efforts to safeguard the flag are constrained by the guarantee of free expression in the First Amendment; and concluding that, because of the First Amendment, the interest of government "in preserving the flag as a symbol of nationhood and national unity" is insufficient to allow government, under a statute that criminalizes desecration of the flag, to punish an individual who burns the flag in order to express dissatisfaction with a government policy). *Cf.* Larry D. Barnett, The Place of Law: The Role and Limits of Law in Society 60 (2011) (discussing federal law that evidences the symbolic importance to Americans of the U.S. flag).

Of course, even if a constitution-based ruling by the federal judiciary or a proposal to amend the Constitution has an unwelcome social side effect, it may still produce a net gain for society and be socially worthwhile. Where such a ruling/proposal does so, it would have a social benefit that outweighed its social cost. Unfortunately, however, scholars who focus on law have shown little interest in, and a seeming reluctance to look for and evaluate, negative social side effects of law. While the institution of law is undoubtedly not the sole societal institution that generates negative social side effects, it has been studied by scholars who have exhibited an inclination to turn a blind eye to such side effects, at least when these scholars have examined law content that embodies the belief that during the last few decades has been ascendant in the places where the scholars are mainly located, viz., colleges and universities.[12] This belief puts the short-term desires of the individual ahead of the smooth, long-term operation of the social order.[13] But the belief is potentially problematic. A society is a system, and a system requires a minimum degree of internal cohesiveness. Social atomization, insofar as it is promoted by the belief, is harmful to societal cohesiveness, and the resulting societal inefficiency is wasteful of limited resources.

At the moment, however, my concern is with the ramifications of the individual-over-society belief for the thesis of the instant book. Adherence to any belief without a willingness to entertain an alternative to or a modification of the belief can hinder progress in scholarship and, hence, in understanding phenomena being studied.[14] For the thesis of the book, the individual-over-society belief may pose an obstacle. The thesis is that law content manifesting this (or any other rigid) belief can bring about negative social consequences, including significant long-term societal stress. The thesis, therefore, may be less than warmly received by advocates of the belief.

---

[12] See Sect. 1.5 in *supra* Chap. 1.

[13] Robert C. L. Moffat, *Cloning Freedom: Criminalization or Empowerment in Reproductive Policy?*, 32 VAL. U.L. REV. 583, 603 (1998) (contending that the concept of individual freedom is now defined as "licentiousness" and that "[r]ampant individualism is the product of a culture which idolizes 'freedom from' but which wishes at the same time to avoid all responsibility for the exercise of unconstrained freedom"); Elisabeth Zoller, *Citizenship After the Conservative Movement*, 20 IND. J. GLOBAL LEG. STUD. 279, 283 (2013) (writing that "[c]ontemporary discourse on citizenship never starts with responsibilities, but with rights").

The belief, by giving priority to the individual, may be the foundation for the "cancel culture" movement in which all socially defined groups of people are evidently assumed to possess equal qualifications for all tasks. For a discussion of the "cancel culture" movement in U.S. colleges and universities, see David Acevedo, Nat'l Ass'n of Scholars, *Tracking "Cancel Culture" in Higher Education* (2022), https://www.nas.org/blogs/article/tracking-cancel-culture-in-higher-education.

[14] *E.g.*, note 12 in *supra* Chap. 1; Robert Hogan & Robert Sinclair, *Intellectual, Ideological, and Political Obstacles to the Advancement of Organizational Science*, 32 J. APPLIED BEHAV. SCI. 378, 381–85 (1976). A case study is in Jay Schalin, *We Need to Talk About Bruce* (James G. Martin Ctr. for Academic Renewal, 2020), https://www.jamesgmartin.center/2020/page/5/. In addition, see Sect. 1.5 in *supra* Chap. 1.

Despite this clash (or perhaps because of it), the thesis warrants consideration. Novel ideas seem often to receive a cool reception.[15] The thesis, however, has a firm basis in credible social science theory and brings into social science a concept (viz., stress) that has benefited biological science. The thesis is also aided by its ability to make sense of a prominent occurrence in the history of the United States, viz., citizen support for a socially divisive, if not seditious, U.S. president, viz., Donald J. Trump.[16] The thesis is, I believe, made further attractive by the research that was undertaken in Chaps. 2 through 4, because this research suggests a way in which the subject of law-produced social stress may be studied with quantitative data and a multivariate statistical technique. Notably, this research yielded plausible findings. I look at these findings next, i.e., in Sect. 5.2, where I summarize the findings of the preferred regression models in Chaps. 2 through 4 and draw inferences from the summary that bring the findings under the roof of the concept of societal stress.

5.2 The Studies of Societal Stress and Law: A Synthesis of Findings

Through empirical observation and abstractions from empirical observation, science seeks to establish that "if variable X changes in a certain direction, then variable Y changes in a certain direction," with the direction of change in Y (the effect) not necessarily being the same as the direction of change in X (the cause). "If–then" statements can describe the findings of empirical research, and they can also, through abstractions from these findings, constitute theory. The findings of the studies that

---

[15] Jennifer S. Mueller et al., *The Bias Against Creativity: Why People Desire but Reject Creative Ideas*, 23 Psychol. Sci. (2012).

[16] Mr. Trump is the only president of the United States who has been impeached twice. States News Service, *US House Impeaches Trump for Inciting Deadly Capitol Riot*, Jan. 14, 2021. The House of Representatives is authorized by the U.S. Constitution to impeach the president. U.S. Const. art. I, § 2, cl. 5; art. II, § 4. A case of impeachment brought by the House is tried by the Senate. U.S. Const. art. I, § 3, cl. 6.

In its first impeachment of President Trump, the House charged Mr. Trump with (1) abusing the powers of the office of the presidency and (2) obstructing Congress. H. Res. 755, 116th Cong. (2019). The Senate concluded that Mr. Trump was not guilty of either charge. The text of House Resolution 755, and the dates of the actions by the House and the Senate on this resolution, are available at https://www.congress.gov/bill/116th-congress/house-resolution/755.

In its second impeachment of President Trump, the House charged Mr. Trump with "inciting violence against the Government of the United States." H. Res. 24, 117th Cong. (2021). Mr. Trump was not convicted of this charge by the Senate, which tried the case after Mr. Trump was no longer president. The text of House Resolution 24, and the dates of the actions by the House and the Senate on this resolution, are available at https://www.congress.gov/bill/117th-congress/house-resolution/24.

Subsequently, Mr. Trump described the United States as a country that is "Rigged, Crooked, and Evil." Donald J. Trump, Truth Social (Oct. 30, 2022, 8:44 AM), https://truthsocial.com/@realDonaldTrump/posts/109257284173667925 (last visited Nov. 3, 2022).

are reported in the preceding three chapters can, therefore, be used to build theory on the macrosociology of law content. To this end, I extract "if–then" statements from the results of the regression models that were selected as the "best" in the three chapters, viz., from Model 2A in Chap. 2, from Model 2B in Chap. 3, and from Model 1 in Chap. 4. Because each of the three selected models had two causal (i.e., X) variables, each model yielded two "if–then" statements, and the three models together yielded a total of three sets of two statements. The statements identify the X variables that increased, and the X variables that decreased, the odds that a state was in the category of the dependent variable that had been coded 1, i.e., the category for states (i) that had in their law a ban which the U.S. Supreme Court invalidated under the national Constitution or (ii) that did not want to add the Equal Rights Amendment ("ERA") to the Constitution. The sociological variables that increased the odds that a state had adopted such law or failed to ratify the ERA are considered to have been responsible for the occurrence of social stress from the Court rulings and the ERA proposal. Conversely, the sociological variables that decreased the odds that a state had adopted such law or failed to ratify the ERA are deemed to have lessened the occurrence of social stress from the Court rulings and the ERA proposal.

The empirical findings from the preferred regression models in the three chapters yield the following six "if–then" statements. The findings of Model 2A in Chap. 2 were:

(1) If nonconformity with the traditional family ideal increased, then law had lower odds of prohibiting marriage between a member of the dominant race and a member of a minority race.
(2) If race-based fragmentation increased, then law had higher odds of prohibiting marriage between a member of the dominant race and a member of a minority race.

The findings of Model 2B in Chap. 3 were:

(3) If nonconformity with the traditional family ideal increased in a state, then the state had higher odds of not ratifying the Equal Rights Amendment.
(4) If the foreign-born share of the population increased in a state, then the state had lower odds of not ratifying the Equal Rights Amendment.

The findings of Model 1 in Chap. 4 were:

(5) If nonconformity with the traditional family ideal increased, then law had higher odds of prohibiting same-sex marriage.
(6) If the foreign-born share of the population increased, then law had lower odds of prohibiting same-sex marriage.

Let me now synthesize the findings above that have the same causal variable. Finding #2 will be skipped for the moment but will be used later to develop propositions of formal theory. Findings #1, #3, and #5 imply that greater deviation from the traditional family ideal in American culture expanded acceptance of social paths for individuals defined by their race but reduced acceptance of social paths for individuals defined by their sex. The two effects presumably occurred because the essence of the American family structure was not societally perceived as jeopardized by cross-race marriage but was societally perceived as undermined by change in the social definition and treatment of the sex attribute.[17]

Findings #4 and #6 imply that greater diversity in culture created a stronger inclination to reject traditions involving the biological characteristic of sex: An increase in the fraction of the population that was foreign-born diminished acceptance of both conventions regarding sex roles (finding #4) and conventions regarding the sex of a person who an individual is permitted to marry (finding #6). The foregoing effects probably happened because greater cultural diversity expands the range of social viewpoints in a society and demands, in the interest of societal stability, more tolerance of heretofore absent (or minimally present) viewpoints.[18] A culture is loosened by immigrants, at least insofar as the immigrants hold viewpoints that are outside the established mold.

The above six statements are not, by their very nature, theoretical propositions because they merely summarize research findings. A theoretical proposition differs from a statement of research findings in a fundamental way—it abstracts from the empirical indicator of its causal variable and/or from the empirical indicator of its effect variable, and by doing so it includes numerous observable phenomena under the variable(s). To take a step toward theoretical propositions, I employ statements #1 through #6 and tie them to the concept of social stress. In addition, I simultaneously take into account the standardized regression coefficients for the empirical indicators of the independent variables in each of the preferred regression models, and thus incorporate the expected *net* change in the frequency of occurrence of social stress when there are equivalent increases in the two causal (i.e., independent) variables that comprise the model. The resulting theoretical propositions, which are listed below, have been labeled A, B, and C: Proposition A combines and extends findings #1 and #2; Proposition B combines and extends findings #3 and #4; and Proposition C combines and extends findings #5 and #6.

A. If race-based fragmentation and a nontraditional family form increase and the increases are equivalent in degree, then social stress caused by the elimination of law against interracial marriage will happen more often.
B. If a nontraditional family form and the range of social viewpoints increase and the increases are equivalent in degree, then the frequency with which social stress happens due to proposed law on sex roles will not change.
C. If a nontraditional family form and the range of social viewpoints increase and the increases are equivalent in degree, then social stress caused by the elimination of law on the sex attribute in marriage will happen less often.

[17] For a discussion of how culture might mold the content of law, see the paragraph accompanying notes 80 to 83 in *supra* Chap. 2; the first paragraph of Sect. 3.2.4 in *supra* Chap. 3; and the third paragraph of Sect. 4.3 in *supra* Chap. 4.

[18] For a discussion of how cultural heterogeneity might mold the content of law, see the paragraph accompanying notes 84 & 85 in *supra* Chap. 2; the second paragraph of Sect. 3.2.4 in *supra* Chap. 3; and the second paragraph of Sect. 4.3 in *supra* Chap. 4.

Readers should notice that propositions A, B, and C include the qualification that the increases in two causal variables are "equivalent in degree" (which in the studies in the prior chapters was one standard deviation in the quantitative indicator of each causal variable). When the changes in causal variables are equivalent in magnitude, the net change in the frequency of stress can be anticipated. However, during a given period of time, the amount of change in one causal variable will not necessarily be the same as the amount of change in the other causal variable. In situations where such differentials exist—which situations are undoubtedly common—the frequency of law-induced societal stress will not be predictable without major advances in the macrosociology of law. These advances will require not only empirical research but also progress in theory. I thus discuss possible paths that research and theory may wish to follow.

5.3 Societal Stress and Law: Topics for Future Inquiry

In previously published studies, I found that an average of four state-level sociological-demographic characteristics accounted for differences between almost eight out of ten U.S. states in the content of state law on societally important social behaviors.[19] The studies reported in Chaps. 2 and 4 of the instant book found that, for substantially more than eight out of ten U.S. states, just two sociological-demographic characteristics explained state differences in the content of law on these kinds of social behaviors. Since the studies in this book were designed to test the utility of the concept of societal stress, their findings suggest that the concept adds to the ability of macrosociology to explain cross-jurisdiction and cross-time variations in the content of law. This evident gain in explanatory power, even apart from other considerations, warrants including the concept of societal stress in scholarship focused on persistence and change in law content.

However, reasons beyond the improvement in explanatory power recommend the concept of societal stress. For scholars, a new concept is useful when, inter alia, it opens new lines of inquiry in research and theory. On what fresh paths can the concept of societal stress take scholars who want to expand what is known about the sociological sources and consequences of the content of law?

To start, scholars should consider sequencing effects because the degree to which change in law content affects the frequency of occurrence of society-level stress may vary with the particular succession of multiple law contents in a society. Let me illustrate. Assume that, within a given jurisdiction, law content on a society-significant social activity has shifted between proscriptions (or prescriptions) A, B, C, and D. The frequency of societal stress generated by the sequence C to B to A to D, for instance, may differ from the frequency of societal stress generated by the sequence D to B to C to A. Complicating matters, the frequency of societal stress that

[19] SAIL VOL. 1, *supra* note 4, at 116–17.

is produced by a given sequence may not be the same across all sociological-demographic conditions. As an example, law may induce societal stress more often in sequence C–B–A–D when condition #1 is present than when condition #2 is present. The situation will be even more complex if both conditions involve numeric phenomena that are dispersed in amount and the amounts of the phenomena in the two conditions can to some extent overlap. The frequency of societal stress from sequence C–B–A–D may be higher (and differ over time) when overlap occurs than when overlap does not occur, and when overlap occurs, the frequency of societal stress may vary with the degree of overlap.

Besides the sequence of law contents, several other factors may account for the frequency of societal stress that is due to actual and proposed modifications in the content of law. One is the cultural importance of the society-significant activity that law content addresses. Quite plausibly, change in law content on a topic will produce societal stress more often when the topic is of high cultural importance than when the topic is of low cultural importance. A further possibility is that the frequency of societal stress stemming from change in particular law content will be affected by interaction between the law content and a simultaneous non-law event or arrangement. The interaction may reduce or amplify the frequency of societal stress that would be produced by change in the law-content alone. Similarly, the frequency of societal stress due to a modification of law content on a specific social topic may be affected by interaction between change in this law content and concurrent change in law content on an entirely different social topic. That is, changes in law content on two matters may work together and result in a different frequency of societal stress than a shift in either law content by itself would yield.

The impact of the passage of time on the frequency of occurrence of societal stress also merits consideration, and in a number of respects. First, how often societal stress is generated by changes in a given law content may decrease over time. If so, law content that changed recently will be responsible, ceteris paribus, for more widespread cases of societal stress at a particular time than law content that changed earlier. However, all temporal decreases in cases of law-triggered societal stress may not be the same in frequency over a specific number of time units, e.g., months or years. In some cases of law-triggered societal stress, the frequency of stress during a given time unit may decrease more than in other cases of law-triggered societal stress. If so, sociologists should identify the factors that cause the differentials. Second, even after diminishing to the point where the frequency of stress is zero, societal stress from a previous change in particular law content may leave a society with a sensitivity to further social stress. When this happens, the lingering sensitivity may exacerbate the frequency of stress that is generated by the appearance of new law content on the same topic, by the appearance of new law content on a different topic, or by an event outside the institution of law. Whether such synergies occur and the circumstances in which they occur thus merit study. Third, an ongoing increase or decrease in the frequency of law-triggered social stress may be halted or reversed by the occurrence of a certain type of event or by the emergence of a certain type of situation. Scholarship on the macrosociology of law, accordingly, should identify the conditions under which secular increases and decreases in the occurrence of law-induced social stress stop and the conditions under which they turn in the opposite direction. Furthermore, how long a reversal in direction lasts, and how far the reversal goes, warrant investigation to uncover the factors that bear on such reversals. These factors are important to understanding how the institution of law operates in a society.

Lastly, let me not neglect an important point. The studies whose findings are reported in the prior three chapters measured their independent variables using data on U.S. states for the year 1960. Around this time, tradition had a relatively firm grip on the American population[20] presumably because the period was sociologically a reaction to the lengthy economic depression and war that preceded it.[21] The then-existent level of tradition is seen in the following:

(a) During the years 1950–1965, married-couple households comprised three out of every four households in the United States, a fraction that was little changed from earlier points in the twentieth century but was noticeably higher than at the end of the twentieth century.[22]
(b) During the years from 1949 to 1962, the median age for first marriage among women in the United States was at its 1890-to-2021 bottom.[23]
(c) In 1960, more than seven out of ten children in the United States resided with two parents who were in their first marriage, but in 2014, less than half of all U.S. children lived in such a setting.[24]

Importantly, World War II did not bring about substantial cultural change in the United States, at least in terms of aspects of culture that are pertinent to the studies in Chaps. 2, 3, and 4. To illustrate, the war had little impact on the overall views of whites toward blacks,[25] and just a minimal impact on the post-war extent to which women were economically engaged outside the home.[26] Data for 1960, in short,

---

[20] See the paragraph accompanying notes 80 to 83 in *supra* Chap. 2; the paragraphs accompanying notes 8 to 12 in *supra* Chap. 3; and the text accompanying Fig. 3.1 in *supra* Chap. 3.

[21] Jesús J. Sánchez-Barricarte, *Measuring and Explaining the Baby Boom in the Developed World in the Mid-20th Century*, 38 DEMOGRAPHIC RES. 1189, 1221–22 (2018); Jona Schellekens, *The Marriage Boom and Marriage Bust in the United States: An Age-Period-Cohort Analysis*, 71 POPULATION STUD. 65, 75, 77 (2017).

[22] James R. Wetzel, *American Families: 75 Years of Change*, MONTHLY LAB. REV., March 1990, at 4, 5, 6 chart 1.

[23] U.S. Census Bureau, Historical Marital Status Tables – Table MS-2. Estimated Median Age at First Marriage: 1890 to present (2021) (reporting, for men and for women, median age at first marriage), https://www.census.gov/data/tables/time-series/demo/families/marital.html.

[24] PEW RES. CTR., PARENTING IN AMERICA 15 (2015).

[25] Steven White, *Civil Rights, World War II, and U.S. Public Opinion*, 30 STUD. AM. POL. DEV. 38, 58 (2016).

[26] Evan K. Rose, *The Rise and Fall of Female Labor Force Participation During World War II in the United States*, 78 J. ECON. HIST. 673, 678, 709–10 (2018) (measuring the effect of World War II on the labor force participation rate of U.S. women in 1950; describing the effect as "small")

Another study concluded that the war increased by about 20 percent the labor force involvement of women, but that the effect was limited to women who had completed high school. Claudia come from a period marked by a relatively high degree of social stability in the United States. As a result, sociology-grounded independent variables, when measured as of 1960, may furnish an unusually good test of the utility of structural-functionalism theory[27] for understanding the relationship between law content and societal stress.

5.4 China and the "One-Birth" Policy

The instant book has put forward the proposition that change in the content of certain law in the United States had significant unintended social consequences for the country and that the consequences included societal stress. Does the proposition apply solely to the United States and jurisdictions like the United States that have (1) a multifaceted societal structure and (2) a democratic form of government? A plausible argument can be made that a change in law in an autocracy is at least as likely as a change in law in a democracy to generate negative, stress-manifesting social side effects, because in an autocracy, law content may not be shaped by societal needs and values but by the idiosyncrasies of the individuals who are its political leaders. Put in other words, the proclivities of a society may not be adequately taken into account by personalities in the political arena when they write new law. The argument raises an issue that warrants investigation even though the issue cannot be definitively resolved at the moment.

To pursue the issue, I note that Chinese society is structurally complex[28] and that the Chinese nation is an autocracy because it has a single-party political system.[29] China, in other words, possesses one but not both of the above attributes, namely, it

---

Goldin & Claudia Olivetti, *Shocking Labor Supply: A Reassessment of the Role of World War II on Women's Labor Supply*, 103(3) AM. ECON. REV.: PAPERS & PROCEEDINGS 257, 259, 261 (2013). Women who had finished high school were, notably, a minority of all women: Fully 71 percent of all females aged 20 or over in the United States in 1940 had gone no further than three years of high school; only 29 percent had completed four years of high school or one or more years of college. Calculated from data in U.S. BUREAU OF THE CENSUS, SIXTEENTH CENSUS OF THE UNITED STATES: 1940. POPULATION. VOL IV: CHARACTERISTICS BY AGE. PART 1: UNITED STATES SUMMARY 78 tbl. 18 (1943).

[27] See Sect. 1.2 in *supra* Chap. 1.

[28] *E.g.*, Shenjing He, *Evolving Enclave Urbanism in China and Its Socio-Spatial Implications: The Case of Guangzhou*, 14 SOC. & CULTURAL GEOGRAPHY 243 (2013); Ye Lu & Yajie Chu, *Media Use, Social Cohesion, and Cultural Citizenship: An Analysis of a Chinese Metropolis*, 5 CHINESE J. COMM. 365 (2012). *Accord*, Zhanwei Zhang, Law, State and Society in the PRC: A Case Study of Family Planning Regulations Implementation at Grassroots Level in Rural China 18 (Jan. 2015) (unpublished Ph.D. dissertation, London School of Economics & Political Science) (noting that the implementation of the "one-birth" policy of the Chinese central government was delegated to provincial and municipal governments because China was characterized by "uneven economic development" and a "diverse cultural milieu").

[29] John J. Chin, *The Longest March: Why China's Democratization is Not Imminent*, 23 J. CHINESE POL. SCI. 63, 64 (2018) (observing that China was among twenty-one autocracies worldwide in 2015).

has attribute (1) above but not attribute (2). As a result, the widely known "one-birth" policy of the government of China may provide evidence regarding whether the proposition that I have advanced applies outside the United States and similar jurisdictions. The policy, which was adopted in 1979, sought to curtail domestic population growth by imposing a one-birth maximum on each Chinese woman who belonged to the majority (Han) ethnic group.[30] The one-birth policy, which lasted more than thirty years[31] and may have been "the largest social experiment in human history,"[32] may not, surprisingly, have appreciably reduced the fertility rate in China.[33] On the other hand, while the policy may not have had a substantial impact

---

[30] Wei Huang, *How Does the One Child Policy Impact Social and Economic Outcomes?*, IZA World of Labor, Sept. 2017, at 1, 2–3 [hereinafter *Outcomes*].

[31] Francisco Zamora López & Cristina Rodríguez Veiga, *From One Child to Two: Demographic Policies in China and their Impact on Population*, 172 Revista Española de Investigaciones Sociológicas 141, 142 (2020).

[32] *Outcomes*, *supra* note 30, at 9.

[33] López & Veiga, *supra* note 31, at 144–46. *See* Junsen Zhang, *The Evolution of China's One-Child Policy and Its Effects on Family Outcomes*, 31 J. Econ. Persp. 141, 151 (2017) (observing that social science research has yielded inconsistent findings as to whether the one-birth policy decreased fertility in China; proposing that the inconsistent findings may indicate that the "policy accelerated the already-occurring drop in fertility for a few years, but in the longer term, economic development played a more fundamental role" in determining the level of child-bearing in China).

Two recent studies constructed a "synthetic" country as a control group whose estimated childbearing was compared to recorded childbearing in China; the impact of antinatalist Chinese government policy was computed from the difference, in each post-policy year, between the level of posited childbearing in the synthetic country and the level of recorded childbearing in China. Each of the studies thus examined year-specific, side-by-side differences between an artificially constructed country and an actual country. Because this "synthetic control method" (or "SCM") is a relatively recent innovation, its strengths and weaknesses in various types of situations are not yet known. Janet Bouttell et al., *Synthetic Control Methodology as a Tool for Evaluating Population-Level Health Interventions*, 72 J. Epidemiology & Community Health 673, 677 (2018).

According to one of the SCM studies, an antinatalist policy (the "initial" policy) that preceded the one-birth policy kept a large number of births in China from happening, and the one-birth policy had a much smaller effect; together, the policies were estimated to have prevented between 164 million and 268 million births. Liu Qiang et al., *Is China's Low Fertility Rate Caused by the Population Control Policy?*, at 5, 25-26 & fig. 7, 31 (Levy Econ. Inst., Working Paper No. 943, 2020) (designating 1971 as the first year of the initial policy; estimating from the crude birth rate the number of births prevented). According to the other SCM study, the initial policy reduced births in China by 85 million, and the one-birth policy did not alter the number of births. Stuart Gietel-Basten et al., *Assessing the Impact of the "One-Child Policy" in China: A Synthetic Control Approach*, 14(11) PLoS ONE 9 fig. 1, 11 (e0220170) (2019) (specifying 1973 as the first year of the initial policy; using the total fertility rate to estimate the number of births avoided). The effects estimated by the two SCM studies are based on different demographic measures: Qiang et al. employed the crude birth rate, which is the annual number of live births per 1000 population; Gietel-Basten et al. employed the total fertility rate, which is explained in Sect. 1.4.3 in *supra* Chap. 1.

Notably the crude birth rate and the total fertility rate in China had started to decline in the late 1960s, i.e., before the initial policy was implemented. Qiang et al., *supra*, at 3 fig. 1; Gietel-Basten et al., *supra*, at 9 fig. 1. The pre-policy decline in childbearing may have been the reason that Qiang on the domestic fertility rate, it produced an array of social side effects in China.[34] These side effects are logically indicants of societal stress. According to available research, the one-birth policy raised the overall crime rate[35] as well as the female crime rate.[36] Additionally, the one-birth policy (1) affected the rate of marriage and the choice of marriage partners,[37] (2) led more families to engage in direct private adoptions of children whose biological parents found themselves in violation of the policy,[38] and (3) was responsible for the abandonment, surrender, and abduction of

---

et al. opined that antinatalist policy in China "may only have contributed to a small part of the birth rate decline." Qiang et al., *supra*, at 32.

To assess the impact of an antinatalist policy intervention that has been implemented by a jurisdiction ("treatment jurisdiction"), an alternative research design involves mainly the comparison of (1) repeatedly measured pre-intervention childbearing levels in the treatment jurisdiction to (2) repeatedly measured post-intervention childbearing levels in the same jurisdiction. Through this "interrupted time-series design" (or "ITSD"), the intervention is evaluated against already occurring rates of childbearing and, hence, against the sociological, demographic, and economic forces responsible for the already occurring rates. A "control" jurisdiction, if similar to the treatment jurisdiction in every relevant respect other than the adoption of the intervention, allows investigators to determine whether a before-after difference in childbearing rates in the treatment jurisdiction is unique; if the before-after difference in the treatment jurisdiction also occurred in the control jurisdiction and at about the same time, the policy intervention did not have an effect on the dependent variable (here, the frequency of childbearing). Chester L. Britt et al., *A Reassessment of the D.C. Gun Law: Some Cautionary Notes on the Use of Interrupted Time Series Designs for Policy Impact Assessment*, 30 Law & Soc'y Rev. 361 (1996). An ITSD study of antinatalist policy in China, however, does not seem to have been conducted. When such a study is done, the investigators will need to take into account that the pre-intervention period in China was characterized by rising rates of childbearing and then declining rates of childbearing. See Qiang et al., *supra*, at 3 fig. 1; Gietel-Basten et al., *supra*, at 9 fig. 1. An accurate estimate from ITSD of the impact of the policy intervention in China requires, therefore, a determination of the degree to which the course of the post-policy childbearing-rate declines deviated from the course of the pre-policy childbearing-rate declines. Inclusion of pre-policy years in which childbearing rates were increasing could inflate the baseline to which childbearing rates in the post-policy years are compared, and the result could be an artificially high estimate of the effect of the policy intervention on number of births.

[34]The one-birth policy has evidently produced instances of human-rights abuses in China. Ying Chen, *China's One-Child Policy and Its Violations of Women's and Children's Rights* 1, 57–65 (2009). To the extent that such abuses occurred, the abuses would have increased social alienation, and decreased social integration, in China. See note 52 and accompanying text in *supra* Chap. 1.

[35]Lena Edlund et al., *Sex Ratios and Crime: Evidence from China*, 95 Rev. Econ. & Stat. 1520, 1533 (2013) (using data combining violent and property crime).

[36]Tina Wang, *Fewer Women Doing More Crime: How Has the One-Child Policy Affected Female Crime in China?*, 61 Sociol. Q. 87, 94, 98–99, 101 (2020).

[37]Wei Huang & Yi Zhou, *One-Child Policy, Marriage Distortion, and Welfare Loss* 4–5, 16 & n.22, 18–19, 21, 26–28 (Inst. for the Study of Labor (IZA), Discussion Paper No. 9532, 2015).

[38]Xueyao Ma et al., *Family-to-Family Child Migration Network of Informal Adoption in China*, 7 Human. & Soc. Sci. Comm. art. 48, at 1, 2, 3, 9 (Aug. 2020), https://doi.org/10.1057/s41599-020-00542-7.

children.[39] Moreover, since the probability of being overweight or obese is higher in China for an only child than for a child in a multi-child family[40]—a situation that results from an only child having an employed mother as well as an employed father who are more likely to make monetary expenditures on the child than to devote time to the child[41]—the policy also reshaped the internal dynamics of the Chinese family. Other social effects have been unearthed, too.[42] The policy was responsible for a material increase in the sex ratio, i.e., the number of males per 100 females,[43] and thereby prompted unmarried, low-income men to spend more money on a publicly salient product (viz., automobiles) in order to improve their social status and, in turn, their appeal to unmarried women.[44] If the sociological experience of China with the one-birth policy is generalizable, in brief, sociologically important social side effects, including society-level stress, emanate from socially oriented law in all structurally complex nations, irrespective of their form of governance.

---

[39] Xiaojia Bao et al., *Where Have All The Children Gone? An Empirical Study of Child Abandonment and Abduction in China* 13–14, 24, 26–27, 31–32, 35 (Nat'l Bureau of Econ. Res., Working Paper No. 26492, 2020).

[40] Jungwon Min et al., *Are Single Children More Likely to be Overweight or Obese than Those with Siblings? The Influence of China's One-Child Policy on Childhood Obesity*, 103 PREVENTIVE MED. 8, 13 (2017).

[41] Jie Zhang et al., *One-Child Policy and Childhood Obesity*, 59 CHINA ECON. REV. 1, 11–12 (art. 100938) (2020).

[42] Not all of the social side effects of the one-birth policy in China were negative. At least one was positive: The policy significantly raised the probability of high-school graduation among Han-ethnicity females who were aged 10-19. Wei Huang et al., When Fewer Means More: Impact of One-Child Policy on Education of Girls 4–5, 32 (2016) (unpublished manuscript). In addition, the policy increased schooling among children who, by virtue of their age, were not required to be in school. Yue Huang, *Family Size and Children's Education: Evidence from the One-Child Policy in China*, 41 POPULATION RES. & POL'Y REV. 317, 327, 334 tbl. 3, 339 (2022). *See also* Laura M. Argys & Susan L. Averett, *The Effect of Family Size on Education: New Evidence from China's One-Child Policy*, 85 J. DEMOGRAPHIC ECON. 21, 25–26, 40–41 (2019) (finding that the policy increased the educational attainment of Chinese-born youth).

[43] Hongbin Li et al., *Estimating the Effect of the One-Child Policy on the Sex Ratio Imbalance in China: Identification Based on the Difference-in-Differences*, 48 DEMOGRAPHY 1535, 1554–55 (2011). *See generally* Emily A. Stone, *Does Mate Scarcity Affect Marital Choice and Family Formation? The Evidence for New and Classic Formulations of Sex Ratio Theory*, 55 MARRIAGE & FAM. REV. 403, 417–18 (2019) (concluding from a review of research that, ceteris paribus, a high ratio of men to women raises the rate of marriage and also increases the marriage of women to men who are higher in socio-economic status).

The larger number of males may not have been responsible for the higher overall crime rate found by Edlund et al., *supra* note 35. Indeed, the rate of violent crime may be lowered by an increase in the sex ratio. Ryan Schacht et al., *Marriage Markets and Male Mating Effort: Violence and Crime Are Elevated Where Men are Rare*, 27 HUM. NATURE 489, 490, 497 (2016) (using data on the United States).

[44] Kevin B. Grier et al., *Marriage Market Matching and Conspicuous Consumption in China*, 54 ECON. INQUIRY 1251, 1255–56 & tbl. 3, 1258–59 & tbl. 5, 1260–61 (2016).

5.5 Some Final (But Important) Points

There is no such thing as a free lunch.[45] (American adage)

The present book has taken a sociological path to understanding state law and Constitution-based U.S. Supreme Court rulings that dealt with race restrictions and sex restrictions on the eligibility of individuals to marry. The book also sociologically examined state reactions to the proposed addition of the Equal Rights Amendment ("ERA") to the Constitution. The ERA, given its potential breadth and uncertain ramifications,[46] divided women[47] and even feminists,[48] and it thus may have been at least as socially unsettling as the Court rulings that invalidated race and sex bars to marriage in state law. Whether that is so, an important sociological effect of both the rulings and ERA proposal would have been societal stress in the United States, and such stress would not have been socially cost-free. Indeed, societal stress may be socially expensive for a society, and this expense requires the attention of scholars.

An important caveat, however, must accompany the line of reasoning in the present book. Although the thesis of the book is that social stress was a by-product of the Court rulings and proposed ERA, the thesis does *not* mean that like rulings should never be sought or that major changes in the text of law should never be advocated and adopted. Such an interpretation would seriously misconstrue the thesis. Once a quantitative indicator of social stress has been developed and sufficient research on the causes of social stress has been done, macrosociology will be able to supply credible estimates of the net impact on the level of social stress that can be expected from a court ruling, from a proposed amendment to the Constitution, and from legislation, and these estimates will be possible *before* the judiciary is asked to examine the constitutionality of existing law or an effort is launched to alter existing law through a constitutional amendment or statutory enactment. The thesis says only that efforts to change the content of law should be carefully assessed and limited, not eliminated, in order to avoid a build-up of social stress to a point where severe, negative consequences ensue. Sociologists can contribute to the commonweal, therefore, by conducting the research and developing the theory that make

---

[45] Wikipedia, *There Ain't No Such Thing as a Free Lunch*, https://en.wikipedia.org/wiki/There_ain%27t_no_such_thing_as_a_free_lunch.

[46] Wolfgang P. Hirczy de Mino, *Does an Equal Rights Amendment Make a Difference?*, 60 ALB. L. REV. 1581, 1582 (1997).

[47] In national surveys that employed probability samples of U.S. residents during the years 1975, 1976, and 1978, interviewees were informed that the ERA "would give women equal rights and equal responsibilities." Among the women interviewed in these surveys, between one out of four and one out of three opposed the ERA, and slightly more than one-half favored the ERA. Rita J. Simon & Jean M. Landis, *Women's and Men's Attitudes About a Woman's Place and Role*, 53 PUB. OPINION Q. 265, 275 (1989).

[48] Serena Mayeri, *Constitutional Choices: Legal Feminism and the Historical Dynamics of Change*, 92 CALIF. L. REV. 755, 762–69 (2004).

possible a cost-benefit sociological analysis of litigation, constitutional amendments, and legislation.

In the meantime, we must keep in mind that research on the societal impact of law and government policy is subject to numerous potential shortcomings that warn against the mechanical embrace of studies that seem to support the use of the tools of government, including the federal Constitution, to engineer social life. As brought out in Appendix 1 to Chap. 1, this line of research has a range of pitfalls that render inadvisable any rush to deploy law and government policy for the purpose of bringing about a substantial change in the incidence of activities and arrangements that are socially defined as problematic. Of course, I am not the first to urge caution with respect to the use of law for social engineering, though not many of those who have done so seem to tie their caution explicitly to defects of design and data in social science research: My position is implicit in scholarly debates[49] as well as in disagreements between judges[50] over the degree of "judicial activism" that is desirable, i.e., over the societal role that is appropriate for courts. An illustration of the latter is found in court orders designed to bring about racial integration in public schools that are segregated by law. As to such orders, a justice of the U.S. Supreme Court expressly admonished the American judiciary against long-term efforts to compel integration:

> The time has come for a thoughtful re-examination of the proper limits of the role of courts in confronting the intractable problems of public education in our complex society. Proved discrimination by state or local authorities should never be tolerated, and it is a first responsibility of the judiciary to put an end to it where it has been proved. But many courts have continued also to impose wide-ranging decrees, and to retain ongoing supervision over school systems. . . . Courts . . . should recognize . . . the limits of effective judicial power.[51]

[49] Gary Lawson, *Conservative or Constitutionalist?*, 1 Geo. J.L. & Pub. Pol'y 81 (2002).

[50] In United States v. Lopez, 514 U.S. 549 (1995), the Court held that the Commerce Clause of the federal Constitution did not authorize Congress to enact a statute that imposed criminal penalties on a person who knowingly had a firearm in an area that the person realized was a "school zone," which the statute defined as the grounds of an elementary or secondary school (public or private) and the area covering 1000 feet from such grounds. 18 U.S.C. §§ 921(a)(25), –(a)26), 922(q)(2)(A) (2020). The Court reasoned that "[t]he possession of a gun in a local school zone is in no sense an economic activity that might, through repetition elsewhere, substantially affect any sort of interstate commerce." 514 U.S. at 567. One justice dissented, arguing that "the Court's previous essays in overriding congressional policy choices under the Commerce Clause were ultimately seen to suffer two fatal weaknesses: when dealing with Acts of Congress . . . nothing in the Clause compelled the judicial activism, and nothing about the judiciary as an institution made it a superior source of policy[,] on the subject Congress dealt with"). 514 U.S. at 611 (Souter, J., dissenting).

[51] Columbus Bd. of Educ. v. Penick, 443 U.S. 449, 479, 487, 489 (1979) (Powell, J., dissenting). *See also* People Who Care v. Rockford Bd. Educ., 111 F.3d 528, 534 (7th Cir. 1997) (three-judge panel) ("[v]iolations of law must be dealt with firmly, but not used to launch the federal courts on ambitious schemes of social engineering. Children, the most innocent of the innocent persons occasionally brushed by draconian decrees, should not be made subjects of utopian projects.").

For social science evidence on the effectiveness of judicially ordered racial integration in public schools, see the paragraph that accompanies notes 33 to 40 in *supra* Chap. 2.

Problems of research design and data in empirical studies that, implicitly or explicitly, encourage social engineering by government should not, however, be the sole reason for caution regarding government intervention in social problems. An additional reason is that an established theory—viz., structural-functionalism theory[52]—explains why law/policy does not exert a material, enduring influence on the frequency with which individuals engage in key social behaviors. That a recognized theory explains a conclusion is important, because an explanation grounded in theory raises the credibility of the explained conclusion. The conclusion that, in a democracy, law and government policy does not appreciably reshape social life, and may produce significant social stress, thus merits serious consideration by judges in discussions about judicial activism, by legislators in debates over pending bills focused on social patterns, and by scholars in studies of the institution of law.

---

[52] See Sect. 1.2 in *supra* Chap. 1; Larry D. Barnett, Demography and the Anthropocene ch. 3 pt. 3.2 (2021).